THE COMPLETE GUIDE TO
MAKING YOUR HOME SAFE

The Complete Guide to Making Your Home Safe. Copyright © 1995 by Dave Heberle and Richard M. Scutella. Printed and bound in the United States of America. All rights reserved. No part of this book may be reproduced in any form or by any electronic or mechanical means including information storage and retrieval systems without permission in writing from the publisher, except by a reviewer, who may quote brief passages in a review. Published by Betterway Books, an imprint of F&W Publications, Inc., 1507 Dana Avenue, Cincinnati, Ohio, 45207. 1-800-289-0963. First edition.

99 98 97 96 95   5 4 3 2 1

Library of Congress Cataloging-in-Publication Data

Heberle, Dave.
    The complete guide to making your home safe / by Dave Heberle and Richard M. Scutella.
       p.   cm.
    Includes index.
    ISBN 1-55870-349-7
    1. Home accidents—Prevention. 2. Dwellings—Security measures. 3. Safety education. I. Scutella, Richard M. II. Title.
TX150.H38   1995
640'.28'9—dc20
                    94-48189
                    CIP

Edited by R. Adam Blake and Julie Wesling Whaley
Designed by Brian Roeth
Illustrated by Susanne C. Wellman
Cover design by Angela Lennert
Cover photos:
   House photo: Superstock, Inc.
   Bathroom Safety: compliments of Kohler Plumbing
      Products
   Electrical Safety: compliments of Leviton Manufacturing
      Company, Inc.
   Fire Safety: Cosmic line, compliments of J.L. Industries
   Vacation Safety: compliments of Intermatic Incorporated

METRIC CONVERSION CHART

TO CONVERT	TO	MULTIPLY BY
Inches	Centimeters	2.54
Centimeters	Inches	0.4
Feet	Centimeters	30.5
Centimeters	Feet	0.03
Yards	Meters	0.9
Meters	Yards	1.1
Sq. Inches	Sq. Centimeters	6.45
Sq. Centimeters	Sq. Inches	0.16
Sq. Feet	Sq. Meters	0.09
Sq. Meters	Sq. Feet	10.8
Sq. Yards	Sq. Meters	0.8
Sq. Meters	Sq. Yards	1.2
Pounds	Kilograms	0.45
Kilograms	Pounds	2.2
Ounces	Grams	28.4
Grams	Ounces	0.04

THE COMPLETE GUIDE TO
MAKING YOUR HOME SAFE

DAVID HEBERLE & RICHARD SCUTELLA

BETTERWAY BOOKS

CINCINNATI, OHIO

ABOUT THE AUTHORS

Dave Heberle has been writing books, columns and articles for over 20 years and specializes in home construction, home maintenance, real estate, and safety. He is a member of the National Safety Council and the World Safety Organization, and is the president of Progressive Safety Management, Inc., a company that helps other businesses install and operate effective safety management systems.

Dave also teaches writing at Pennsylvania State University, is the Maintenance Skills and Safety Training Supervisor at a pulp and paper company in Erie, Pennsylvania, and is a member of the Quikrete Home Projects Council of Atlanta, Georgia.

Richard M. Scutella is a Maintenance Planning Analyst for a pulp and paper company in Erie, Pennsylvania. His responsibilities include maintaining equipment and facilities in a reliable and safe condition.

The co-author of books on new home construction, home purchases, home inspections and home maintenance, Richard has also designed and supervised the building of new homes.

His training includes: American Red Cross Adult CPR Certification, American Red Cross Standard First Aid Certification, OSHA General Industry Seminars, MSHA General Industry Seminars, Safety Management Services Certification, Safety Management Audits and Inspections Certification.

Richard is a member of the American College of Sports Medicine Fit Society in Indianapolis, Indiana and a member of the Quikrete Companies Home Projects Council in Atlanta, Georgia.

Table of Contents

Introduction

Nowadays, as always, people want to live as long as they can. And they want to stay healthy. Of course, different routes are taken to achieve those ends. Some individuals tend to coast through life, relying on medical science to cure what ails them. Others try to exercise and diet their way toward tuning their bodies to the highest level of fitness they can reach. Of course, many obvious roadblocks are out there along the way—health concerns such as smoking, high cholesterol, AIDS, and even driving without a seat belt.

It's generally felt that the healthier you are, the longer you'll live. So the object seems to be to keep as fit as possible over the long haul.

At the same time, the health care crisis has been brewing, with spiraling medical costs, workers compensation court battles, hospitals trimming layer after layer of services, and huge out-of-pocket deductibles in health insurance policies. And where will Medicare and Medicaid end up? Indeed, business, industry, government, retirees—all of us have to be concerned about providing medical coverage for ourselves and our families.

These topics have been written about extensively in consumer magazines. A walk through any bookstore or supermarket will take you past magazines advertising articles such as "Eight Ways to Stay Healthy All Winter," or "Finally, a Diet You Won't Quit." Lots of diets. Lots of healthy eating. Lots of medical reports about what not to eat. A flurry of healthy sex stuff.

Yet, with all of this to think about, there is another aspect of health that—while being recognized for years by management in business and industry—is largely ignored by most people. In the typical household, there are no safety policies or procedures in place. Family members are just supposed to know how to behave in a safe manner. Indeed, when was the last time you had a safety meeting at home? If you have young children or grandchildren, when was the last time you audited your own home for hazards, such as staircases without handrails, tools without safety guards, sharp corners on furniture, or poisonous cleaning products stored within reach of tiny hands?

That most forgotten about aspect of health is safety. Yet who can deny that by safeguarding yourself and your family you can tip the odds in your favor, especially if you also keep yourself reasonably fit and avoid the most obvious health hazards.

But how to proceed? You've got a life to live. You've got to work. The lawn needs mowing. The children need a ride to soccer practice—three nights a week. You like to socialize. It's tough to find the time. Days pass. Weeks pass. Months turn into years. How do you work all of the components of health and safety into your schedule?

This book was written to help fill the safety gap. It's meant to impart safety information a little at a time. It recognizes that the home—be it a trailer, high-rise apartment, condominium, city flat, middle-class house in the suburbs, or a farm home miles from the nearest neighbor—is where most of life unfolds, and consequently is also where a person is more likely be injured, accidentally or otherwise.

HOW TO GET THE MOST OUT OF THIS BOOK

This book presents a wide range of ideas, suggestions, examples, tips and alternatives for you to consider to help make your home a healthier, safer place to live in. Feel free to take any idea here and call it your own. Put a special twist to it if you wish. Try it one way, then another. There's a lot of material here—pick out what you feel will work for you. Share the information with others, too, family, friends and co-workers.

Here are some suggestions:

- Start Out Small. You can't do everything at once. Attempt too much too fast and discouragement will set in. You could end up abandoning improvements before they are fully in place.
- Put the Book Where You Can Frequently Pick It Up. In a bathroom, perhaps, or on a kitchen

counter, near the phone. The sections are short, and can be read in only a few moment's time. You can skip around, too. There's no rule that says you've got to read everything in the order presented.

- Keep a Highlighter Pen Handy. Attach it to the book by a string. Mark sections or passages that apply to you. Along with the highlighter, keep a pen and small pad of paper with the book to jot down notes.
- Get Interactive. To gain the most from this book, it should be an interactive experience. In other words, you'll need to take action on various suggestions and ideas. Encourage family members to read the book as well. Use the checklists as reviews.

The book is a comprehensive, simple to follow, practical guide that will help anyone achieve a safer household. Some of the material may sound like common sense, but for thousands of people every year who are injured or even killed at home by everything from falling off ladders to heat exhaustion while gardening, was it a lack of common sense or disregard for elementary safety rules that caused the injuries? If it saves you or a family member only one trip to your doctor, one ambulance ride, one anxious visit to an emergency room, it's done its job.

GENERAL SAFETY

Being mindful of the safety basics covered in Part One could save your life or the life of a loved one, or at least prevent serious injury. Certainly this book does not need to be read in order, but please do read the chapters on fire and electrical safety so you'll know how to avoid dangerous situations and what to do in case of an emergency.

Above all, remember that safety is as much attitude as it is procedures, behaviors and conditions. Develop a habit of thinking about activities or tasks in individual steps. Identify potential hazards to each step, then plan a way of completing the step so you'll eliminate or avoid the hazards.

CHAPTER 1

FIRE SAFETY

Individuals who have lived through a massive house fire, and who have suffered the pain of third-degree burns—or have seen family members or friends affected the same way—take fire prevention seriously for the rest of their lives. To experience a tragic fire gives new meaning to the importance of installing smoke detectors and checking detector operation frequently. It gives new meaning to the relevance of home fire drills in which all household members are schooled in what to do if they encounter smoke or fire. It gives new meaning to what goes on in hospital burn units, and how long it takes burn injuries to heal. Unfortunately, once a fire rages through a home, destroying contents and scarring the inhabitants, it's too late to make a difference for that household.

Ask any fire fighter and they'll tell you what they've run across. How a child playing with a candle in an attic caused the loss of not only his home, but his entire family as well. They'll tell you about improperly installed stoves and fireplaces, and electrical wiring systems that were woefully substandard. Once pressed, their list of tragedies goes on and on.

If you follow only a handful of points from this book, take the basics of fire prevention found in this chapter and make them yours. It's a case where a few hours' worth of prevention a year—even if the methods may sound like overkill—are a lot better than days, weeks or months of cure. Indeed, if a major fire ever affects your residence, your posses-

sions, yourself and your family, the consequences could be overwhelming for years to come.

Contact your local fire department. Those individuals are knowledgeable and dedicated and will always share prevention information with interested citizens. In many cases, they'll provide you with pamphlets, children's fire-safety coloring books, recommended procedures, and the names and phone numbers of other helpful sources you can follow up with. Some fire department officials will even help inspect your home for potential hazards, and assist you with preparing a plan to correct deficiencies.

THE BASICS OF FIRE

Two basic forms of fire exist: flaming (including explosions) and flameless surface (including deep-seated glowing embers). The flameless surface variation of fire is a surface fire in which combustion is occurring from a combination of the three sides of the fire triangle (source of fuel, temperature and oxygen—see Figure 1-1), but the fire has not yet reached a stage where flames begin to burn the vapors given off by the fuel. You may not always see a fire that's started somewhere in your home. A fire could smolder within a wall for days before bursting into flames. The important thing to remember is that a fire cannot burn without all three elements of the fire triangle; the removal of any one of them will effectively cause extinguishment.

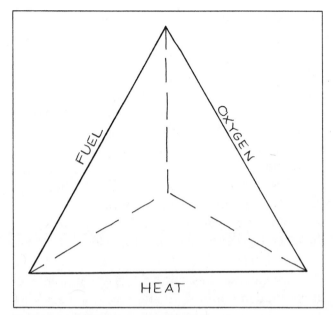

Figure 1-1. The fire triangle.

The fire triangle, however, represents only the smoldering mode of combustion. When a fourth element is added—a chemical chain reaction that occurs with flames—the fire triangle turns into a "fire tetrahedron" (see Figure 1-2) or four-sided pyramid (the fourth side is the bottom of the pyramid), when the fuel becomes hot enough that fuel vapors are created, which the flames consume.

And don't rule out spontaneous combustion, where the heat is caused by chemical decomposition. Oily rags, solvent-soaked swabs, paint wipers and other flammable rubbish—even though used and discarded—can still be active fire hazards that ignite spontaneously in a confined space when enough oxygen is present. Spontaneous flame generation can also occur when wet hay is stored in a barn.

Flaming, then, is a direct burning of a gaseous or vaporized fuel. The rate of burning is high and a high temperature is produced.

There are also, for our purposes, three basic types of fires: types A, B and C. Type A fires are the burning of wood, paper, cloth, trash and other ordinary materials. Type B fires involve flammable liquids such as gasoline, oil, paint and lubricants. And type C fires occur with live electrical equipment. Another type of fire is type D, which involves "exotic" metals that can catch fire and burn—a situation that generally does not occur in residential dwellings. Because the most common fires are types A, B and C, the best all-around fire extinguishers to have at home are the multipurpose dry chemical (ABC) kind.

HOUSEKEEPING

Everyone knows the importance of good housekeeping, but occasionally it falls to the bottom of

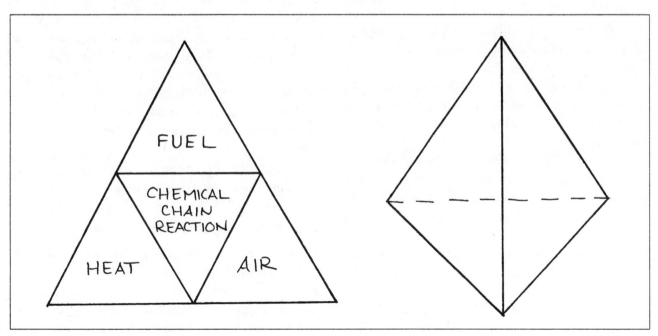

Figure 1-2. The fire tetrahedron.

the list of things to do. In a time when jobs and careers are becoming more demanding, when single parents wear any number of hats, when children are becoming involved with sports and a wide range of other extracurricular activities that need parent taxi services, when adults are working two jobs and flocking to exercise classes, corners of the house, garage or yard can tend to be let go.

There are remedies for common household conditions, that could directly or indirectly lead to fire hazards. For instance, dispose of rubbish and trash regularly. Why let it accumulate? The fewer materials in your house, the better. Avoid missing a week's worth of trash removal. Keep wastebaskets emptied. It's important not so much from the standpoint of preventing a fire from starting, as from removing fuel that would help a fire to spread quickly. Trash burns well. Store rubbish and trash away from heat sources, preferably in metal cans with lids. An open wastebasket next to a stove or cooktop is asking for trouble. Keep piles of newspapers, books and magazines away from water heaters, space heaters and furnaces. Consider keeping these materials in sturdy cartons, and when a carton is full, take it to a recycling center for disposal.

Sell, donate or recycle old clothes, books, toys and other "treasures" that you can't remember using and don't know if they'll ever come in handy again. Don't let them accumulate into a fire hazard.

Either use up or dispose of partially emptied cans of paint, thinner, solvents and other flammable liquids, especially if you have no plans for them in the near future. Ones you will need should be closed tightly and stored away from sources of heat. Some of these liquids may not be flammable, but their vapors can be.

Clean up spills immediately, especially sawdust, flammable liquids, oil or grease. Clean work areas after each use. Oily rags that are allowed to sit around for weeks and weeks could start a fire all by themselves—through spontaneous combustion.

Keep escape routes clear. Make sure windows and doors aren't blocked, and can be opened easily in case of an emergency.

If you smoke, or allow others to smoke in your home, use deep, sturdy, heavy ashtrays. Never flick or dump ashes in wastebaskets or garbage bags without making certain the ashes are extinguished. In fact, it's best to douse full or partially full ashtrays with water and let them stand in a sink before disposing of ashes and butts. Check the floor, rugs and furniture after smokers leave your household. Never smoke in bed or while reclining on a couch where the possibility of falling asleep exists. Avoid leaving cigarettes, cigars, pipes or candles burning unattended.

Close the cover of a matchbook before lighting a match. Discard matches carefully, making sure they are cold before you throw them away. Never use matches to search in dark attics, closets or other closed places.

Store all matches and lighters away from children, hidden out of sight and reach in metal containers. Teach children to give matches they find to an adult. Children as young as two years old are capable of lighting cigarette lighters and matches. Never encourage or allow a child to play with a lighter, even when in your presence. Once a child has seen fire, and learned to start it, the urge to do so again can be great. Studies have shown that telling a child not to play with fire is not enough, and neither is punishment. The National Fire Protection Association has estimated that children who have recently been punished for playing with fire are likely to do so again. And if the children play more than once, a fire will result over 80 percent of the time. Again, the only realistic way to prevent children from playing with fire is to keep fire-starting implements out of their sight and reach—that means hidden somewhere above the height of an adult's shoulder—and where the items cannot be reached by simply climbing on top of a cupboard or handy piece of furniture.

And lastly, if you don't smoke, consider a "No Smoking" policy for your home.

HEATING EQUIPMENT FIRE HAZARDS

Fireplaces and wood stoves can be wonderful. They provide warmth and a comforting atmosphere complete with sounds, odors, and the sight of flickering flames or glowing embers. But they can also mean trouble. Space heaters can provide temporary respite from the cold, but they too can be dangerous.

Misuse of all three have caused and continue to cause many tragic fires.

Furnaces and Main Heating Plants

Inadequate inspections and servicing are the culprits in most furnace and main heating plant fires. Some deficiencies can be found only by experienced technicians who need to carefully look at critical components from the inside out.

Have a heating/cooling specialist inspect your heating unit at the beginning of each heating season. Ask for a complete tune-up with this visit and have internal parts cleaned and calibrated.

Inspect flue pipes. They should be the right size for your furnace, as short as possible, well supported about every three feet, tightly connected, not touching any combustible materials, and free of rust or weak spots.

Make sure pilot lights and burner flames are adjusted to burn efficiently: blue instead of orange or yellow.

React immediately to the smell of natural gas and other fuels. Find the cause and have it corrected. If a gas main supply is interrupted, turn off all gas appliances, and see that they remain off until you are ready to relight them. Remember to relight the pilot lights.

Baseboard heaters should have nothing combustible touching them, including furniture, draperies, curtains, blankets, carpeting or electrical cords. A baseboard heater can become hot enough to ignite or melt things that are in prolonged contact with it.

Fireplaces and Wood Stoves

Has your fireplace or wood stove been properly installed and inspected by professionals? Amateur installations are a chief cause of house fires. Someone knowledgeable of local building codes should inspect the completed installation.

To avoid creosote buildup, burn only dry, seasoned hardwood such as hickory, maple, elm or oak. Avoid pine, spruce, and wood that is green and moist. Burn coal only in heating appliances designed for that fuel. Follow the manufacturer's instructions when burning artificial logs.

Never burn trash, plastic, or large amounts of paper in a wood-burning fireplace or stove. Colored newspapers, gift wrap and magazines can all contain chemicals or inks that create unhealthy fumes; aerosol cans can explode. Also avoid burning charcoal in stoves and fireplaces—it produces deadly carbon monoxide and the fire may not get hot enough to cause a draw up the chimney to get rid of the gases.

Have separate flues for each major wood-burning appliance.

Inspect chimneys for creosote buildup. Creosote is a natural by-product of burning wood, a highly flammable tar-like residue. When exposed to very hot or tall flames, creosote can ignite in a flash and cause a dangerous chimney fire. The best way to prevent chimney fires is to have chimneys cleaned once a year or as often as they need it. A quick visual inspection can reveal a lot. If you find an accumulation of creosote that's more than one-fourth-inch thick, it's a real fire hazard.

Watch out for chimney obstructions such as bird nests, leaves, or even bee and wasp nests. Look for crumbling mortar, broken tiles or liners, cracks and holes. Is the chimney adequately supported? Is the mortar and brick hard, as it should be, or can you push a knife between the bricks? Has the chimney base deteriorated? Failing to clean out the bottom of the flue for an extended period of time can cause base deterioration. Look up and down each flue with a light and mirror through any available opening (see Figure 1-3).

Vertical or horizontal cracks in brick, especially at offsets, can mean a dangerous condition. Check the chimney where it passes through the attic, too. Look especially below the roof line for deterioration—it's an easy place to overlook. Finally, look on the roof, where the chimney rises above the shingles. Is the chimney top at least three feet above the roof and two feet above any portion of the building within ten feet? Is there a mesh cover on top of the chimney to keep sparks from flying out onto the roof, and birds and animals from entering (see Figure 1-4)? Missing mortar or loose bricks should be repaired. If your roof is steep and you don't want to risk a fall, have a contractor do the inspecting, or use a pair of binoculars from the ground to examine all four sides of the chimney.

Figure 1-3. Inspecting a fireplace flue.

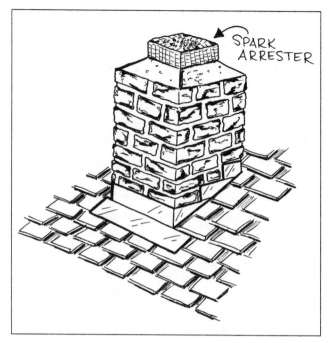

Figure 1-4. A chimney spark arrester.

Signs of a chimney fire include loud roaring, popping noises, or humming, sucking sounds. Stovepipes can glow red and rattle, and sparks or flames can shoot out from the chimney. If a chimney fire starts and begins burning rapidly, know what to do:

- First, get everyone out of the house.
- Cut off the air supply to the chimney. Put a metal cover over the front of the fireplace, if possible. On a stove, shut the damper.
- Douse any flames on the roof, bushes and trees if you can do so safely.
- Call the fire department from a neighbor's house.

Wood Stoves

Wood stove installations are critical. Their flue pipes should be kept as straight and as short as possible. Each flue pipe joint should be secured with at least three metal screws. Places where a flue enters a chimney should be protected by a tile or metal sleeve. A wood-burning stove should rest on a heat-resistant pad or brick or stone that extends at least eighteen inches beyond the stove in all directions.

Wood stoves *must* be inspected and cleaned at the beginning of each heating season, and stove pipes and chimneys checked regularly during the rest of the season.

Burn smaller, hotter fires. Add fuel often instead of packing the firebox full of wood. Chimney fires can result from attempting to burn too much wood at a time (which is called "overfiring"). Or a pile of burning wood could dislodge and push screens or glass doors open.

Avoid carrying hot coals from one fire to light a fire in another room. And never use lighter fluid, gasoline or kerosene to start a fire.

Store wood and other combustibles at least three feet away from the firebox. Clear the area directly outside of the hearth of all combustibles, especially rugs. Keep drapes, curtains and other accessories away from heat sources.

Use a spark screen or heat-resistant glass doors in front of the hearth (see Figure 1-5). Avoid drying clothes too near an open fire, even if the fire has a screened opening.

Figure 1-5. Glass fireplace doors.

Never leave an open fire unattended, and avoid leaving children unattended while a fireplace is in operation. Make sure a fire is extinguished before you go to bed or leave the house.

Don't let ashes accumulate in the firebox. Try to remove them after each fire. Dispose of ashes and soot after they have cooled down. Place them in a metal can with a cover, never in cardboard or wooden boxes, and dispose of them in a safe place outside the house.

Lock away heavy or sharp fireplace tools when children are around—the temptation children have to play in a fire with them can be almost overwhelming.

Keep a multipurpose ABC fire extinguisher handy.

Portable Kerosene and Electric Heaters

When portable kerosene or electric heaters must be used, accept only those models certified as safe by a well-known testing laboratory, such as Underwriters Laboratory (UL). Gas heaters should also be approved by the American Gas Association (AGA).

Is a portable heater the only answer? Or can you modify your existing heating system to cover the area in question instead? If you do purchase a kerosene heater, you introduce hazards related to fuel storage and handling. And you'll find the convenience of a kerosene heater is exaggerated. You'll need to allow time for buying fuel, fueling the heater, and taking care of frequent maintenance chores. The wick will have to be inspected every week or so during the heating season, and cleaned if it's dirty. Take care to use the right fuel. Kerosene heaters require 1-K grade kerosene. When colored or cloudy kerosene is burned it will give off an odor, it will smoke, and it will increase pollution levels because the fuel's higher sulphur content will result in a higher sulphur dioxide level than is emitted by the recommended 1-K fuel. Don't overfill the tank, and never refill a heater while it is still hot or burning. Keep kerosene in well-marked safety cans designed for storing fuel. Avoid using containers marked "kerosene" for gasoline or other fuel or oil storage.

Kerosene heaters have constant flames while burning. For that reason alone, they should not be operated in a room where solvents, aerosol sprays, gasoline, oil, or other types of vapor-producing flammables are stored. Adequate room ventilation is also a must.

Never, never attempt to move a lighted kerosene heater. The carrying handle could be hot and could cause a burn, and just think what would happen if you dropped it along the way. Play it safe by extinguishing the flame and letting the heater cool before you transport it somewhere else.

Avoid using a kerosene heater while you're sleeping. Turn it off before you go to bed. Use goose down comforters instead, or turn up your central heating system.

When taking a kerosene heater out of storage in the fall:

- Install batteries and inspect the shut-off mechanism and wick for proper operation.
- Fill the tank with fresh kerosene. Never use kerosene from a previous season—it could have biodegraded. Never, ever use gasoline to power a kerosene heater. Even small amounts of gasoline mixed with kerosene can greatly increase the likelihood of explosion and fire.
- Review the operator's manual to make sure you remember all of the operating and safety features.

When putting a kerosene heater into storage after the heating season:

- Remove all fuel from the tank—or burn the heater until it runs out of fuel. Kerosene can change its chemistry and become "stale" while in storage over the summer.
- Clean the wick if it's dirty. If it's worn out, replace it according to the heater manufacturer's instructions.
- Clean the heater, discard worn batteries or store good batteries in a dry place, covering both ends with masking tape.
- Place the unit and accessories in a dust-free, moisture-free container—possibly the box the heater came in.

If a kerosene heater doesn't seem quite right for you, and an electric heater seems a better alternative, you'll need to keep some commonsense advice in mind. But first, is the wiring in your home adequate to supply safe electric power for an electric heater? Their demands can be quite heavy on a circuit that may already be pushing its limit.

Avoid using extension cords with electric heaters, if possible. If there's no other option, make sure the cord is marked with a power rating at least as high as that of the heater itself. Keep the cord as straight as possible, and not buried under carpeting or wrapped tight around furniture legs.

Remember to keep heaters away from curtains, drapes and other combustibles, and never leave children alone with portable heaters.

APPLIANCE FIRE SAFETY

Most appliances rely on electricity to run as they should. In some units, electricity plays a "minor" role—to operate a timer or other component. But when electricity plays a major role—as it does in heating appliances and electronics—there is a greater opportunity for malfunctions that could help start accidental fires. To keep a fire from starting, keep in mind the following points.

Unplug heating appliances such as irons, toasters, hot plates and space heaters after each use. Remove accumulated lint from the clothes dryer filter (see Figure 1-6) after each load is dried. The dryer should be vented to the outside (see Figure 1-7) and plugged into its own outlet.

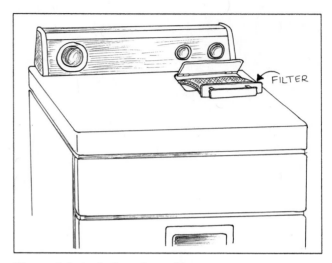

Figure 1-6. A clothes dryer filter.

Figure 1-7. A dryer's outside vent.

Keep oven/range interiors, exteriors and vent fans clean and grease free.

Repair or replace any appliance that gives shocks, smokes, sparks, or gives off "burnt" odors.

Although a seal of approval from a testing service such as Underwriters Laboratories means the appliance has been put through rigorous tests, that doesn't mean the appliance cannot be misused. No seal of approval will, of course, prevent an electric radio that has fallen into a bathroom sink full of water from shocking the unfortunate individual who reaches in after it.

Television sets, stereos, computers, and other appliances that need proper ventilation to keep from overheating should not be "built-in" to a confined space or other area where appliance ventilation slots or screens cannot breathe.

Never turn an electric blanket on if it is wet, and do not switch it on to help it dry out either. Let electric blankets dry naturally. Keep them dry and flat because folds and creases can cause overheating. Avoid using a hot water bottle at the same time you're using an electric blanket; water and electricity are dangerous companions.

To extinguish electrical fires, unplug the offending appliance or component, if possible, or shut off power to the circuit it's on. Never use water to attempt to extinguish an electrical fire—you could receive a shock. Use a multipurpose ABC dry chemical extinguisher instead.

KITCHEN FIRE SAFETY

All told, the kitchen is one of the most likely places in the typical household for accidental fires to start. There are some prevention pointers to consider when working in the kitchen. First, put only what you want to heat or cook on a stove top. An electrical coil can reach a temperature of 800 degrees Fahrenheit; a gas flame can go over 1,000 degrees. A dish towel or pot holder can catch fire at 400 degrees Fahrenheit. And so can your bathrobe, apron or shirt sleeve.

Use potholders and insulated mitts to handle hot pans and pots—never towels or other cloths that can dangle onto electric or gas burners and catch fire. A number of serious fires and accidental burns are caused each year by individuals who cook at the stove top while dressed in flowing robes or other clothing with long, loose sleeves. Such sleeves can catch on pot handles and overturn pots and pans, causing scalds, and they can come in contact with electric or gas burners and catch fire.

Don't store candy, cookies or other youngster attractions over or near range cooktops. The temptation for children to climb onto a counter and reach for the goodies can be too great, and can be deadly if done while things are cooking. They can easily burn their hands, knees or hair, or their clothes could catch fire.

Never leave the kitchen unattended while something is cooking. It's easy to forget that cooking oil is heating on a stove top. If oil gets hot enough it can burst into flames. Fires involving fats or oils are especially dangerous because they happen so suddenly, with flames that burst out of control in seconds. One of the most frequent causes of oil fires is a person being called away from the stove to answer a doorbell or phone. The person becomes involved in conversation and before long—fire! The best way to avoid this is to remove hot oil from burners before you leave the kitchen.

Clean stove exhaust hoods, filters and ducts regularly. Wipe up spilled grease as soon as the stove surface cools down.

Use back burners whenever possible. Keep all pan handles pointed to the back sides of the stove; avoid letting them extend over the front of the stove where children can pull the handles and the pans' contents onto themselves.

Keep an all-purpose dry chemical ABC fire extinguisher nearby. Never pour water on a grease fire—it will only scatter the flames and spatter hot grease. To extinguish a grease fire contained within a pan, carefully cover the pan with a lid and turn the burner off. Lack of oxygen will put out the fire.

Another alternative for putting out small kitchen fires is a fire blanket made of tightly woven fiberglass and fireproof Kevlar thread. Its tight weave prevents oxygen from getting to the fire. (A fire blanket can also be used as a fire shield to exit a burning building. They come with quick-access containers that can be wall mounted or stored in a cabinet.)

SMOKE DETECTORS

Surprisingly enough, smoke is responsible for about three out of every four fire deaths. That's why smoke detectors can provide such an effective defense against household fires. At the first hint of smoke they warn occupants by emitting a loud, piercing siren alarm. Some of them also have small light bulbs that will illuminate the nearby space to help people get their bearings. Make sure all family members know what the smoke detector alarm sounds like. It should be considerably different than the sounds made by other alarms—burglar alarms, for instance. You don't want your family hiding from a burglar when they should be running from a fire.

There are two basic smoke detector designs— those that are battery operated, and those that rely on the house electricity. The battery-powered models (see Figure 1-8) are simple to install and are operable as long as a charged battery is in place. Naturally, the batteries need regular checking and replacement. The unfortunate truth is that of all battery-operated smoke alarms in place, about a third of them are inoperable at any given time because of worn-out batteries or batteries that have been removed to stop the annoying warning signals produced by some detectors to let people know the batteries are about to fail. Sometimes children even remove smoke alarm batteries to power their battery-operated toys.

detector with a battery backup, if the battery supplying the backup is changed at regular intervals.

Purchase only models that carry a testing laboratory seal of approval. The alarm must be loud enough to wake a sleeping person behind a closed door.

If you have any special requirements, consider what they are and select a detector that will best satisfy your needs. For example, a number of more sophisticated detectors are available that are programmable, that will not only sound an alarm but will *tell* people how to proceed in a calm, authoritative voice. They can be especially valuable for chil-

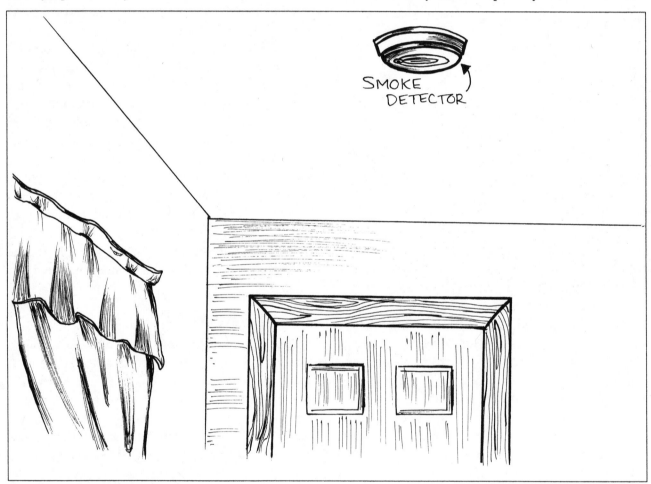

Figure 1-8. A smoke detector.

Household-current smoke detectors—the ones wired directly to the home's electric system—need to be put in place by an electrician and need far less attention once they are set up. On the other hand, they may fail without battery backup in the event of a blackout. The best of both worlds is a wired-in

dren, the elderly and the sight-impaired. Similar devices, with flashing strobe lights, can be installed to help the hearing-impaired.

Try to purchase detectors with at least five-year manufacturer's warranties. There should be a malfunction signal on each unit. It will warn when batteries or light bulbs need replacement.

Maintaining and cleaning detectors should be a simple task, not requiring a lot of tools or complete removal.

Sleeping areas need the most protection. A single detector in a typical hallway outside bedrooms is usually adequate. But take the individuals' physical health characteristics into account as well. If the people sleeping in a bedroom do not hear well, perhaps a single detector directly outside of each bedroom door is necessary.

For maximum protection, sleep with doors closed and install detectors in each bedroom, as well as in the hallway. Place a smoke detector at the top of each stairwell and at the end of a long hallway. Bedroom hallways longer than thirty feet should have a smoke detector at each end. Don't forget, smoke rises easily through stairwells.

Smoke detectors positioned in living areas should be kept away from fireplaces and wood stoves to avoid frequent false alarms, which could lull a family into a false sense of security during a real fire. Kitchen and dining area detectors should be kept away from cooking ranges and ovens for the same reason.

In basements, mount a smoke detector close to the stairway but not at the top of the stairway or near the furnace exhaust. On the ceiling above the bottom step is usually a good place.

Battery-powered detectors are simple to install, but those connected to household wiring should have their own separate circuit and should be installed by a professional electrician.

Ceiling mounts should be kept at least four inches away from the dead air space near walls and corners. It is best to install detectors as close to the center of a room as possible.

Wall mounts should be placed four to twelve inches below the ceiling and away from corners. Keep detectors high on a wall because smoke rises.

Avoid placing smoke detectors near air supply registers. Keep them at least three feet away, or the register could prevent smoke from reaching the detector.

Avoid installing smoke detectors on uninsulated exterior walls or ceilings. Temperature extremes can affect batteries, and temperature differences could keep smoke from reaching a detector.

Replace smoke detector batteries at least every year—usually in response to a tell-tale chirping sound that means the battery power is running low, or sooner if needed. Keep spare batteries on hand. Some people like to change batteries whenever daylight savings time comes around.

Replace light bulbs every three years, or as needed. Keep extras handy. And replace damaged parts as soon as they break.

Check the alarm on a smoke detector every thirty days by pushing the test button or releasing smoke in the detector's vicinity. Also test the device if you have been away from home for more than a few days.

Clean a detector's face and grillwork at least once a month (usually at the same time you test the alarm) to remove dust and grease. Use a vacuum cleaner tool to get rid of dust and cobwebs that could impair a detector's sensitivity.

FLAMMABLE LIQUIDS

Flammable liquids are especially dangerous because they give off vapors that burn. That's why you shouldn't use flammable liquids to clean equipment or floors. The vapors collect and can be set off by a single spark, a lighted cigarette, or even a gas appliance pilot light.

Gasoline is the main cause of serious flammable liquid fires. Its frequent use with recreational vehicles, lawn mowers, and power tools is the primary source of troubles. Many of the accidents result from refueling equipment that is still hot enough to ignite gasoline vapors. Let lawn mower, garden tractor, weed trimmer and other gasoline engines sit and cool before refilling their tanks. Always handle gasoline fueling outdoors if possible, where the vapors can easily disburse, instead of inside a closed garage or shed where vapors can collect and create fire and explosion hazards.

Store gasoline in approved safety cans and, whenever possible, keep it in an outside shed or separate storage building other than in the house or in an attached garage. The shed should have good ventilation.

Other liquids emit vapors that can easily catch fire or explode, including kerosene, paints, thinners, strippers, adhesives and acetone. Try to limit the amounts you have on hand to only enough to do the jobs they are planned for.

OUTDOOR FIRE PREVENTION

Clean up debris on your property. Dead tree limbs, tall weeds, and shrubs or bushes that have lots of dry grass and leaves caught in their branches can cause the smallest fire to spread to your home in a matter of seconds. Anyone who has experienced grass fires or forest fires during a draught can attest to just how serious a situation this can be. Look at your yard. If a fire were to approach from any direction, what would its path encounter? If the answer is a lot of dry, dead vegetation and other flammable materials, you'd better revise your landscaping into a more fire-resistant plan.

For barbecues, use an electric starter or barbecue starter fuel designed for that purpose. Avoid using gasoline, kerosene, or other flammable liquids. Never, never try to "freshen" a fire by squirting more starter fluid onto hot coals. Never leave a grill unattended. You never know who could enter your yard. A child could wander in, or a pet could dash by, knocking a flimsy barbecue grill to the ground. Store unused charcoal in a cool, dry place because damp coal can ignite itself.

Reactions to outdoor fires should include calling the fire department and wetting down buildings and materials that may be near or adjacent to flames—if it can be done safely—and closing windows and doors. Keep the wind direction in mind and never get trapped with the flames between you and your only means of escape.

If a vehicle catches fire while you're inside of it, turn off the ignition, get out of the car, and move away—in case of a possible explosion. Call the fire department.

HOLIDAY FIRE PREVENTION

More on holiday fire prevention is found in the chapter on holiday safety, but remember that the two weeks comprising the Christmas and New Year's holidays bring electrical, heating system, wood burning stove, fireplace and open candle-flame fires each year.

To keep your home safe, use fire-resistant decorations; use only lights that carry a testing laboratory safety seal of approval. Water cut evergreen trees daily, and keep them away from heat sources. Be sure to turn out tree lights and other electrical decorations when you go to bed. After the holidays properly dispose of used wrapping paper and rubbish as soon as possible—don't burn them in the fireplace.

Halloween is another holiday that can spell trouble—with open candles in pumpkins and other decorations. Costumes should be made of fire-resistant materials. Use flashlights or other lights, never candles, for illumination effects indoors and out. Don't leave pumpkins with candles burning inside while no one is at home or while you are sleeping.

FIRE EXTINGUISHER USE

Fire extinguishers look easy to use, but during a real emergency, things happen fast. Household members should read instructions on how to use an extinguisher *before* it is needed. Here are some points to consider about fire extinguisher use.

If only one fire extinguisher will be purchased, it should be a multipurpose ABC dry chemical extinguisher, to cover the possibility of all three basic types of fires.

Inspect fire extinguishers at least every month. Keep records of the inspections by fastening a durable tag showing the inspection dates and any recharges that may have been necessary (Figure 1-9). Look at the pressure gauge to make sure the extinguisher hasn't developed a slow leak that has partially discharged the tank. Does the gauge still read in the safe zone? It should. Is the extinguisher pin still in place? Lift the extinguisher off its bracket to check its overall condition and to make sure it's easy to remove in case of an emergency. Weigh carbon dioxide extinguishers every six months to see if the contents are leaking. Don't expel contents of regular or multipurpose dry chemical extinguishers in an effort to check them. Once any amount has been used, they should be recharged. If repairs or adjustments are needed, have them made by a professional fire equipment company technician.

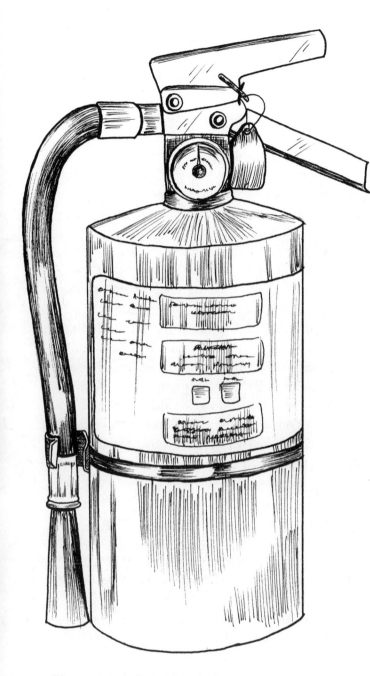

Figure 1-9. A fire extinguisher.

Place fire extinguishers so there is at least one per floor, near exits and in full view so they can be reached quickly and easily. Consider placing extinguishers in the garage, at the head of the basement stairs, near the kitchen, and near any wood-burning appliances or portable heating units that are in service.

Use the extinguisher only if everyone is out of the area and the fire is still small. If there is any doubt as to whether the extinguisher will do the

trick, get everyone out of the house and call the fire department. Never let a fire get between you and the only escape route.

To use the extinguisher, pull the pin, aim the extinguisher nozzle at the base of the flames, squeeze the handle, and use a rapid, sweeping motion vertically or horizontally from about six to eight feet away from the fire, covering from the base of the flames to just above the top or from side to side, making sure to start in front of the flames and to end just beyond the flames.

FIRE ESCAPE PLANNING

Despite the best prevention efforts, an accidental fire is still possible. Household members should discuss what to do in case of a fire, including how everyone will escape. Draw a floor plan of your residence. Indicate where doors, windows, bedrooms, stairways, hallways, ledges and roofs are. Mark the exits and alternate escape routes. Stress the importance of staying calm. Panic will increase a person's chance of breathing in smoke or toxic gases—and making a bad judgement call that could injure someone.

Rooms should ideally have at least two escape routes. Windows should unlock and open easily. Escape ladders may be needed upstairs if there is no nearby roof. Chain ladders (see Figure 1-10) are available through mail order catalogs and in lock and security shops, hardware stores or building supply centers. Store them near the windows or under beds. Practice using them.

Remember that smoke and poisonous gases rise with hot air from the flames. Instruct family members to crawl along the floor where smoke and fume concentrations are the lowest. It's best to hold a wet cloth to your face and take short breaths.

In the event of a fire, bedroom doors should be closed to prevent the flames from spreading. Feel the door before opening it. If it's cool, brace yourself against it, turn your face away, and open it carefully. Slam it shut again if you notice any smoke or heat coming from the opening. Don't open a door that feels unusually warm or hot to the touch; get out a different way.

Escape routes such as doors, windows, stairways and hallways must be kept clear. People might

Figure 1-10. An escape ladder.

need to negotiate them in the dark. Never paint windows shut so they can't be opened.

If you must break a window that can't be opened, first make sure all doors to the room are closed (in general, open doors and windows will help spread a fire). Then stand to the window's side as you swing an object such as a chair or unplugged floor lamp base toward the glass. Carefully remove sharp pieces of glass from the frame, then place a double-folded blanket or other thick cloth over the windowsill.

If you can't escape through the window open-

ing, signal for help by waving a sheet or other light-colored article in the window.

Jump from a window only as a last resort, especially if you are two or more stories from the ground. If jumping is your only option, first hang by your hands from a windowsill, then let go. Bend your knees to help cushion your landing.

Decide on a meeting place outside where every household member knows to gather. Hold practice drills, some of them at night so everyone will know what to do and be able to act quickly in an emergency. Assign a family member to help the elderly or very young escape. In the event of a real fire, *do not go back into a burning house* for personal belongings or a pet. Fire fighters have a far better chance of rescuing trapped people.

If you're trapped, try to get to a room with a window, then seal doorways and vents from smoke and gases (stuff clothing or other soft material under the door). Call the fire department if a phone is available. Open a window toward the top of the room to let out smoke; open a window toward the bottom to breathe fresh air and signal for rescue. If smoke is rising from a lower floor, however, don't open a window—stand at the window and signal with a sheet or brightly colored cloth if possible.

If your clothes catch fire, stop, drop to the ground with your arms folded across your chest, and try to roll the flames out—in a blanket, heavy coat or rug if possible, to smother the flames—until someone can spray you with water.

Teach children how to warn others, leave the house, and call for help if a fire occurs. Each member of the family should have his or her own flashlight.

Make sure everyone in the household knows that preserving life is the first consideration and that no action—even calling the fire department—should be taken until all family members are warned of the fire. The most important job is getting everyone out first.

Inform baby-sitters what to do in case of a fire. The fire department phone number should be posted at every phone in the house.

✓

FIRE PREVENTION
QUICK CHECKLIST

☐ Remember that fire needs three elements to exist: fuel, oxygen, and a source of heat or ignition.

☐ See that no electrical hazards are present.

☐ Maintain good housekeeping; eliminate clutter.

☐ Never smoke in bed; dispose of butts carefully; and secure matches, lighters and candles from children.

☐ Follow all safety procedures when using furnaces, fireplaces, wood stoves and space heaters.

☐ Use portable kerosene or electric heaters only if main heating systems cannot be modified to heat areas in question.

☐ With kerosene heaters, use the correct fuel, provide adequate ventilation, don't refuel a hot unit, and keep flammables and combustibles away. Turn kerosene heaters off when you go to sleep or leave the house.

☐ If possible, avoid using extension cords with portable electric heaters or, at the very least, use extension cords with power ratings heavy enough to handle the job.

☐ Have fireplace and wood-burning stove systems installed by professionals, and inspected yearly by the same. Look for and correct dangerous levels of creosote in chimneys.

☐ Burn only dry, seasoned hardwoods and other materials manufactured explicitly for clean wood-burning use.

☐ Burn small, hot fires in fireplaces and wood-burning stoves. Don't "freshen" a dying fire by squirting flammable liquid into a wood-burning unit.

☐ Regularly inspect fireplace and wood-burning stove chimneys and flues.

☐ Always use a spark screen or a set of heat-resistant glass doors in front of a fireplace. Never leave a fire unattended.

☐ Unplug heating appliances such as irons, toasters, hot plates and space heaters after each use.

☐ Don't cook on stove tops while wearing loose, long-sleeved clothing. Keep combustibles away from stove-top burners.

☐ If you're called away to answer a door bell, phone, or child's request while cooking with oil, temporarily remove the oil from the stove top.

FIRE PREVENTION QUICK CHECKLIST
(continued)

☐ Use back cook-top burners whenever possible; keep pan handles from extending over the front.

☐ Keep multipurpose ABC fire extinguishers near high-risk areas. Make sure all family members know how to use the extinguishers.

☐ Use good smoke detectors, and keep fresh batteries in them. Test detectors at least every month or after the household has been vacant for a few days.

☐ Store gasoline in outbuildings or sheds, in approved safety containers. Handle all fueling and refueling tasks outdoors, if possible.

☐ Try to purchase only as much flammable liquids as you need for a particular job.

☐ Clean dry leaves, dead branches, and other tinder-like vegetation from your yard.

☐ Never start or freshen charcoal fires by squirting flammable liquid on the briquettes. Don't let a charcoal fire burn unattended.

☐ During holidays, be especially cautious with decorations, candles, Christmas trees and jack-o-lanterns.

☐ Household members should know how to use a fire extinguisher *before* the extinguisher is really needed. Inspect the gauge on the extinguisher every few months.

☐ Use a fire extinguisher only if a fire is still small and everyone else is out of the area.

☐ All household members should know what to do in case of a fire. Practice fire drills several times per year.

☐ Rooms should have two reasonable means of escape.

☐ In the event of a fire, crawl on your hands and knees on the floor. Feel doors before opening them—if they're very warm or hot, keep them closed.

☐ Keep all escape routes such as doors, windows, stairways and hallways clear.

☐ Post the fire department phone number at every phone in the house.

☐ Teach children how to warn others, leave the house and call for help.

CHAPTER 2

ELECTRICAL SAFETY

All things considered, electricity is our most valuable energy resource. Can you think of a residence that can do without it? Electrical energy does it all: It powers equipment from the simplest electric shaver to the most complex heating and cooling systems; it provides light; it even helps transmit sounds. Where would your television or stereo be without it?

Although we use electricity day in and day out, few of us truly understand what electricity is and how it works. It's invisible. That's one problem. Unless sparks are flying or smoke is coming from somewhere it shouldn't, an electrically charged wire, component or piece of equipment can appear to be harmless. And because electricity is such a common, everyday part of life, people tend to forget how dangerous it really is.

A common perception is that "normal" electricity, the kind available at typical household outlets, is not very dangerous. In fact, at one time or another, most people have experienced mild electrical shock and never considered it to be harmful or even dangerous. Nothing could be further from the truth. *All electricity should be considered dangerous*. It doesn't take much electricity to kill someone.

WHAT IS ELECTRICITY?

Put simply, electricity is an energy source created by an imbalance of electrons in tiny building blocks of matter called atoms. As the electrons try to "correct" or "balance out" their unequal distribution, they're driven by a force or electrical pressure called "voltage" to move in what's known as an electrical current. A higher voltage can force more current through your body easier than a lower voltage can. A higher voltage can cause violent muscular contractions, often so severe that the victim is thrown clear of the circuit. Although low voltage also results in muscular contractions, the effect is not so violent. Low voltage, however, often prevents the victim from freeing him or herself from the circuit. This is what makes contact with low voltage dangerous. In fact, 120 volts (common household electrical service) is the most common voltage that electrocutes people today. A lower voltage might appear to be harmless, but it can be deadly if a victim is exposed to it over a long period of time.

Current flow is the factor that causes injury in electrical shock. In general, the longer a current is allowed to flow through a body, the more damage is done. A person's resistance to current flow is found mainly in his or her skin resistance. Callous or dry skin has a fairly high resistance, but a sharp decrease in resistance occurs when the skin becomes moist or wet.

Electricity can be "manufactured" or generated for our use in a number of ways. Nuclear power plants can produce it, and so can hydroelectric power plants, which are constructed along rivers and other bodies of moving water where water currents are used to drive rotating equipment that generates electricity. But most electricity is produced at large power stations that burn coal or oil to heat water. The water is heated until it creates steam, and the steam then spins turbines that generate electricity. The resulting electricity is carried along thick wires from the power plant. To send the electricity over long distances, the voltage is increased by transformers. When the electricity reaches cities or towns, the voltage is reduced by other transformers for home use.

Electricity travels through a system of wires much like water travels through pipes. One main difference, however, is if a water pipe breaks, the water continues to flow and will spill out from the break. Not so with electricity. If a wire breaks, the flow of electricity will stop because electricity needs a complete circuit to flow. A circuit is a path that returns to its power source or point of origin, in a circular fashion. A broken wire, a loose connection, a switch in the off position, or a short-circuiting of the circuit by some other electrical conducting material can all cause the original circuit to be broken.

Metals such as copper and aluminum are used to transmit electricity because those materials are good conductors—electricity flows through them easily, and does not meet with much resistance. Water is another good conductor of electricity, and so is the human body, by virtue of its watery nature. Most non-metals, such as rubber and plastics, glass and wood are poor conductors of electricity. That's why they're often referred to as insulators. An extension cord is a good example of both: a metal conductor (the copper wires) protected by an insulator (the rubber coating or exterior).

ELECTRICAL HAZARDS

There are three basic types of electrical hazards: fire, shock and burns.

Fire

In chapter one on fire safety, the three ingredients of fires are discussed: For each fire there must be a source of fuel—something has to be burned or consumed to sustain or feed the fire. There needs to be enough oxygen to keep the burning going, and there must be a source of heat or ignition to start the fire. Electricity is a source of heat. The delivery systems, such as your home's wiring and electrical fuse or circuit boxes, are engineered to prevent electricity from building up enough heat to start fires. Controls and safeguards such as fuses, circuit breakers, ground fault circuit interrupters (GFCIs) and insulators are designed to prevent electricity from being a heat source for fires. A system should shut itself down before temperatures reach the critical level and produce a fire.

Some electric-related fires can be prevented by using safe installation and operating practices. Fires have been associated with electricity use in the following appliances and installations, and others:

Electric cooking appliances
Electric wiring, installation
Radios and televisions
Electric blankets
Electric water heaters and washers
Electric lighting
Electric welding and cutting equipment

To prevent electrical fires, carefully inspect electrical systems, outlets and cords. Follow good housekeeping practices; keep potential fuel sources away from electrical equipment. Perform maintenance on electrical equipment. Faithfully follow manufacturer's recommendations for component replacements, cleanings, filter changes and all repairs, and don't overload circuits and outlets. Never operate equipment that has greater energy demands than your electrical system is engineered to supply.

Shock and Burns

Shocks and burns are often related. Accidental contact with electricity can cause a variety of health consequences, from minor tingling feelings to internal organ damage, burns and even death. Factors that affect the seriousness of injury include:

The type of circuit and voltage. A shock resulting from just enough power to cause a slight tingling, to make your hair stand on end, or to cause an involuntary movement can be harmless. Or it could cause you to lose your balance and fall. Or it could—if the right path is followed through your body—affect a pacemaker or trigger a delicate heart condition. A "medium" shock may result in a loss of muscle control that could prevent you from letting go of or pulling away from the source of shock.

The longer the electricity runs through your body, the more harm it will likely do. Strong shocks can cause internal organ damage, internal and external burns, cardiac arrest and respiratory failure.

PERSONAL PROTECTIVE EQUIPMENT

Naturally, the most effective way to avoid accidental contact with electricity is to de-energize a system you are working on or to just stay away from "live" electrical parts. If that isn't possible, consider hiring a qualified electrician to do the work. At the very least, wear personal protective gear, and follow established safety rules and procedures.

Non-conductive personal protective equipment should be worn when working with or around electricity. Leather gauntlet gloves can be worn over rubber insulated gloves. Rubber is an insulating material and leather is a non-conductive material that will prevent the rubber gloves from being punctured or ripped. Non-metal hard hats can offer protection whenever there's potential for your head coming into contact with an energized source. Safety glasses with side shields should be worn when there is the possibility of sparks and small particles flying through the air.

Metal jewelry such as watches, rings, chains and earrings shouldn't be worn when working around exposed energized parts. The metal items could cause serious burns to the skin.

ELECTRICAL POWER BOXES OR PANELS

A home's main power panel or box can be either a modern circuit-breaker box or an older fuse box. You may eventually need to shut off the home's current through the electrical box for any one of a variety of reasons, for a flooded basement, for instance, or a smoking wall outlet, light switch, fixture or appliance. Never stand on moist or wet soil, concrete, or other floor surfaces while working at a main power fuse or circuit box. (That means if you can't approach the main power box because of a flooded basement, don't attempt it. Call the power company at once, from a safe location.) Always be sure your hands are dry, too. Wear rubber-soled shoes, and keep one hand at your side so you are less likely to inadvertently create a circuit from the panel box through your own body. For the same

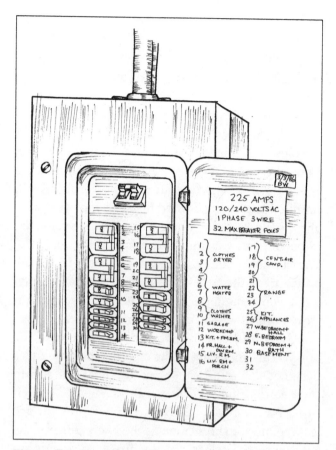

Figure 2-1. An electrical box.

reason, never touch any other grounded metal object such as a freezer or refrigerator while one hand is in contact with the main power box.

To determine when your home's electrical system was last inspected, look at the door or cover of your home's main electric panel box. The panel should contain a label or tag with a date, signature or initials on it (see Figure 2-1). If there is more than one date, the most recent one should be the date of the last inspection. If your last inspection was forty or more years ago, the inspection should be done again—it's long overdue. If the inspection date was more than ten years ago, have it done again, too, especially if substantial electrical loads have been added or overload warning signs are occurring.

Label circuit breakers or fuses according to what they control, so you'll know which ones need attention in case of problems in the system.

If your main circuit breaker or fuse box is within children's reach, lock the box up. Most electrical boxes are equipped with a place to padlock the door.

Fuses

An electrical fuse is a device designed to act as the weakest link in an electrical circuit. When too much electricity is drawn through the system the fuse is connected to, a small strip of metal visible through the glass window of the fuse "burns through" or "blows." Afterward, the fuse may look burned or discolored. A burned fuse cannot be reset. Instead, it must be replaced in the same manner as an electric light bulb. After shutting the main power switch off, simply unscrew the burned fuse and replace it with one of the recommended amperage—usually the same amperage as that of the fuse being replaced. The "bottom" rim of a fuse is insulated and is the only part of the fuse or fuse box you should touch when replacing a damaged fuse. Always stand on a dry surface when accessing the fuse box.

Using a fuse with a higher amperage than the one you are replacing or the one that the circuit was designed for could cause enough heat buildup to start a fire. Some electricians can "read" broken fuses. For example, when the fuse window surface is discolored, a short circuit is the likely cause. If the fuse window is clear and the broken fuse wire inside can be seen, an overloaded circuit is often the cause. After unplugging some of the appliances that were on the circuit when the circuit failed, replace the fuse. If it blows again with fewer items drawing power, there may be an appliance with defective wiring that is causing the power drain. Check each appliance on the circuit for visibly defective wiring or plugs.

Again, the greatest danger with ordinary fuses is that they can be replaced with fuses of heavier capacities. That, of course, defeats the purpose of a correctly rated fuse, which is supposed to blow before an overloaded circuit starts a wiring fire. For that reason it is recommended that only fuses of the correct size be kept on hand to prevent the temptation to put a larger fuse in place "just to get by" until one of the correct capacity can be obtained. In short, never tamper with fuses, or circuit breakers, in an effort to keep them from blowing or tripping.

The clothes washer, dryer, refrigerator, dishwasher, water pump, and other major appliances should have circuits to themselves, usually 20 amps or more each.

Circuit Breakers

Circuit breakers are more modern, improved versions of fuses. If a circuit breaker turns off (or "trips") because too much demand or draw is placed on the part of the wiring the individual circuit breaker represents, simply follow the resetting instructions on the electrical panel box where the breakers are located. Usually that means just flipping the thrown circuit breaker switch back on. The nice thing about circuit breakers is they can't be defeated or altered as easily as fuses. Even so, a tripped circuit breaker means something has overloaded that part of the electrical system. The cause of the overload should be identified and corrected or prevented from happening again. Most often an overload results from too many appliances being operated at the same time, or from running defective electrical equipment. A malfunctioning switch, a worn appliance cord, or a broken plug can all cause circuit breakers to trip.

Sometimes a household can go for years without having a circuit breaker trip. Because of that likelihood, it's a good idea to trip breakers manually a few times per year to make sure the contacts are in working order. To see if they work, simply check the appliances on the circuit while the breaker is tripped. If the appliances still operate while the breaker is tripped, there is something wrong—the breakers aren't providing the safety measure for which they were intended. Circuit breakers can be reset by first switching them off, and then back on.

Remember, if a circuit breaker trips:

1. Unplug whatever appliance you believe caused the problem.
2. Reset the circuit breaker according to the instructions. That usually means just turning it back on.
3. If it trips again and you can't figure out what the problem is, it's time to contact a qualified electrician.

WIRING

Wiring should always be installed and inspected by qualified electricians. All of it should meet or exceed local and national code standards. Typically, a home's main electrical panel or box should be rated for at least 100 amps. If the box or panel isn't clearly labeled, or if the household power is delivered through ungrounded outlets designed for the older style of two-pronged plugs, the wiring system should be upgraded or replaced.

Wiring, and all electrical equipment for that matter, should be "grounded"—connected to the ground through contact with a ground wire in a three-pronged plug, or, as many clothes washers have, by a wire that acts as a ground by being fastened to a copper cold-water plumbing line. The grounding helps prevent electricity from taking a shortcut through a person who touches a "live" wire or appliance.

If a circuit breaker becomes overloaded because it is trying to draw more electricity than it was designed to provide, this is a major wiring concern. Overloads frequently occur when something that requires a lot of energy—a toaster or clothes iron, for example—is plugged in and operated while a number of other appliances are being run from the same circuit. Sometimes an overloaded circuit may not blow a fuse or trip a circuit. It could manifest itself in other ways—light bulbs may dim, toasters and irons may heat slowly or never reach their potential, or electric motors may change speeds when other appliances are turned on. Plus, if the fuses or circuit breaker switches don't function properly, the appliances being run on an overloaded circuit may be damaged beyond repair.

Again, in many older homes the electrical systems are hopelessly outdated and should be replaced entirely. Knob-and-tube wiring and limited fuse-box services should be pulled out in favor of more modern, heavy-duty wiring. If you have doubts about the safety of any wiring system, warning signs include warm cover plates on switches and outlets, dead outlets, flickering lights, or smoke coming from outlets or appliances. Also watch out for live wires hanging from the ceiling, or switches, outlets and junction boxes without covers—revealing bare wires within.

ELECTRICAL OUTLETS

If you have young children at home, or children visit your residence occasionally, use safety caps—plastic inserts—on all unused electrical outlets, including extra ports on extension cords. Toddlers are otherwise likely to touch an open outlet with their finger, a coat hanger, a paper clip or anything else they find, which could result in a serious electrical shock.

Make sure all plugs are completely inserted into outlets, so no part of the plug's prongs are exposed. Have an electrician replace any outlet that doesn't hold a plug firmly. Contacts in an outlet can wear out, causing uneven operation of an appliance or overheating inside of the outlet. An outlet with nothing plugged into it can still run hot if it is passing current through to other outlets on the same circuit. Outlets that feel warm or hot, that emit smoke or sparks, or in which plugged-in appliances turn on and off, flicker, or fail to work at all, must be replaced or taken out of service completely.

Face plates on all outlets should be present and intact so wiring won't be exposed. Sometimes plastic face plates will crack in half (see Figure 2-2) and be kept in place in a loose manner, falling apart whenever someone uses the outlet. A new face plate costs only a few cents.

Simple test kits are available to make sure your outlets are properly grounded. Ungrounded outlets are a safety hazard and can wreak havoc with expensive electronic equipment such as computers and stereo systems. You can't tell just by appearances—even modern-looking three-pronged outlets are not necessarily grounded.

To prevent damage to outlets, appliances should be turned off before they are unplugged. Avoid unplugging cords by yanking them out of an outlet. It's tough on the cord and plug, and the sideways pressure can crack the plastic face plate, exposing live parts of the outlet.

GFCIs should be installed in outlets where electrical appliances will be used near moisture or water—in outdoor outlets, near swimming pools, and in basements, bathrooms and kitchens, for example. The GFCI quickly detects a fault, short-circuit or electrical leak, then shuts off the power to prevent accidental shocks. To make sure that GFCIs will work when you need them, test them once a month. To check a particular unit press the *test* button. The interrupter should then indicate *open* or *off* and should disconnect the power from the circuit in question. Start the *reset* switch to restore power. If

Figure 2-2. Face plates.

you have a home without GFCIs, have a qualified electrician install them where needed—in bathrooms, kitchens, garages and basements. If you want to install GFCI protection yourself, plug-in units can be purchased to safeguard individual outlets.

EXTENSION CORDS

You've probably noticed that all extension cords are not alike. Some are short, some are long. Some are thin, and some are thick. Some are well made, others are flimsy. To get the right cord for the job, ask yourself what you'll be using it for.

If an extension cord is needed for outdoor duty, for running an electric hedge trimmer or lawn mower, for example, you'll need a heavy-duty cord rated for outside use. If you'll be using it to operate a small electric radio, for listening to a baseball game while playing cards, an inexpensive, lightweight cord will do the trick. If you need a cord to run more than one appliance, a model with a double or triple socket may be just right. The cord's plug should also match your home's outlets; three-pronged receptacles should use only three-pronged plugs. Whenever possible, avoid using adapters to plug three-pronged plugs into two-hole outlets. Never remove

the third prong on a plug to create a two-pronged plug.

Remember that the sum of the electrical loads connected to an extension cord must never exceed the electrical capacity of the cord. How can you tell? The cord should have its electrical capacity marked in amperes or watts. Appliances and other electrical components or equipment should be marked with the same information.

If there are no markings on a cord, and you suspect it can't safely handle what's on it, feel the cord. If it's warm or hot to the touch, it's overloaded. Heated cord insulation can eventually harden and crumble, or it can melt. The insulating plastic on many extension cords will melt at about 250 degrees Fahrenheit. If the wires inside eventually touch each other, or touch something on the outside such as a metal floor lamp, sparks or electrical shock could result.

Avoid using extension cords as permanent fixtures. They should not be run beneath carpets, through doorways, or stapled to a wall. Either install additional permanent outlets or arrange appliances so existing outlets will suffice.

Unplug and remove extension cords that aren't being used, especially if babies and toddlers are at home. Crawling babies, infants, and even pets in the teething/chewing stages could be attracted to bright-colored extension cords and may treat the rubber-coated cords as chew toys. If the cord is plugged in, the child's or pet's saliva could cause a short circuit between the metal parts of the cord's outlet. The short circuit could heat up enough to cause severe burns to the child or pet's mouth and throat.

For safer extension cords, purchase models that come with safety caps that seal off any unused receptacles on the cord.

APPLIANCE CORDS AND PLUGS

Check all cords and plugs for damage. A worn, cracked, twisted, knotted or kinked cord can cause electrical shock if touched, with short circuits causing heat and possibly fires. Replace worn or cracked appliance cords and plugs—don't just tape up the damaged parts.

Avoid wrapping cords around or draping cords over hot furnace pipes, space heaters or radiators. The heat may dry out or scorch the cord's insulation.

An arrangement where an appliance cord dangles from the front or side of a table or counter is not a safe one. A pet, child or adult could snag the cord and pull the appliance onto the floor. To reduce the risk of a child chewing or playing with a cord, try to run electrical cords behind furniture—while making sure the cords are not beneath carpeting or trapped under the leg of a sofa or easy chair.

Newer plugs and electrical outlets have one metal prong that's wider than the other, and one outlet slot that can accommodate the wider prong. This is called polarization. Polarized plugs help prevent electrical shock. The wider prong can only be inserted in the "neutral" side of the outlet. Electricity flows from the narrow-prong side which is attached to the hot or "live" wire. The hot wire is the wire that's actually attached to whatever switch is being used for the electrical appliance or piece of equipment. At the same time, for example, a lamp plug is situated so the neutral wire "takes control" of the lamp to prevent someone from getting a shock while replacing a light bulb.

If you have to push very hard to fit a plug into an outlet, make sure you're not forcing a wide prong into a narrow hole. You'll defeat the safety benefits achieved through polarization.

ELECTRICAL APPLIANCES AND FIXTURES

All electrical appliances, including units wired directly into a household's electrical system, such as water heaters and furnaces, should display a seal from a certified testing laboratory. One commonly found testing laboratory symbol is UL, representing Underwriters Laboratories.

Never operate electrical appliances while touching metal objects (especially plumbing) or other good conductors, while standing on a wet surface, or while your hands are wet. If an appliance smokes, smells, sparks or gives a shock at any time, unplug it or turn off the electricity, then have the appliance inspected and repaired or replaced, if necessary.

Keep electric motors free from buildups of dust, dirt, lint, and lubricating oil. Space heaters, toasters, irons, and other heat-producing electrical appliances and components require extra care to minimize fire hazards. Never place combustibles such as paper, drapes or furniture near them. Keep heating appliances clean, in proper condition, and out of high-traffic areas. Unplug these appliances, if possible, after each use. Let them cool before storing them in a safe place. Avoid using lightweight extension cords with heat-producing appliances. If an extension cord must be temporarily used, select a heavy-duty model with enough capacity to handle the appliance, so the cord will not get warm to the touch.

Space heaters should be equipped with thermostats so they won't just run on and on by themselves, despite the room temperature. Another important feature is an automatic shut-off in case the unit is accidentally tipped over.

Unless you're skilled in electronic appliance repair, never attempt to troubleshoot or fix malfunctioning appliances yourself. Touching parts inside of a television set or other electronic unit could cause a severe shock, even when the power cord is unplugged. And an error in reassembly may result in radiation emissions.

Ventilation openings in electronic appliance

cabinets and computer cases allow heat generated during operation to be released. If those openings are blocked, heat buildup within the unit can cause failures that could result in a fire hazard, so:

- Never block the ventilation slots of a portable television by placing the set on a bed, sofa, shag rug or other cushioned surface.
- Avoid putting the unit in a built-in enclosure such as a wood cabinet unless proper ventilation is provided.
- Don't put electronic appliances over a heat register or near a radiator.

Caution children about dropping or pushing objects into television and other electronic cabinet openings. Again, some internal parts carry hazardous voltages and contact can result in electrical shock.

Never operate an electronic appliance if liquid has been spilled into it. Rain or excessive moisture may cause electrical shorts that could result in fire or shock hazards. Unplug such a unit and have it inspected by a service technician before further use.

Water and electricity can be a deadly combination. Plugged-in bathroom, kitchen or other appliances can cause shock and electrocution if they fall into a bathtub or sink when you're taking a bath or washing up—even if they're turned off. It's nice to listen to a radio or to have an electric clock in the bathroom or kitchen, just keep them away from water sources and out of the reach of wet hands. If an appliance that is plugged in falls into water, never reach in for it. Cut the power first—throw the bathroom circuit breaker or pull the correct fuse. When you're certain the circuit is shut off, open the tub drain, then unplug the offending appliance and pull it out of the tub.

Inspect electric blankets to make sure there are no cracks in their wiring, plugs or connectors. Avoid folding an electric blanket while the blanket is turned on—it may overheat and catch fire. Use an electric blanket as the top cover; never place other coverings or anything heavy on top of an electric blanket. Also avoid tucking any wired parts of an electric blanket beneath a mattress. The plug or connector joining the control to the electric blanket or pad should be fully inserted and firmly connected.

Always unplug appliances before cleaning them, removing parts, and repairing or adjusting components. Never leave electrical appliances running when you're not home, especially appliances that generate heat with their operation, including stoves, clothes dryers, irons, dishwashers and space heaters.

As children mature and begin to use more electrical appliances, remind them that fish tank accessories, a radio, a lamp, a clock and a clothes iron cannot all be plugged into the same socket. Teach your children to look for frayed cords, warm wires, sparks, or anything that looks, smells, sounds or feels suspicious. Emphasize zero energy—that no item should be fooled with while it's plugged in—even if it's turned off at the time.

Always follow the manufacturer's instructions when using electrical fixtures. If a lamp comes with a label specifying that a 40-watt bulb is the maximum-rated bulb to use, don't try a 60-watt model. The label is saying that the 40-watt bulb runs at the maximum current the lamp can safely handle.

Never leave light-bulb sockets empty in wired-in lighting fixtures or when portable lamps are plugged in. The urge for a young child to stick his or her finger in the vacant socket can be too tempting.

Recessed lighting fixtures should be positioned within vented metal cylinders, cages or protectors to shield surrounding insulation and construction materials from the fixture's heat. Some recessed lighting fixtures are available with a device that interrupts electrical power to the unit when it overheats for any reason. Inquire at building material stores and specialty lighting shops.

Before working on any fixture, be sure that the electrical supply to that unit has been shut off.

During a storm, lightning that strikes near power lines may cause brief high-voltage spikes or surges in your home's electrical system. These surges, if allowed to course through your wiring system, could damage appliances such as televisions, stereos, computers, and other units with solid-state circuitry. Protect electronic equipment from lightning by either unplugging it during electrical storms, or by using surge protectors (see Figure 2-3). Surge protectors are devices that reduce unusually high voltages before those power bursts can enter an appliance.

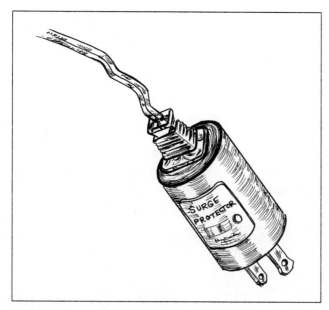

Figure 2-3. A surge protector.

When using power tools, the operator should dress properly. Rubber-soled shoes and rubber gloves should be worn when working in wet areas. Avoid loose-fitting clothes that could become entangled in rotating equipment. Remove rings, bracelets, wristwatches and other jewelry while operating power tools. Sawdust, shavings, rags and other debris should be kept from piling up where they could create a fire hazard or cause tools to overheat by blocking proper ventilation.

If you have any life-sustaining equipment at home, such as respirators, kidney machines or monitors, register them with your local electric utility company. Your physician or medical equipment supplier should agree on what measures to take to provide a backup power supply in case of a power outage.

OUTDOOR ELECTRICAL SAFETY

A few commonsense guidelines will help you make the most of outdoor electrical use. First, make sure outdoor electrical outlets are weatherproof and protected by GFCIs. All outdoor lighting fixtures, extension cords, holiday decorations and other accessories should be designed for outdoor use.

Avoid using electric lawn mowers or other power tools during wet conditions, if possible. Never operate any electrical equipment while bare-

foot. Wear rubber-soled shoes or boots instead.

Turn off circuits or unplug extension cords before hanging or adjusting outdoor lighting fixtures and decorations.

Antennas should be properly grounded and wired to lightning arresters. Homes in locations subject to frequent electrical storms should have lightning rods professionally installed.

Keep away from power lines, especially when performing tasks where equipment could come into contact with electrical lines, such as working with ladders, dump trucks, roofs, gutters and antennas. Touching power lines with antennas, metal ladders, kite line or metal poles are major causes of electrocution associated with "household" outdoor electrical shock. In most antenna accidents, the antenna hits an overhead power line when the antenna is being removed or installed. Victims fail to notice where the power line is, misjudge the distance to a line, or the antenna and mast assembly is too heavy to be controlled, and it falls onto the line. Metal ladders are notorious for electric shock fatalities. Contact often occurs when the victim, while painting or doing roof or gutter work, fails to check the location of the power line in relation to the work area. Some people believe a covering on the power line will protect them, but coverings can't be trusted. A metal ladder scratching through a covering and touching the bare wire could easily cause a fatal shock.

To prevent power line troubles:

• Locate antennas a safe distance from power lines, a horizontal distance of at least twice the length of the antenna should separate the antenna from the nearest point of the power line.

• When taking down or installing antennas, line up enough help to safely control the structure. It's also a good idea to designate an official observer, whose job it is to watch the work and help if needed.

• Avoid installing or working with antennas during windy or wet weather.

• When working with a ladder near power lines, use a non-conductive ladder made of fiberglass or wood.

• Fly kites in open areas, far away from power lines. Avoid kite flying in wet, stormy weather. A wet kite string is a good conductor of electricity and may cause electrocution if it touches a power line. If a kite gets caught in a power line, don't attempt to remove it. Notify the electric utility company instead.

If arcing (when a luminous bridge is formed between two separated terminals or conductors of electricity) or sparks occur anywhere outside your home, from wires rubbing against trees or parts of the house, don't try to correct the problem yourself or touch any of the affected items. Call the electric company immediately. They, or emergency personnel such as firemen, are the only ones authorized to turn off the power and inspect the damage to that part of your electric service.

Locate underground wires before digging. Contact your local electric utility well in advance of the excavation or digging day. One call will usually result in the different utility companies all coming to flag where any of their underground lines are located. These can include cable television, electrical, natural gas, water and phone lines.

Monitor the status of trees in relation to power lines and your electric "drop" lines (a line that connects or drops down toward your home from the main power supply). Keep foliage trimmed away from power lines. Contact the electric company if major pruning work is needed.

IF SOMEONE CONTACTS ELECTRICITY

If someone comes in contact with electricity, bystanders must be extremely careful with rescue attempts. Although every second of contact with the electrical source may cause more serious consequences, avoid actions which could result in a rescuer being injured as well.

First, the victim's contact with the source of current must be broken in the quickest and safest way possible (while this is occurring, someone else should be calling 911 for emergency help). Don't touch the victim or anything the victim is in contact with in a manner that could "freeze" you into the same position as the victim's. If the victim is in contact with a ladder or antenna, those items are probably electrically charged, too. Disconnect an appliance plug or pull the main switch at the fuse or circuit box. If the source of current is from a utility power line, call 911 and the power company at once,

because there is no safe way for you to shut off the current. Keep everyone away from the victim and from downed power lines until professionals arrive.

If you have broken the flow of current, check the victim for breathing and pulse, bleeding and burns. Don't move a victim unless absolutely necessary. If you must move an injured person for safety reasons, move the body lengthwise (not sideways) and head first, with the head and neck firmly supported.

PRECAUTIONS

Certain everyday events having to do with electricity can easily turn into tragedies you'll never forget. Here are some:

For instance, electric shavers have dropped into sinks that were partially full of water and electrocuted people who tried to retrieve them without unplugging them first. Make sure your face and hands are dry and do not shave with water in the basin. Leg-shavers should stick to the same principles.

If a toaster becomes stuck in the down position with food inside, turn off and unplug the unit before trying to dislodge the food. Let the toaster cool somewhat, then remove the item with a wooden tool—a spoon, fork or spatula.

When an overhead electric light bulb needs changing, turn off the electricity at the switch. Switch off table or standard portable lamps and unplug the lamp before you change a bulb or clean a lampshade. Allow time for the bulb to cool if it's still too hot to handle. If you can't tell if the light switch is on or off—due to more than one switch operating it—then simply throw the correct breaker or pull the proper fuse to the room or circuit before changing the bulb.

Renovations need to be carried out carefully. Never just chisel or saw or drill away into a wall. You could accidentally strike electric wiring. Since it's difficult to know where electric lines run behind walls, turn off the electricity at the main box for the brief time it takes to cut or drill through the wall.

And finally, never hesitate to call a certified electrician if you have any doubts of which way to proceed. Electricity is nothing to take chances with.

ELECTRICAL SAFETY QUICK CHECKLIST

☐ Remember that electricity is invisible and dangerous. Even common "household" electrical current can kill.

☐ Electrical systems must be installed and periodically inspected by professional qualified electricians.

☐ Avoid trying to draw more power than your system or any of its parts are designed to provide.

☐ Prevent electrical fires by developing good housekeeping habits, keeping flammables away from heat sources, and making sure that electrical appliances, equipment and components are inspected and well maintained.

☐ Wear non-conductive personal protective equipment when the possibility of accidental contacts with electrical components exist. Never use equipment made of metal.

☐ Avoid wearing metal jewelry or other accessories around electrical wiring or components.

☐ Never attempt to access a power box, wiring, or even appliances that are turned off but plugged in, while you're wet or standing on a wet or damp surface.

☐ Circuit breakers and fuses should all be labeled as to which areas and major appliances they service.

☐ Avoid replacing blown fuses with fuses of higher-rated capacities.

☐ If a circuit breaker trips, attempt to find out why. Call a certified electrician for help if needed.

☐ Make sure your electrical system is properly grounded, and your outlets are all grounded as well.

☐ With older electrical systems, watch out for trouble symptoms such as warm cover plates on outlets and switches, flickering lights, motors running at erratic speeds, dead outlets, and smoke coming from outlets or appliances.

☐ Use plastic safety caps on all unused electrical outlet ports.

☐ Turn appliances off before you pull their plugs out of electrical sockets.

☐ Install ground-fault-circuit-interrupters in outlets where electrical appliances will be used near damp or wet conditions. Test the GFCI units monthly.

ELECTRICAL SAFETY QUICK CHECKLIST
(continued)

☐ Be especially careful with electricity when you're near water or moist environments.

☐ Follow manufacturer recommendations for extension cord usage. Extension cords should not be "permanent" electrical solutions.

☐ Never break the third prong off a three-pronged plug so it will fit in a two-pronged receptacle.

☐ An extension or other electrical cord should not be warm or hot to the touch—if it is, there are too many appliances or too large a draw on the same cord.

☐ Unplug and remove extension cords that aren't being used.

☐ Inspect appliance and extension cords and plugs frequently. Keep all cords out of the sight and reach of babies and toddlers.

☐ Insist on knowing that an electrical appliance has been given a seal of approval by a recognizable product safety testing service such as Underwriters Laboratories (UL).

☐ Unless you're thoroughly qualified, don't try to repair televisions, stereos, or any parts of your home's electrical system.

☐ Avoid cleaning or doing any work on appliances or electrical components that are plugged in or energized. Unplug them or shut power down so you can't be accidentally shocked or electrocuted.

☐ To protect electronic equipment from high-voltage spikes caused by lightning or other abnormal situations, use surge protectors.

☐ Be aware of the location of outdoor power lines. Be especially careful with antennas, metal ladders, dump trucks, and while working on roofs, siding or gutters.

☐ Keep tree branches and other foliage trimmed away from power lines.

☐ Be extremely careful if trying to separate someone who is being shocked from the source of electricity they are touching.

CHAPTER 3

SAFE MATERIAL HANDLING

I n one way or another, material handling tasks account for many of the typical household hazards.

Most material handling concerns revolve around avoiding slips, trips and falls, around lifting/back injury prevention, around hand and arm safety, and around the use of ladders.

SLIPS, TRIPS AND FALLS

Have you ever said something you know you shouldn't have, only to regret it moments later? That's known as a slip of the tongue. Or talking before you think. "What a homely little baby," you say to a woman standing next to you on a pediatrics floor in a hospital. Seconds later you learn that the newborn you made fun of behind the viewing glass is the lady's granddaughter. You've made an enemy for life. Or "I hear our new boss is a real blockhead," you remark to a stranger you meet at a winter cocktail party—right before you find out that he's the new guy's brother from Cleveland.

Offhand comments like those can get a person in trouble. They might seem minor at the time, but they can have long-range implications and do long-term harm.

It's a simple fact that many things in life that which *seem* minor can easily develop into major problems. Take people slipping, tripping and falling down, for instance. That may sound humorous, but it's not. In fact, every year in the United States alone, falls kill about thirteen thousand people at home,

at work or at play. On top of that, about fourteen million others are injured enough to need medical care.

Most of these incidents are not dramatic "fall off a bridge" type incidents. Most of the falls that injure people result from slips and trips that happen at or near floor level. Slips are caused by a wide variety of conditions, but most can be attributed to hurrying and walking carelessly on uneven, slippery or unstable surfaces. Trips also contribute heavily to accidental falls. They're usually caused by hurrying or carelessness while walking through cluttered, dark or unfamiliar territory.

Like a slip of the tongue, a slip of the body can best be prevented in a similar fashion: by thinking before you act.

Here are some pointers to think about:

Wear sturdy shoes with low, non-skid soles and rubber (not leather or hard plastic) heels. The lower the profile, the better.

Use a ladder, not a stack of boxes or a swivel chair to reach high places. Know how to use ladders safely.

Allow yourself plenty of time to get places or perform work so you won't have to hurry.

Be alert. Watch where you are going and what you are doing. Anticipate slippery and difficult conditions such as:

- Slippery linoleum, tile or wood flooring
- Carpeting that isn't fastened down
- Throw rugs on landings

- Bathtub and shower surfaces
- Wet, oily and greasy surfaces
- Poor housekeeping
- Crowded storage areas
- Poorly lit staircases
- Furniture placed in odd positions
- Electrical cords not positioned securely
- Toys and other items on floors and steps
- No night lights in bedrooms

LIFTING AND BACK INJURY PREVENTION

Your back. It's often a mysterious, forgotten area of your body that you see only in photos or mirrors. Unless it's bothering you, it's probably taken for granted. Rare is the individual who does preventive maintenance on his or her back.

If our ancestors hadn't started walking erect on two feet instead of on all fours, our backs wouldn't be in the situation they're in today. Our lower backs support our upper body weight, and are continuously subjected to poor posture, overeating, lack of exercise, and the stresses of daily living.

Contrary to popular belief, the typical back isn't all that tough; it's one of the most injury-prone parts of our bodies. Studies indicate that almost 70 percent of the population will suffer back pain at some time during their lives.

Being ready for anything can save a lot of time, aggravation and injuries—especially when it comes to work that requires twisting and turning or lifting heavy, bulky or even light objects. Have you ever had to get into an awkward position—under a desk or bench, perhaps, to unscrew some fasteners from a fixture or other piece of equipment—only to find that three of the fasteners were straight screws, but one was a Phillips-head? Next time, before you get into that situation, you'll probably take both kinds of screwdrivers along.

You could have the straightest back in the world. You could strengthen it through exercise, weight lifting, proper diet and posture. Yet a single careless action, an action that results from not thinking before you attempt to lift or move an object, can throw it out of whack for life.

You may already be aware of the proper procedures for manual lifting:

- Test the object's weight.
- Stand close to the object. Try holding a gallon of milk near your side, at waist level for one minute. Easy, isn't it? Now, still holding the milk, extend your arm straight out in front of you. Notice the difference? Likewise, the more distance between you and the object, the more difficult the lifting becomes.
- Lift with your legs, not your back. With both hands, clasp one of your thighs, halfway above the knee. Tense your thigh muscles. Feel how big and strong they are? Perfect for providing lifting power.
- Bend your knees, not your back. Your knees are custom made for bending. Let them bend. Your back has more important things to do. Keep it straight.
- Pull instead of push. Think of weight lifters, and how large their biceps are. They're a lot bigger than the triceps. You've got more power in your biceps, too. And biceps are made for pulling. During a lift, when you push instead of pull, your back has to supply the difference in power.
- Maintain good balance. Avoid lurching, jerky motions. Plan ahead to avoid sudden load shifts, and be sure of your footing. Take smaller steps if you have to. Turn with your feet instead of your back.
- See that you have a clear path, with no tripping hazards.
- Get help when in doubt. Enlist the aid of others, or use a mechanical device.

Sometimes people forget about these procedures. They may think the object is lighter than it really is. Or that the floor is not slippery when it really is. Or that twisting with a load can't hurt anything, when it certainly can. Lifting is not just physical. It's mental as well. Think before you lift, because lifting is not something that comes naturally. Look at each lift as a new lift, and prepare yourself for anything. Back injuries are a lot easier to prevent than to correct.

Beyond the proper procedures for lifting, there are other ways you can keep your back healthy and help prevent injury:

Begin a sensible exercise program. Back experts contend that 80 percent of back pain can be traced to lack of exercise. Strengthened back, upper leg and abdominal muscles will increase your spine's support. Stretching exercises increase flexibility and will decrease the possibility that you'll sprain your back when lifting objects or moving materials. About fifteen minutes worth of back exercises four or five times a week can do wonders to strengthen and increase flexibility in the muscles and joints that support your back. Exercising your stomach muscles is also very important.

Keep excess pounds off. Okay, okay, it's easier said than done. But a potbelly exerts pressure on your backbone and encourages spinal curvature. Ten extra pounds on your abdomen puts about a hundred pounds of extra strain on your discs!

Learn how to relax, and then do it regularly. This eases muscular tension that builds from stress. Avoid excessive caffeine. Also, prevent or relieve fatigue and strain by changing positions frequently, by stretching and deep breathing, and by adjusting work heights.

Develop good posture. Straighten up while sitting, standing and walking. Keep your head high, chin tucked in, pelvis tilted forward. Sit with your back pressed against the back of the chair, feet flat on the floor.

HAND AND ARM SAFETY

For a moment, hold your hands out about ten or twelve inches from your face, palms down. Study your wrists first, then the backs of your hands, and finally move along the knuckles to your fingertips and nails. Anthropologists claim that our fingernails are nothing but vestiges of claws used thousands of years ago by ancestors too primitive to be called men and women. Back then, claws—and the rough, strong hands they were on—supplied practically all the skills those speechless creatures had. If anything disabled one of their hands or arms, chances were they would perish in their hostile world.

We've come a long way since then. Although we no longer depend solely on our hands to gather food and fashion clothing and shelter, just try living without one or both of them for a day. Our hands are valuable to almost every kind of task, and because they're used so much—day after day—they're vulnerable to injuries, especially to injuries involving material handling.

Several kinds of injuries are most prevalent to the hands and arms, but a few precautions can prevent even these:

• Cuts, punctures and abrasions can be prevented by wearing proper gloves for the job and by not exposing hands or arms to hazardous conditions.

• Heat and chemical burns can also be prevented by wearing proper gloves and by not taking chances while working with or near hot surfaces or harsh chemicals.

• Sprains can be prevented by never attempting to lift, pull or push an object that's too heavy for you and by not attempting to move a heavy object while your body is off-balance.

• Pinch-point injuries are among the most painful and serious types of injuries. Smashed fingers, amputations and even fatalities have resulted from pinch-point accidents. They're common in households, in workshops, in recreational activities, and at various work places. Sample pinch-point injuries include fingers caught against a doorframe while carrying furniture and fingers injured when a file cabinet or other drawer closes on them.

The way to prevent hand and arm injuries is to recognize the potential hazards and practice awareness and avoidance. Gloves should be used whenever possible. Always keep hands away from moving machinery. Equipment guards should always be in place. Follow manufacturer's instructions for using tools and equipment, and check materials for sharp edges, burrs or splinters before handling them. Store tools so sharp edges are not exposed. Make sure you know how hot or cold an object is before handling it, and wipe off greasy or slippery items before handling them. Lift objects so your hands are not near pinch points; whenever possible, keep your fingers on the sides of objects you are lifting, not the tops or bottoms, especially when you are stacking materials. Put items down carefully so you won't smash your fingers. Carry awkward materials with a palm-down grip whenever possible.

LADDER SAFETY

Respect for the proper use of ladders and knowledge of the potential hazards involved in their use can go a long way toward reducing or eliminating the possibility of ladder-related injuries.

Ladder Selection

Just because you have one or two ladders at home doesn't mean that every situation will be covered by them. For each task you plan that requires a ladder you need to consider the work site, the physical demands of the job, and the potential hazards in the area. How much weight must the ladder support? What length of ladder is needed? How will the ladder be set up? Is the surface uneven or soft? Are there overhead obstructions? Electrical hazards? Is the area congested?

There are many different types of ladders available. They can be straight, extension, or self-supporting step models. Most are made of either wood, aluminum or fiberglass. Whatever kind of ladder you choose, be sure to examine it each time you use it, especially if it's been stored over the winter. Test all parts of a wooden ladder to make sure they are sturdy. Check rivets and brackets on aluminum and fiberglass models. Never use an aluminum ladder near electrical lines or equipment, or outdoors during electrical storms.

Ladder Duty Ratings

Each ladder has a duty rating based on the maximum weight capacity that the ladder has been designed to hold. There are four rating categories:

Category	Weight Limit	Rating
Type IA	300 lbs.	Heavy Duty Industrial
Type I	250 lbs.	Heavy Duty
Type II	225 lbs.	Medium Duty
Type III	200 lbs.	Light Duty

Naturally, exceeding the rated weight capacity of a ladder can break the ladder and cause injury. Make sure that your own weight, together with that of any supplies or tools you may be carrying, does not exceed the rated capacity.

Selecting the Proper Ladder Length

Using a ladder that is too short or too long is unsafe. A ladder is too long if you have to extend forward more than an arm's length to reach the area you are working on. A ladder is too short if you have to stand any higher than the second step from the top of a stepladder or the third step from the top of a straight or extension ladder.

For a straight or extension ladder, the bottom of the ladder must be one foot away from the wall or other working surface for every four feet from the base of the work surface to the spot where the ladder rests against it. Of course, the further the ladder is from the base of the work surface, the longer the ladder must be to reach the necessary height. If you intend to climb onto a roof safely, the ladder must extend at least three feet beyond the roof line. When working on an extension ladder, never stretch it out completely; the base and upper sections must overlap at least one-twelfth of the total working height of the ladder. Of course, because of the angle involved with the placement of a straight or extension ladder, if you are painting or scraping a wall, you may be too far away to reach the center portions safely from the ladder. At that point, you might need a smaller stepladder.

Ladder Footing Support

Self-supporting stepladders should be set up so that all four legs are on solid ground or surfaces, and the spreaders can be locked into place (see Figure 3-1). Never use a stepladder as a straight ladder by leaning it against a wall or other surface.

Ladders with two feet (straight and extension models) must also be placed on firm, even surfaces whenever possible. If the ladder must be used on uneven ground, it's far safer to use a ladder leveler—a device that attaches to ladder rails and can be adjusted to balance the ladder—than boards, bricks or other items. Rubber feet can be attached to a wooden ladder to help prevent slipping on a concrete or other smooth surface.

Ladder Misuse

Avoid placing ladders on boxes, boards, tables or other objects to gain height.

Never lean an extension ladder against a

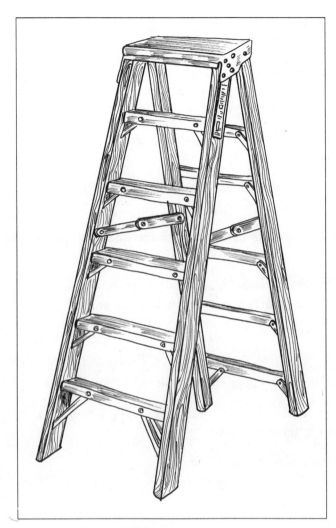

Figure 3-1. A stepladder.

"shaky" surface such as a tree branch, a pile of boxes, or a phone or electric line or cable.

Don't attempt to tie several short ladders together to make one long ladder. Never try to move a ladder while standing on it.

Don't leave ladders standing unattended. They can be very tempting to young children who may climb to a height from which they could fall or be afraid to climb back down.

Store ladders properly. Extension and straight ladders should be hung horizontally and supported at least every six feet to prevent warpage. Keep ladders away from excessive moisture, heat and cold. Wood ladders can be treated with clear wood preservatives, but should not be painted. The paint may cover up cracks or other defects, and could also result in slippery rungs.

Avoid working high in the air by yourself. If you will be working more than six feet off the ground — measured from the ground to your feet, be sure someone is holding the ladder to prevent it from slipping backward or to the side. If no one is available to help, you could tie off the top, middle and bottom of the ladder to something stable that could hold the weight of you and the ladder.

Avoid facing anywhere but toward the ladder while climbing or descending, and keep a three-point contact with the ladder at all times: one foot and two hands, or two feet and one hand.

Avoid carrying materials or tools up or down a ladder with your hands. Instead, have a helper hand you the items, or pull them up with a rope or rope and basket after you've climbed and taken a balanced position on the ladder.

When climbing high on a ladder, have a partner or helper on the ground hold the ladder so it can't slip backward or slide left or right.

SAFE MATERIAL HANDLING QUICK CHECKLIST

☐ Take potential slip, trip and fall hazards seriously. Take the preventive steps: wear non-slip shoes, avoid using "makeshift" ladders, allow enough time to get places or perform work at an unhurried pace, and anticipate slippery and difficult conditions.

☐ Be aware of and practice proper manual lifting and carrying techniques.

☐ Safely exercise your back to develop additional strength and flexibility.

☐ Wear appropriate gloves for tasks having hand and wrist hazards.

☐ Be aware of pinch-point hazards, and plan ways to complete work without putting hands and other body parts at risk.

☐ When a ladder is needed, select a properly rated model that's best for the job; borrow or rent one if you have to.

☐ Avoid using metal ladders near electrical lines or components.

☐ Avoid working more than six feet off the ground by yourself. In fact, use a helper whenever possible.

☐ Take no shortcuts when working from ladders.

CHAPTER 4

CHILD SAFETY

No class of individuals can be so creative when it comes to accidental injury as can babies and young children. Perhaps it's their curiosity, their way of exploring, their unfamiliarity with how things are supposed to work. In any event, make sure your child—or a visiting child—isn't among the one out of every four who will suffer an accidental home injury serious enough to require medical attention. Children are usually a lot smarter than people think they are. Teach youngsters to look before they leap. Emphasize the importance of safety. Don't just tell them "No!" Explain the reasons they shouldn't run out in the street without looking both ways. Tell them why they shouldn't get into a stranger's car, or why they shouldn't approach a dog they don't know. Explain the hazards of different activities they're involved with, and the importance of using safe procedures to stay healthy.

Use this chapter to survey your residence and to help you recognize conditions that could lead to common childhood accidents. It's not intended to be a catch-all for child hazards—that would be an impossible mission. Use it to help you recognize some dangerous conditions, to reinforce safe behaviors, and to help your children develop safety awareness. Some of the points in this chapter are elaborated on in other chapters. That's not accidental; it's by design. We'd be remiss not to emphasize in each chapter the most likely ways children could be injured.

When child-proofing a home, remember that it's important to observe potential accident situations from a child's perspective. And be aware that the kinds and numbers of injuries a child may receive change as the child grows and matures. A crawler can only reach so high off the floor, but a toddler standing erect, opens up a whole new range of "reachable" hazards.

If you don't have young children, should you continue reading the rest of this chapter? The answer, we think, is yes. There's always the possibility that a snippet of information learned here might save an innocent youngster from harm—be it your grandchild, nephew or niece, a neighbor's child, or even a total stranger.

CRIB SAFETY

Cribs are mini-worlds for babies. What could be safer than a child's crib? How about crossing a freeway at night, in dark clothing? Or teasing a strange Doberman pinscher during an August heat wave? In other words, cribs can be downright dangerous, even fatal, if not designed, constructed and used properly.

If you assemble a crib yourself, make sure all the nuts and bolts are firmly secured so they can't be loosened by someone's fingertips, then periodically check them. Test the crib by raising and lowering the side rails before putting it into service. Push, pull and shake the crib by its end panels and sides to see how strong the construction is. If it's wobbly, or leaning one way or another, either repair what's loose or get a different crib.

All of a crib's slats and posts should be solidly attached and spaced no more than two and three-eighths inches apart from one another. That also includes the space between a crib's corner post and sliding rail. If slats are further apart, a baby's body may slip through—while the head may not—resulting in a possible strangulation.

A crib mattress should fit snugly. If you can fit the width of two of your "average size" fingers between the mattress and sides, the mattress is too small or the crib is too large. A baby could slip into the gap and suffocate. Also make sure the crib's end panels extend below the mattress support at the support's lowest position, so, again, a baby can't get caught in the gap between a panel and the mattress.

Mattress support hooks should stay firmly in their brackets when the mattress is maneuvered or jostled about, such as when you're changing the crib's sheets.

The top rail of a lowered drop side should be at least nine inches above the mattress support at its lowest setting, so an infant can't fall out. The top of a raised side should be at least twenty-six inches above the support at its highest setting.

Avoid a crib with a drop side that can be released too easily or that can be opened with only a single motion for each lock. If you can adjust the side that easily, maybe the baby could too.

All cribs should have bumper pads around the entire crib interior, attached by snaps and no less than six straps.

Fancy decorations that can come off and break apart are not safe. A child can choke on the pieces. Cutouts in the panels are also unsafe; they can trap a baby's arms or neck.

Corner posts or "finials" that protrude above the tops of the end panels can snag garments and strangle a baby. And never hang anything on a string or ribbon around a baby's neck—such as a pacifier. The string could get caught on a bedpost or rail. As a rule, avoid hanging blankets, towels, bags, toys, dolls with strings or ribbons or anything else on a crib.

Avoid placing a crib near draperies, curtains, furniture, heating vents, wall lamps, electrical out-lets, windows, doors or even the wall. It's best to have at least a foot or more of safety space between the crib and its surrounding walls or furnishings so a baby can't reach anything from the crib.

Avoid leaving large toys in the crib. A baby could use them as steps to climb out.

Keep the crib sides up. Never use cribs or play-pens with the sides down. The baby could crawl out and fall, or in a mesh playpen, an infant could roll into a loose pocket formed by the mesh and suffocate.

OTHER INFANT FURNITURE

Many pieces of baby or nursery furniture are constructed sturdily, and can be passed along from generation to generation if properly cared for and stored between uses. When selecting furniture, shy away from inexpensive, cheaply made models. Look for pieces that will last. Avoid high chairs, playpens and cribs with exposed screws, bolts or other fasteners that could scratch delicate skin. Avoid materials with sharp edges or points, and avoid scissor-like mechanisms that could crush toes or fingers, and watch out for cut-out designs that could trap a child's arms, legs or head.

High Chairs

High chairs get their name, naturally, because they prop a baby high off the floor, higher even than some adult dinner tables. Consequently, it's a long drop if a baby happens to wiggle out of his or her seat. So always use the safety belt or strap to secure a child in place: The straps should be easy to attach and unfasten so you won't avoid using them (see Figure 4-1). Next, place the high chair so the baby's feet and hands cannot reach your dining or kitchen table, cabinets, counters, or other furniture the baby could use to push off from, because babies have surprisingly strong legs.

When attaching the eating tray to the high chair, make sure the baby's fingers don't get pinched. Double check that the tray is firmly locked in place before you step away from the high chair. The tray should lock in some manner so the baby cannot figure out how to lift it open by him or herself.

Figure 4-1. A high chair with safety strap.

Walkers

Walkers are wonderful inventions that give babies mobility way before they (or we) are ready for it. Parents who have never unleashed an infant in a walker are invariably amazed at where those walkers can go. Over rumpled carpets, Labrador retriever tails, bare feet, and practically any sort of item that's left on the floor.

Never leave a child in a walker unattended. And keep walkers out of rooms where there are stairs, even if a stair guard is in place. Also keep walkers out of areas that have uneven surfaces.

Look for potential hazards that the walker will allow the child to access, such as a hot radiator, lamps on table tops, artwork or glass items on coffee tables, and similar objects. Either remove the hazards or keep the walker out of that room. Throw rugs, edges of carpets, or raised thresholds can sometimes cause a child to tip a walker over.

Changing Tables

Changing tables should include safety straps to prevent the baby from rolling off and falling. The table should also have drawers or shelves you can reach easily while tending the baby. Avoid leaving safety pins laying around on the top of the table, or lotions or powders that the baby could accidentally spill on herself.

Naturally, a baby on a changing table—even if strapped to the top—should never be left unattended. Babies are strong. They can kick and squirm out of restricting straps in a way that would make Houdini jealous.

Toy Chests

Never keep toys in a toy chest, trunk or other container with a hinged lid that could fall or close on a child's body, causing injury or death. The chest must not be airtight either, nor should it have a lock or latching mechanism—in case a small child climbs inside. If the chest does have a heavy, free-falling lid, remove the lid (see Figure 4-2). It's better to have a chest with sliding panels or a lightweight removable top. Some very practical models are made of brightly colored canvas. Avoid using the toy chest as a catch-all for blankets, books, tools and other household items.

TOYS

Years ago, toys didn't come with age recommendations on their packages. Now they do. When selecting toys for babies, toddlers and other young children, pay attention to age recommendation guidelines. Although most read something like "Recommended for children three to five years old," you should also consider the level of maturity of the child you are buying for.

When buying toys for babies and toddlers, think big! And think solid! The main hazards with toys are small parts that can be pulled or bitten off and

Figure 4-2. An open top toy chest.

swallowed. Small removable parts can also become lodged in a child's ears or nose. Again, children can be very creative. They have a way of yanking button eyes or noses from dolls, or extracting bells and squeaking mechanisms from the insides of squeeze toys.

Wooden toys should not have screws, nails, bolts, nuts or metal brackets that are prone to loosen. Edges should not be sharp, and there shouldn't be any points either. Surfaces should be round or gently curved. Paint must be nontoxic.

There should be no strings, ropes, chains or strong ribbons attached to a toy. They could strangle or choke a child.

The safest and most popular toys often come from reputable manufacturing companies that make the toys according to the voluntary safety standards of the Toy Manufacturers of America and the requirements of the U.S. Consumer Product Safety Commission. But don't automatically take the toy manufacturer's word. Carefully inspect any toy before you buy.

After purchasing a toy, inspect it from time to time to make sure nothing's broken or coming apart at the seams. The stuffings—sometimes small pellets in stuffed animals or other toys—can be choking hazards.

In addition to small pieces of toys, make sure you don't let other small items come within easy reach of babies and toddlers. Coins, pins, buttons, small batteries, marbles and numerous other commonplace items have all been removed from the stomachs of children.

HOUSEHOLD FURNITURE AND FURNISHINGS

Many antiques and old pieces of furniture were put together during times when neither manufacturers nor the buying public were overly concerned with "safe" designs. Even today, there's nothing to say that a coffee table must have round edges instead of pointy corners. If toddlers and babies live in or frequent your home, look at your furniture for hazards.

Inspect the drawers in all pieces of furniture and in built-in cabinets. Make sure they have safety catches or latches to prevent the drawers from being pulled all the way out.

Inspect the contents of low-level drawers everywhere in the house. Remove sharp, pointy and small items such as scissors, knives, marbles, screws and any objects with which children could injure themselves.

On tables with glass tops, make sure the top cannot be pulled or toppled from its base. Also remove heavy objects that a child could use to crack or smash the glass. Never, for example, leave a claw hammer within a toddler's reach. If the child has seen you using the hammer, the attraction to it may be too much to resist.

Don't keep breakable objects on coffee tables or other low-to-the-floor pieces of furniture.

Furniture with sharp edges should be protected with "safe" corners available at department stores and from a variety of mail order catalogs.

Look at furniture from the child's point of view. What's *under* that dining room table? Any bolts, screws or nails sticking out? Or sharp edges where metal brackets fasten one half of the table to the other? Protect children from such hazards by creatively covering the hazard with child-friendly materials such as cushioned corner and edge protectors or tape foam strips.

Tablecloths should be secured or folded so they don't dangle far enough from the table's edges for a child to pull them down.

Ironing boards should be stored in a closet. If you don't have enough closet space, set the board up in an out-of-the-way place. Avoid folding and leaning it against the wall in an open room—it could easily be knocked down onto a child. If you keep the ironing board set up all the time, keep the iron somewhere else, unplugged and out of a child's sight and reach. A hot (or cold) iron jarred off a board can be a lethal weapon to a baby or toddler.

Never put thin plastic material over mattresses or pillows. Plastic sheathing can cling to a child's face, causing suffocation.

Don't forget that children love to climb and explore. Inspect your furniture for small or narrow openings. Youngsters have strangled when their heads or necks became caught in open V-shaped cutouts in pieces of furniture.

Wall mirrors should be securely fastened. A child should not be able to twist the fastening tabs so a mirror can fall from the wall. Protective films are available in window stores that can be applied over mirrors and windows to prevent splinters of glass from falling and flying through the air in case of breakage.

Large paintings, drawings and similar artwork should likewise be firmly hung on the wall, especially artwork located above couches and chairs that toddlers could climb.

Keep heavy, breakable objects out of reach. Know a piece of furniture's center of balance. Some lamps, stools or even tables can be pulled over with surprisingly little effort. Make sure bookshelves and other tall pieces of furniture are sturdy or secured to a wall. Floor lamps can be especially dangerous. If a child can pull a piece of furniture over, either anchor the piece to the wall or floor, or remove it until the child is older.

Make a habit of closing all drawers. Open drawers can act as steps that can be climbed to reach items that shouldn't be touched by youngsters.

Remember to keep all basement doors closed so crawlers, toddlers and walkers can't fall down steep stairways.

Rocking chairs and recliners can easily pinch or cut a child's fingers. Show youngsters the hazards and train children to keep away.

Screen off hot radiators.

Install child-proof latches (see Figure 4-3) for cabinets that hold potentially dangerous items such as bleaches, detergents or disinfectants. Keep all poisonous materials off countertops in the locked cabinets. Know where all dangerous items are, such as medicines, toxic bleaches, oven and drain cleaners, paints, solvents, polishes and waxes. Hazardous items in child-resistant containers should still be placed out of sight and out of reach, never under a sink or in plain view in a garage.

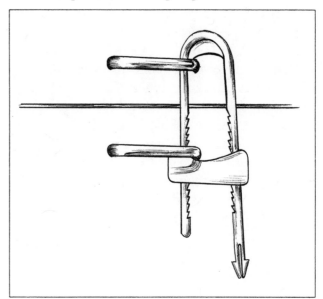

Figure 4-3. A child-proof cabinet latch.

Remember to protect your electronic equipment. Televisions and VCRs can become popular playthings with toddlers. They love to push buttons, change channels, and turn up the volume. They also love to spill soda, cereal and crumbs of all kinds inside the delicate machinery of video and audio units. A VCR locking mechanism available at electronics stores will help protect control buttons and knobs from sticky, sturdy, curious little fingers.

Loose, worn and frayed carpeting should be removed or replaced. Make sure area and throw rugs have nonskid backing.

Keep cords for draperies and blinds out of reach. Hide lamp cords, or at least tuck them away along wall and floor edges. If you use clotheslines in a basement, laundry room, attic or outdoors, make sure they are high enough to be out of a child's reach. Wrap or cut off any excess line.

A night-light should be able to glow indefinitely without getting hot enough to scorch or melt anything that happens to touch it. When purchasing a night-light, make sure it's certified by Underwriters Laboratories (UL approved). Don't use anything else. And make sure there's a cover that protects the bulb. Don't place the light where bedding, draperies or other materials could come in contact with it.

POISONS

What to do in case of an accidental poisoning? Call your community's poison control center. It's very important that you know their number. You might be surprised to know that about 80 percent of all poisonings can be successfully treated at home. But first you have to be sure yours is one of these and not one of the other 20 percent. If the poisoning you describe can be safely managed by you at your residence, the poison center staff will tell you, step by step, exactly how to do it. Give the nurse or operator your name, phone number and address. Give the name, age, sex and weight of the child or person that has ingested the poison, and what the poison was if you know it. Then the poison center nurse will:

- Tell you what to do immediately to help the poisoned patient. You may be advised to administer ipecac syrup to induce vomiting, so keep a bottle of it handy in your medicine cabinet.
- Ask what hospital you wish to take the patient to, if it is necessary.

- Quickly give you any necessary additional instructions.
- Contact the hospital and send complete information by telecopier or fax regarding the type of poison ingested, and instructions for the proper antidote. The hospital will then be waiting for the patient's arrival and have the proper antidotes available for immediate treatment.

Remember that you benefit by calling the poison center first because you'll not only be told what corrective actions you can take, but you may avoid the trauma of rushing a young child to the emergency room—which is a very scary trip indeed for a little, frightened child. And you may avoid having to pay for the cost of an unneeded hospital visit.

If there isn't a poison control center in your area, try phoning your doctor. If that fails, call the emergency room of your local hospital. If the symptoms are violent and increasingly severe, rush the victim to a hospital.

Seasonal Poisoning

If you ask down at your local hospital's emergency ward, or any poison control center, you'll find that due to activities that occur every spring, summer, fall and winter, cases of particular poisonings become more common than others at those times. In general, they are as follows.

During Spring:
    carbon monoxide
    medications
    chemical combinations from cleaning products
    gasoline siphoned for lawn mowers
    holiday hazards

During Summer:
    fumes from outdoor grills used inside
    gasoline siphoned for lawn mowers
    kerosene ingestion
    pesticides, herbicides, insecticides
    contact dermatitis, such as poison ivy
    snakes and insect bites or stings
    outdoor plant ingestions
    pool products
    food poisonings
    chemical skin irritation from wearing less
        clothing

poisonous berries

During Fall:

carbon monoxide

chemical combinations from cleaning products

paints

vitamins left out by older children taken before going to school

mushrooms brought home by mushroom hunters

During Winter:

carbon monoxide from furnaces and fireplaces

medications, such as cold medications left out on counters

holiday plants

holiday hazards

Remember that simply keeping hazardous materials out of sight could eliminate up to 75 percent of all poisoning of small children. Small children are incredibly curious and resourceful, but they can't ingest what they can't see.

While you may not call a penny, a marble, an ink eraser or other items "poisons," to children they can be all the same. Tots will often first swallow small items they explore.

Plant Poisonings

Toddlers are the worst. They tend to pick, pull, prod and try to chew on anything they can. Serious illness and even death can result if a child swallows the leaves, flowers and or fruit of some common indoor and outdoor plants and trees. Lily of the valley, iris, sweet pea, daffodil, crocus, elephant ear, choke cherry, morning glory and rhododendron are prime examples.

Try to enlist a knowledgeable florist or agronomist to tour your home and yard and identify your various plant specimens. Even if he doesn't know if the plants are poisonous, at least you'll have the correct names so you can look up the information yourself. Lists of poisonous plants—both cultivated and wild—are available through local hospitals or poison control centers, or can be found at any library.

If dangerous plants are found inside, remove them from a child's reach, or loan the offending plants to a friend or relative until the child grows out of the nibbling stage. Outdoors, fence off poi-sonous plants and also plants having wicked prickers or thorns that could injure an eye or cause other damage, trim them to levels beyond a child's reach, or have the plants removed.

Until your children are old enough not to "taste" plant leaves, flowers or fruit, check the poison characteristics of all plants before you purchase them, either by asking a florist or by looking through a book that includes both clear, specific photographs and descriptions of the plant you're considering.

Before planting seeds or bulbs, keep them locked away from tiny hands they might otherwise play with the plant parts and put them into a curious mouth.

Frequently remind children that they should never pick and eat flowers, berries or other fruit without adult supervision. Sure, blueberries are fine to eat, but what about those hard little berries that don't taste so good? A young child may react to a berry with a bitter taste by swallowing it instead of spitting it out.

Consider that children are not the only victims of plant poisonings. Adults who are trying to get "back-to-nature" by foraging for edible wild plants and mushrooms can easily run into trouble with dangerous look-alike specimens from afield. Unless you know someone who has been picking wild plants and mushrooms for years—without adverse effects—you're best off to decline an invitation to a "wild" dinner. You wouldn't want to accidentally partake in a side dish of poison hemlock or deadly mushrooms. In all cases, let children eat only safe, store-bought or farm-raised foods.

STAIRWAY SAFETY

If balusters on stairs and balconies are more than four inches apart, a barrier of some kind should be installed to prevent a child from either falling through or getting stuck.

Stairways should have sturdy handrails (see Figure 4-4). Consider installing temporary handrails at a lower level so a toddler learning how to use stairs can lean on the rails. Instruct children never to carry sharp objects up or down the stairs.

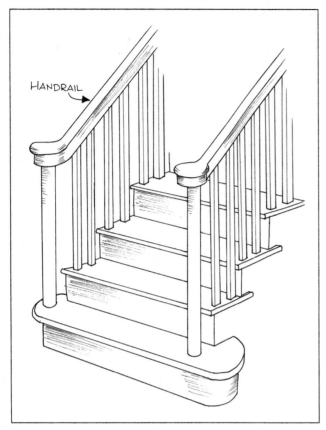

HANDRAIL

Figure 4-4. A stairway handrail.

Safety gates should be installed at the top and bottom of all stairways. Avoid using accordion-style gates that a child can stick his or her arm, leg or neck through.

Painted wooden stairs can be very dangerous for youngsters (and adults) who frequently run around the house in their stocking feet. Consider carpeting stairways to ease the impact of possible falls. Never place a throw rug at the top of a stairway.

Keep toys, shoes, clothing, and all other tripping hazards off the steps. Repair uneven or broken steps.

When carrying a child up or down the stairs, be sure you can see clearly where you are stepping and always use a handrail for support.

KITCHEN SAFETY

To small children, a kitchen is where the action is. They may spend more time in their playpens and cribs, but the kitchen is where they have breakfast, lunch (when not at day school or a sitter's house),

supper and various snacks. Parents are generally hanging out there, too, working at a kitchen table or counter, preparing food, or doing the dishes while watching television. A kitchen is full of interesting items, from automatic can openers, dishwashers and microwave ovens, to drawers full of foodstuffs and implements.

But it's also chock full of dangers for babies and youngsters. Keep small appliances such as toasters, coffee makers and food processors toward the backs of counters. Keep them unplugged when they're not in use, and don't let their cords dangle from or near the edge of the counter—they could be tempting for a child to pull. You don't want a child to be able to turn on an appliance, and you don't want the possibility of electrocution if an appliance is pushed or pulled into a sink full of water. Too, all kitchen electric outlets should be kept covered with plastic inserts when they're not being used.

Keep a dishwasher's door latch in a locked position. Put soap in the dishwasher only when you run it, not before. And never walk away from a dishwasher when the washer's door is open.

If you have a trash compactor, make sure it won't run when the door is open and that it can be turned on only with a key, and then keep the key well hidden.

An electric disposal is nothing for a child to play with. If yours works by a switch on the wall or counter, a safety-lock switch should be installed so the disposal can be operated only with a key. Be especially cautious with a disposal that runs continuously after the switch is thrown. That means a child could throw the switch, then put objects or her hands down into the whirring blades.

It's a lot safer when stoves and cooktops have control knobs on their tops, not on their front sides. If your stove control knobs are on the front, consider removing them when you won't be around. Cook on rear burners whenever possible, and never let pot or pan handles stick out past the front of the cooktop. When frying foods that tend to spatter and pop, use a splatter screen over the pan or keep the lid at least partially on, blocking the front of the pan. As an added precaution, keep children away from the stove altogether.

Keep boxes of aluminum foil and plastic wrap

out of children's reach because the boxes are likely to have sharp cutting edges. The plastic film can also be inhaled and choked on. For that same reason, keep plastic grocery bags away from babies and toddlers.

While children are young, collect all sharp knives and implements and store them out of reach in a hard-to-open container. Be careful when the knives are in use or they're out on a counter or in the dishwasher (pointed ends down, of course).

Cabinet and drawer latches are available to keep children from easily opening drawers and rummaging through the contents. Don't forget to lock up matches and hazardous materials such as cleaning supplies.

Avoid storing cookies, candy, gum or other favorite items high up in cupboards or on top of refrigerators—it's too tempting for a child to try to crawl up on counters and appliances while trying to get to the goodies. Keep goodies away from the stove, too.

Dangling tablecloths can be yanked by young children, bringing whatever's up there crashing to the floor or onto the children themselves. Use anti-slip place mats instead.

Make sure all of your child's drinking glasses, plates and cups are made of unbreakable plastic or paper, not glass or ceramics.

Refrigerator magnets can be dangerous. Many of them are fairly small and shaped like cookies, candy or other edible items. Use larger magnets that do not resemble foods and keep them high enough to be out of a child's line of sight or reach.

Don't rush babies onto hard foods. And be particularly careful when feeding toddlers hot dogs, pieces of meat, chunks of hard vegetables, such as carrots and celery, hard candies, nuts, and even raisins. Always cut foods into irregular shapes, not rounds. Any fairly large, round items such as grapes, ice cubes or pieces of bubble gum can also be choking hazards if accidentally swallowed whole.

Don't get into a habit of automatically giving a baby or toddler milk or food that's been heated in a microwave oven without testing the contents' temperature first. It could be scalding hot, or worse yet, have a hot spot hidden away inside.

Keep kitchen trash away from children. Tiny hands can reach into the garbage and get cut on broken glass, metal can tops, or other sharp items, or can pull out tiny things to swallow. Keep the trash out of sight or under a hard-to-open lid. Take extra precautions with dangerous items—such as the sharp metal lids or broken glass—put the pieces in some other container, perhaps an empty orange juice carton, before placing the waste in a trash liner or can.

SAFETY OUTDOORS

Since the number of possible scenarios in which children are at risk of getting injured is infinite, we can only give a representative sampling of outdoor situations and safety precautions.

As soon as they are able to understand, instruct children to stay within the boundaries of your yard, or within the joint boundaries of yours and a neighbor's yard. The number one hazard, of course, is the street. Children should avoid walking in front of or behind idling buses, postal delivery vehicles, and other equipment that might travel your street. Bus drivers and operators of heavy equipment may not be able to see a youngster who has stepped near either end of the vehicle, below the driver's line of sight.

Children should not get into the habit of riding bicycles, skateboards, or any kind of mobile toys from the driveway into the street, especially when there are parked vehicles hindering visibility.

Children should wear approved safety helmets while riding bicycles, motorcycles, snowmobiles or all-terrain vehicles.

Children should not operate any power landscaping equipment, nor should they be in the immediate area when power equipment is being operated.

Playground Safety

A trip to any crowded city playground can be an exciting time for both child and parent. Swings, teeter-totters, merry-go-rounds, monkey bars, slides and sandboxes can be good exercise and a lot of fun. But to prevent an afternoon of fun from leading to a hospital emergency room, consider the following:

Is there protective surfacing beneath and around the play equipment? There should be.

About 75 percent of all playground accidents result from falls. Hard, paved surfaces such as asphalt and concrete may be easier to keep clean and maintain, but they aren't very friendly to children. Hard sod or hard-packed soil are not much better. Small pea-size gravel is preferred. Wood chips have also been used with some success.

Swing sets and other equipment should be installed far enough apart to allow children to move about without getting dangerously close to other "children in motion." Toddlers need a responsible baby-sitter or adult to hold their hand and help them get onto playground equipment.

Do elevated surfaces such as climbing platforms, walkways and ramps have adequate guardrails or protective barriers to prevent falls? Are there any bolts, nails or metal brackets protruding from the equipment? Is the construction sturdy? There shouldn't be loose splinters or obvious decay on wood components. Rust and chipped paint on metal parts could also be dangerous.

Check to see if there are any exposed moving parts that could easily pinch or crush a child's extremities.

GENERAL SAFETY

Teach children not to lean against screens or windows. Windows, especially on upper floors, should be limited as to how far they'll open.

Never tie pacifiers or other items around a baby's neck. Cords, strings, jewelry chains or ribbons can become twisted or can catch on pieces of furniture or other objects.

Young children should not have clothes with drawstrings. Drawstrings could catch on a bus or in a car door as the child is getting out, or become caught in moving equipment youngsters approach.

Clothes washers and dryers can be tempting appliances for a toddler to climb into. Instruct children on the dangers of doing so. Avoid using a dryer that starts when the door closes or that has an automatic-latch door lock. Safer models require a button to be pushed on a control panel on top of the unit, toward the back.

Refrigerators and freezers are not toys. Keep freezers full and locked. If a unit is temporarily out of service, remove the door.

Teach children to treat each household plant as if it were poisonous.

Install bathroom doorknobs that can be unlocked and opened from the outside.

Install protective padding on bathroom tub faucets, and nonslip mats or other surfaces in bathtubs.

Install screens and safety rails on fireplace, stove and heater fireboxes.

Don't let children access garage door openers. Replace or repair electric doors that do not reverse on contact.

Keep power tools unplugged, stored out of a child's reach with safety guards in place.

Kids and Water

Set the water heater temperature in your home no higher than 120 to 130 degrees Fahrenheit.

Never leave a child alone in a bathtub or pool, not even for a few seconds. A drowning can occur in less than an inch of water.

Don't let water stand in laundry tubs or five-gallon buckets. A toddler could fall headfirst into either. Empty tubs, buckets and other containers after each use.

Teach children to swim. See chapter thirteen on swimming pool safety.

Electrical Safety Concerns

Keep babies and toddlers away from electrical hazards. Although you should teach small children not to touch electric plugs or cords, every unused electrical outlet should still be protected by inexpensive outlet safety caps or inserts (see Figure 4-5), so children cannot easily access the outlets with their fingers, utensils, car keys or other items.

Children have been electrocuted when plugged-in hair dryers or other appliances fell into water-filled bathroom or kitchen sinks. Appliances such as hair dryers and electric shavers should be kept unplugged and out of reach. So should kitchen appliances such as hot plates, food processors and mixers.

Keep light bulbs in all fixtures, even fixtures that aren't being used. See chapter two for more on electrical safety.

Figure 4-5. Outlet safety caps.

Children and Eye Wear

Because their eyes are more transparent and delicate than those of adults, children are particularly vulnerable to sunlight's ultraviolet radiation (UV). The damage from such UV radiation, unfortunately, is both cumulative and irreversible. Too much of it can seriously impair a child's vision. So keep babies out of direct sunlight and insist that children wear sunglasses. Look for lenses labeled "Meets ANSI General or Special Purpose UV Standards." The lenses should also be impact-resistant so they won't shatter upon impact. Ask your optometrist if he or she can order children's eyeglass frames with sunglass lenses to fit small heads and faces, if otherwise only cheap, inefficient glasses are available.

BABY-SITTERS

Unless you plan on staying with your children for twelve or thirteen years straight, without ever leaving their sides, you're eventually going to use the services of a baby-sitter. Be sure to use only sitters that you get iron-clad references from. Never, never use a sitter you know little about. If possible, let the child have a say in which sitter you select.

Make sure the sitter knows your household rules. Will you let a friend of the sitter, male or female, stop over while you are gone? Can the sitter talk to friends on the phone at your house? Can your child have friends over? Or talk on the phone? A list of written rules is always helpful, both for the sitter and for you.

Have a list of emergency phone numbers pre- pared, and keep it by the kitchen or other phone. The list should include numbers for the police, fire department, hospital, family doctor, and at least two neighbors who will be home that day or evening. Most important, leave your plans for the evening, and how you can be reached in case of an emergency. Some parents have gone so far as to carry digital beepers, so the baby-sitter can contact them immediately if there's a problem.

Show the sitter where all first-aid supplies are kept. If the sitter will be feeding your child, make sure you have something prepared or tell the sitter what to fix before you leave.

If you have young children who have trouble going to bed with you gone, try taping a bedtime story on an audio- or videotape, and have the sitter play it for the kids right before bedtime.

If the children are old enough, ask them to give a report on your baby-sitters the following morning.

CHILDREN AND PETS

Bringing a new baby into a house for the first time can be a traumatic event for the family dog or cat. Before you bring a new baby home, bring something that holds the child's scent, such as a blanket or sleeper, and let your dog or cat sniff the item. In fact, place the item near the dog or cat's bed overnight. This way the baby's scent will be somewhat familiar to your pet when introductions are made. Since animals sense a change when a baby is brought into the household, try to comfort your pets by keeping to familiar routines, especially with feeding and walking times.

No animal should ever be left alone with a baby or toddler. Although you may have heard of family pets protecting or even saving the lives of babies and young children, never trust even the most docile pet with the safety of a child. The time for interaction between pets and babies or youngsters is when an adult or responsible baby-sitter is present.

While toddlers are usually attracted to dogs and cats, the feelings are not always mutual. Dogs and cats may appear to be friendly, but even the gentlest pets may nip, scratch, snap or jump up on someone if they're frightened, startled or teased by children. Pets accustomed to wrestling or roughhousing with their adult masters can harm children accidentally, using the same behaviors the pets are usually rewarded for.

Keep pet food and water dishes in a place inaccessible to very young children who could choke on hard dog food pellets or drown in a large bowl of water.

PERSONAL SAFETY FOR CHILDREN

It's sad to say, but children must be instructed as early as possible on how to act if they're approached by strangers. Children have been kidnapped from their front yards, from a neighbor's sleep-over party, from a crowded department store, from the end of an amusement park ride line, and, really, from just about anywhere. Their pictures are stamped on the backs of milk cartons and posted on supermarket bulletin boards.

Numerous articles, written by individuals familiar with child abuse, with kidnappings, and with the perpetrators of such crimes, advise parents and guardians to follow any number of preventive measures. They include instructing children never to go into a public restroom alone, to avoid playing in abandoned buildings, and to stay at least six feet away from a car with a stranger in it.

Teach your child that anyone they don't know should be treated like a stranger, even if the person says the child's name or says he or she is passing information from someone the child does know. Assure your children it's OK to say *no* to an adult who makes them feel uncomfortable or wants them to

do something they feel is wrong or bad. No one should touch them where their swimming suit or underwear covers. If anyone is scaring them or making them feel uncomfortable, it's OK to run away and scream *"help."* Some experts recommend a child scream "kidnapper" to clearly distinguish between real danger and a battle of wills with his own parents.

Children should never be forced to hug or kiss or show affection to someone they don't know or like. They should not open doors to anyone they don't know, or give strangers any information over the phone or tell *anyone* if they are home alone.

A child should memorize his full name, address and telephone number, including area code, and know how to use the telephone to call home, 911, the police, and the fire department in an emergency. Teach your children to call and let you know when they will be leaving the house, and where they are going. Have them follow check-in procedures so you always know where they are.

Teach kids where to go for safety if you're not around, and to run to other people and to lighted areas if they are being followed (not to run and hide). They should use the buddy system when walking to school, to the playground or to social functions. They should stay near you in stores and public places. Instruct them never to go out into a parking lot if they get separated from you in a shopping center or other place; go to the nearest check-out counter and ask the clerk for assistance instead.

Teach children if someone grabs them, to scream and try to break free and run to the nearest house or business place. Go over how to describe a person's appearance, clothing and vehicle if they're approached by a stranger.

It's critical that children are told about the possibility of being approached by individuals who may want to harm them, and who may appear to be responsible adults involved in sincere situations. Teach your child the facts of abduction early. Explain the facts simply, just as you would any other coping skill. The "professional" child molester or kidnapper has many ploys that have worked well in the past. They include:

• Pretending to be injured and in need of

assistance

- Asking for directions
- Saying they need help "to find a little puppy or kitten," or offering children a kitten or puppy to play with
- Offering gifts or money
- Saying the child's parents have been in an accident, or that the child's house is on fire and his parents want the stranger to bring the child home
- Asking to take the child's picture
- Asking the child to help carry something or perform some minor task

There are many others. All of these ploys appeal to a child's desire to help others. It's unfortunate, but children must be taught to mistrust strangers. Pure and simple. Go so far as to define the word "stranger." Children often think strangers are only people they have never seen before or people who look or act "funny." They must understand that although they see the ice cream man in their neighborhood almost every day, he is really a stranger.

Get a copy of your child's fingerprints. Take photos of your child. Full facial portraits are best, and to be up to date, take photos of preschoolers at least four times a year because their appearances change so rapidly. Also take photographs of any distinguishing marks, such as birthmarks, moles, scars or deformities.

Practice having your child make long distance phone calls—both with your home phone and with a pay phone. Do your children know their telephone area code? They should. And teach them how to call collect. It's also a good idea to tape enough coins for a phone call inside a child's shoes, or sew them into a jacket lining.

Don't buy items with your child's name on them. Children are more likely to trust a stranger who may claim to know them or their parent.

Know your child's route to school, their friend's house and other places. Establish strict procedures on who will pick your child up from school, and be consistent in following them. Be sure the school, or the child's baby-sitter, will not release the child to anyone but you or someone designated by you. Choose a code word with your child to be used as

a signal if you must send an unfamiliar adult to pick your child up.

Never leave a child unattended in a car.

Teach children to walk toward oncoming traffic so they can see approaching cars. If a car slows or stops, children should run to the nearest home or business.

"Latchkey" Kids

In this time of two-income families, young children who arrive home earlier than their parents are commonly referred to as latchkey kids. There are several ways to help safeguard the latchkey children in your household.

Teach children to pay attention to their surroundings when they get home. A child should not enter the home if he or she notices a broken window, an open door, or anything else that looks unusual.

Teach children to keep the doors and the first floor windows locked. It's best that children never open the door to salespeople, survey takers or other solicitors, or strangers—children or adults.

When children are home alone they should never volunteer information to a stranger over the telephone. Your child should tell callers you are home but unable to come to the telephone. Explain that this is not really lying—it's just a rule that children follow to be safe at home alone. Above all, keep the conversation brief. The same goes in replying to someone at the door.

Children should know to call 911 (or whatever other number is appropriate in your area) in an emergency. Your home address, along with important numbers such as the poison control center, police, fire department, parents' work numbers, and other numbers should be kept near the phone.

Instruct children to leave the house as quickly as possible if a smoke detector sounds, then call 911 from a neighbor's home.

Arrange for a trusted neighbor or nearby relative who is usually home during the afternoon to be available for children who may need help or advice over the phone when you're unavailable.

Make sure children understand what they can't do while they're home alone. That they can't go swimming in a pool by themselves. That they can't use the gas stove burners to cook with. That they can't give the dog a flea bath in the master bathroom.

Children should know where the first aid kit is, and how to perform first aid for minor burns and cuts.

It's effective to turn the teaching into games such as "What if?" scenarios. Ask your children what they would do if faced with a fire in the kitchen, or a little sister who swallowed medicine. Review all of the home-alone safety rules you think apply to your residence.

For Parents

Know where your children are at all times. Know who your children's friends are, where they live, and what their phone numbers are.

Have your child's school or day care center call you immediately if your children are absent. In-struct your children that you expect a phone call from them when they arrive after walking or biking to a friend's house or shopping mall.

Be cautious and extremely conservative when selecting baby-sitters, preschools and day care centers. Insist on verifiable references. Check the references and meet the people you will be entrusting your child to. Listen when your children tell you they do not want to be with someone.

Get to know your neighbors, especially if you've just moved into a new area.

Once again, this chapter is certainly not meant to be an all-inclusive presentation of every possible child safety hazard. There are many, many more situations that the typical child can get in trouble with. A variety of additional situations can be found within other chapters in this section. But at the very least, children should be taught basic safety awareness.

CHILD SAFETY QUICK CHECKLIST

☐ Give household pets advance notice of a newborn's impending arrival by bringing home a blanket or clothing item carrying the newborn's scent.

☐ Babies and toddlers should never be left alone with even the most trusted pets. Instruct all children to avoid unknown pets unless the children receive approval from a responsible adult present at the child's side.

☐ Young children must not have access to pet food and water bowls.

☐ Baby cribs and playpens must be sturdily assembled, with no loose nuts, bolts or fasteners of any kind, and no protruding parts that can snag a baby's blankets or clothing.

☐ Crib slats and posts should ideally be spaced no more than two and one-eighth inches apart.

☐ A crib mattress should fit with no gap between the mattress edge and the bed frame or end panels.

CHILD SAFETY QUICK CHECKLIST
(continued)

☐ Mattress support hooks must be firmly held in place so they cannot be accidentally dislodged by regular bed changing chores.

☐ The top rail of the drop side crib panel must be high enough to prevent a baby from falling out of the crib when the panel is in its lowered and raised positions.

☐ A crib should not have large cutouts in its panels, and a bumper pad should be securely attached to the inside perimeter, at mattress level.

☐ Cribs must be located at least a foot away from walls, furnishings and furniture.

☐ Use security straps to fasten babies into high chairs, and keep the chairs away from walls and furniture.

☐ Babies in walkers need to be supervised at all times.

☐ Avoid using chests, trunks or other containers with hinged lids that could fall or close on a child's body. Avoid containers with locking or latching mechanisms.

☐ Use only trusted, qualified baby-sitters that responsible individuals can vouch for.

☐ Provide a baby-sitter with household rules and emergency phone numbers, plus your itinerary and how you can be reached while you're gone.

☐ If stairway baluster spacings are wider than four inches, a barrier of some kind should be installed to prevent a child from falling through or getting stuck.

☐ Until children can safely negotiate stairs on their own, install safety gates at the top and bottom of all stairways. Consider covering wooden stairs with padded carpeting.

☐ Keep small electric appliances to the rear of counters, unplugged, away from sinks.

☐ Cover unused electric outlets with plastic safety inserts.

☐ Keep dishwasher and compactor doors closed and latched.

CHILD SAFETY QUICK CHECKLIST
(continued)

☐ Dangerous appliances such as disposals and compactors should have safety-lock switches.

☐ Stove and cooktop controls should be located on the top of cooking units, not on the front.

☐ Lids and spatter screens should be used while frying and boiling on stove tops.

☐ Keep sharp and pointy knives and implements, matches, medicines, poisons, small items and other dangerous objects out of a child's reach in hard-to-open containers or in locked cabinets.

☐ Keep kitchen trash away from children.

☐ Follow age-range recommendations on toys. Look out for small parts that could cause choking; strings, ropes or chains that could snag and strangle; and sharp points and edges that can cut.

☐ Avoid or modify furniture that has sharp points or edges, or protruding fasteners, brackets and framework on its underside.

☐ Tablecloths shouldn't dangle off the edge of tables so a child can pull the table's contents down on herself.

☐ Avoid storing clothes irons on set-up ironing boards.

☐ Thin plastic wrap and bags can suffocate children.

☐ Secure mirrors, artwork and all furnishings to walls, doors and other surfaces. Keep drapery and curtain cords above a child's reach.

☐ Screen off hot radiators and fireplace hearths. Prevent children from accessing space heaters, wood stoves and other hot appliances.

☐ Protect your electronic equipment and breakable furnishings and decorations from childhood explorations and abuse.

☐ Keep children away from streets and from the ends of driveways.

☐ Make children wear helmets for bike riding, skateboarding, skating, snowmobiling or all-terrain vehicle riding.

CHILD SAFETY QUICK CHECKLIST
(continued)

☐ Avoid using playgrounds with asphalt, concrete, or extremely hard soil grounds. Inspect play areas with safety in mind before allowing children to visit.

☐ Children playing near or in water must be supervised every minute. Teach children how to swim.

☐ Educate children about the hazards of electricity.

☐ Protect children's eyes and skin during hot weather.

☐ Warn children about the dangers of large appliances they could crawl into. Make sure access is restricted and that children cannot easily start the appliances from floor level.

☐ In the event of a suspected poisoning, call your nearest poison control center first, if one is available. If not, call your doctor, then a hospital emergency room.

☐ Simply moving hazardous materials out of sight can eliminate up to 75 percent of all poisonings of young children.

☐ Understand the hazards associated with common houseplants and outdoor plants that are toxic to children and adults.

☐ Teach children to be wary of all strangers. Review ploys used by child molesters and kidnappers on pages 48-49.

☐ Latchkey children should receive special instructions on what they should and shouldn't do while they're home alone.

☐ Review your safety-away-from-home guidelines with children periodically (see pages 48-49).

CHAPTER 5

PET SAFETY

Pets, as the saying goes, are only human. At least that's how many of them are treated. For additional information on pet safety, just read chapter four again, on child safety, because pets can be treated in similar ways. They're curious and often playful. They explore things by biting or chewing or swallowing them.

For our purposes, there are two parts to pet safety: keeping the pets safe and sound, and keeping the people around them unscathed.

KEEPING PETS SAFE AND SOUND

The pets that do the most interacting with human household members are dogs and cats. There are other mammals kept as pets—including mice, rats, guinea pigs, hamsters, rabbits, chinchillas, ferrets, monkeys, pigs, horses, and additional lesser-known creatures—but we'll concentrate on dogs and cats, because individuals keeping more exotic animals are generally versed (or should be) in the animals' care.

Although certain kinds of dogs and cats have been bred in captivity for literally hundreds of years, their roots still go back to the wilds. What that means for pet owners is that your four-footed friends may not always act completely civilized, nor can household pets survive without your care. In the following pages we will look at a number of ways to keep your pets safe and sound.

Keep Them Where They Belong

The greatest hazards to most pets come when they are turned loose outside to fend for themselves for minutes or hours at a time. This usually occurs because the owners have had some success with such behavior before—it's a lot easier to open the front door on a dark and stormy night, without having to get dressed or having to march up and down a boulevard with a dog yanking on the end of a leash. House pets outdoors on their own are at a greater disadvantage than are pets raised on the street or in a wild environment.

Typical household cats and dogs can fall victim to a variety of dangers. They can get hit by cars, trucks, vans, motorcycles or other vehicles. Black pets are at a distinct disadvantage at night. Ask any commercial breeder of black Labrador retrievers what their number-one non-age-related dog mortality cause is, and the answer will likely be "the streets." White or cream-colored animals can also be at risk on the streets during winter, when they blend into snow-covered terrain.

Pets can be injured in fights with other animals. Some dogs and cats can be very territorial. If your pet happens to wander into the domain of a Siberian husky or pair of Siamese cats, a tussle could result in which your pet could be seriously injured or killed. Pets can also be injured by wild animals such as foxes, porcupines, raccoons and owls.

Pets also can be hurt by heartless people. Some individuals value their yards above anything else. They'll sit up late, in darkened living rooms, peering outside, BB gun in hand, waiting for an unsuspecting dog to come padding across the yard. Other individuals are just naturally cruel—for no reason at all. Since typical pets have no reason for suspecting that strangers could mean them harm, they may let themselves be captured — and even kidnapped — by someone who gets a kick out of seeing living things suffer.

Pets can get lost, too. Sure, you saw the movie where Lassie treks thousands of miles over months and months to get home, and you've heard of cats, dogs and birds that have traveled incredible distances in similar circumstances. But don't trust your own pets to do the same. Many dogs, especially when they are young, simply wander away from home, never to be seen again. Numerous things can happen to a lost dog, including starvation, hypothermia, and even adoption by well-meaning individuals.

Besides chain-link and other landscaping-type fences, invisible fences are also an option to help you keep your pet where it belongs. An invisible fence system consists of a thin antenna wire buried about an inch into the ground around the perimeter of an outside area or yard. The dog wears a collar with a transistorized radio receiver. A radio transmitter in the basement, garage or other nearby location sends pulsed signals through the buried wire "fence." When the dog wearing the collar comes within a predetermined distance of the buried wire, the collar will emit a beeping noise. If the dog doesn't stop, he'll receive a mild shock. The dog is conditioned so it stops and won't go beyond the wire.

Keep Them Properly Fed

Feed your pets the right kinds of foods, in correct amounts. Many, many dogs and cats are overweight. They're fed table scraps, treats and snacks at irregular hours. Fat cats and dogs are more likely to become injured when faced with situations in which mobility is needed, such as avoiding a speeding pickup truck or the snarling jaws of a Doberman pinscher. Too, obese pets run up against many of the same medical ills faced by overweight humans, such as heart problems and cancer. While a table scrap here and there won't cause problems, sharp chicken, turkey or pork bones from leftovers may become lodged in a pet's mouth or throat, or perforate an intestinal tract. Other common foods such as chocolate and salt can also be harmful to pets.

Figure 5-1. A doghouse.

Keep Them Properly Sheltered and Cared for During Winter

Dogs used to sleeping outside in doghouses can withstand most winter conditions, as long as their shelter is slightly raised off the ground with an entrance that faces away from the prevailing wind, and has some insulation and dry bedding (see Figure 5-1). On subzero nights, however, consider bringing them indoors.

Animals, like humans, need extra energy to keep warm in the cold, so consider supplementing your pet's diet with extra portions of food during the winter if it stays outdoors. Check an outdoor pet's water dish every day, and replace frozen water with fresh, warm water. Since indoor pets tend to be less active during the winter months, it's best to decrease their food portions to keep them from gaining excess weight.

Cold is not the only winter hazard your pets face. Keep pets away from your vehicles when you're adding antifreeze. Antifreeze is sweet-tasting but highly poisonous. Clean up any spills immediately, before a dog or cat has a chance to lick them.

Occasionally check your pet's paws for ice balls or pieces of rock salt between the claws or toes that can cause skin irritations and sores, and can result in a noticeable limp. Paws that are cracked and bleeding can also be afflicted with frostbite.

Cats have been known to crawl onto or near warm car engines to sleep. If you or your neighbors have a cat or cats that range the neighborhood, consider opening the hood of your car before starting it, or slap the hood with your hand before starting the engine on cold days to startle any animal sleeping there.

Limit an indoor pet's exposure to freezing weather conditions. Consider putting a sweater on small or short-haired dogs, puppies and older dogs.

Protect Them From Heat

Summer heat and humidity can be deadly to pets. If you haven't noticed, most pets are covered with fur. Their skin can't perspire like ours can. That's why dogs continually pant, with their tongues hanging out, during spells of hot weather. Evaporation of moisture from their tongues and from the pads of their feet help rid their bodies of excess heat. Fresh water should always be available for pets. And on hot days the inside of your car, van or truck can be an extremely dangerous place to leave your pet. A dog or cat "trapped" inside such a vehicle could suffer brain damage or death in a matter of minutes.

A pet's doghouse or other sleeping quarters should be in a cool, shady spot. Avoid tying a pet outside where there is no shade or water, and be careful not to over exercise animals during the hottest parts of the day. It's generally best to leave pets alone during the "dog days" of summer.

Fleas, ticks and other parasites are more prevalent during warmer months. If your dog or cat frequents areas with thick underbrush and tall grasses, or interacts with other pets that may be infested, consider shampooing and treating your pet with spray or powder insecticides recommended by a veterinarian. Look carefully for fleas and ticks around a pet's ears, neck, back legs, "armpits," groin areas and between its toes. One way to remove ticks is to apply rubbing alcohol to them or dab a drop of nail polish remover or animal flea/tick spray on them to shock the hardy insects, wait about two minutes, and then pull them off gently with tweezers. Flea collars and flea-resistant bedding such as cedar shavings may also help control pests. Daily brushing will help keep a pet's coat clean, and will rid fur of dander that will otherwise build up during summer and add to the heat problem. The brushing will also give you an opportunity to inspect your pet's skin for rashes, which are more common during warmer temperatures. If a pet scratches more than usual or develops patches of raw skin, take it to a vet.

Schedule Regular Trips to the Vet

Pets periodically need rabies, heartworm, and a variety of other shots or inoculations, depending on the hazards present where you live. Check with your vet and follow her recommendations.

Other Pet Safety Tips

Avoid giving a cat medicine that was intended for a dog, and vice versa. Cats can be extremely sensitive to flea and tick treatments.

If your pet is an indoor animal, follow poison control procedures similar to those used for children. In other words, keep harmful substances out of a pet's sight and mind. That includes common household cleaning products, cosmetics, garbage and poisonous houseplants. Cats are notorious plant-chewers, so be aware that plants such as mistletoe, dieffenbachia, and Christmas cherry can cause felines severe vomiting, diarrhea and even death. Seedpods and beans of dried tropical plants can be especially toxic.

Keep pets away from areas in which you're working with chemicals. Keep dogs or cats away when you are painting your bedroom, changing your car's oil or antifreeze, or spreading weed killer on the back lawn.

Don't forget that glass surfaces can be hazardous for pets. Countless pets have walked into, run through and flown against glass doors and windows, especially when pets are new to a particular environment. Safety glass, decals, blinds, sheer curtains and other window treatments can help prevent unfortunate accidents, and so can restricting a pet's freedom inside the home until it's used to the boundaries.

If you like your pet's company when you travel, use some good common sense to keep your dog or cat safe. Pets should not ride in the back of an open pickup truck. They can be too easily tempted to leap out of the truck bed. The best place for a pet is in the backseat or the rear portion of a car, van or station wagon. Portable pens or pet carriers of all sizes are also available. If you have a pickup truck, a pen can be secured to the truck's bed. Be careful if your pickup truck bed has a cap or canopy enclosure. Rear exhaust systems or leaking side exhausts can pollute the inside of the bed if carbon monoxide enters through a rusty floor or from between the bed and tailgate. Always make sure there is plenty of ventilation.

PROTECTING YOURSELF AND YOUR FAMILY MEMBERS FROM PETS

There are a number of hazards you should be aware of when it comes to pets. Reading the following pages will familiarize you with those hazards and ways to avoid them.

Most Pets Can Bite or Scratch

Whether your pet bites or scratches depends on the pet, and the situation. Certain breeds are more difficult to handle, are more high strung, nervous, or likely to lash out at someone they don't know. If you're planning to purchase a dog or cat, read up on the breeds you are considering. Golden retrievers, though quite large, are excellent with children. So are Labrador retrievers. But expecting similar personalities from a Doberman pinscher or a pit bull would be asking too much.

Some households elect to obtain pets from Humane Society shelters—dogs and cats that are unwanted by others or caught running loose by animal protection officers. Most such animals do not come with papers—detailed family trees or lineage histories—and many are of unknown mixed breeds. The mixed breeds can be good, all-around, friendly mutts or cats—or they can be miserably mean individuals. Their true personalities may not emerge until the puppy or kitten matures.

If you have a pet already, consider that temperaments can change as animals age. A cocker spaniel that would once put up with children tugging at its ears may not be so forgiving toward the latter part of its life. Young children should be instructed not to approach a pet when it is eating, drinking, chewing on a rawhide bone, fighting or sound asleep. Children should also keep their faces away from a

pet's face and paws. Cats can easily shred skin with their claws, and they have a knack for striking out at any eyes within pawing distance.

And certainly discourage children from attempting to handle unfamiliar animals—there is no way of knowing whether such animals are healthy, and the animals themselves may not recognize such attempts as friendly. Too, avoid adopting animals from the wild—especially if the animals appear to be sick or injured. If you want, report sightings of injured animals to the local wildlife biologist or conservation officer.

In general, trust only the pets you are already familiar with, or ones you gradually get to know.

Pets Can Carry Fleas, Ticks, Other Pests and Illnesses

Pests can cause diseases—some of which can be serious, such as Rocky Mountain spotted fever, rabies, distemper, tetanus, lyme disease and others. Some bacteria and fungi from pet skin conditions can also cause problems for humans.

Pets Can Cause Strains, Trips, Slips and Falls

An untrained large dog, when walked by a small (or regular-sized) person, can yank so hard on a leash that a strained wrist, arm, shoulder or back can result. Either take the dog to obedience school, or use a choke chain that restricts the dog's breathing if it pulls too hard. Be careful not to put the chain over a regular leather collar, though, because the leather collar may impede the workings of the choke chain, preventing the choker from tightening up as it should.

A dog that sleeps anywhere it wants to in a house can also be a hazard at night if it curls up in a dark bedroom hallway at the top of a stairway. Black dogs are especially risky this way.

Pets Can Strain Relationships Among Household Members

A black Labrador living in a home full of white wall-to-wall carpeting, white tile flooring and white furniture, can definitely cause problems. The hair the dog sheds will be noticed everywhere. Pets need to be fed and watered every day. They need to be groomed. They need to be taken out or cleaned up after. They need to be trained and played with. When young they can literally chew and scratch their way through carpeting, wallpaper and furniture. They need medical examinations and from time to time, pills, shots and various medicines. They need to be looked after when the rest of the family goes on vacation. Before your family adopts a pet, consider the responsibilities and inconveniences and decide how to handle these. A little planning now can preserve family harmony later.

Pet Dander and Hair Can Cause Allergies
Some family members may develop allergies to the dander and hair a pet sheds. If they do, several recourses other than going pet-less, are to switch to other kinds of animals—such as reptiles, or to arrange for suitable pet living quarters outdoors.

PET SAFETY QUICK CHECKLIST

- ☐ Don't let pets run loose. Keep them off the streets.

- ☐ Keep pets properly fed; do not overfeed or substitute highly spiced or fatty human food for standard pet fare.

- ☐ Keep clean water available for pets at all times.

- ☐ Cover garbage containers so pets cannot get to chicken bones, pork bones, fish bones or other refuse.

- ☐ Shelter pets from direct sunlight, rain and extreme temperatures.

- ☐ Never keep pets in closed vehicles during sunny or hot, humid days.

- ☐ Guard pets against fleas, ticks and other pests.

- ☐ Schedule your pets for regular veterinarian checkups.

- ☐ Follow poison control precautions similar to those used for children.

- ☐ Don't let pets ride unprotected in the bed of an open pickup truck.

- ☐ Children should keep their faces away from a dog or cat's mouth and paws; should not attempt to handle unfamiliar or wild animals; and should not approach or bother an animal that is sleeping, fighting, drinking, eating, or chewing on a rawhide bone or other item the pet would consider its own.

- ☐ Never bring home or try to adopt sick, injured or "abandoned" animals from the wild.

- ☐ Trust only pets you are already familiar with, or ones you gradually get to know.

PET SAFETY QUICK CHECKLIST
(continued)

☐ Make sure your pets have a clean bill of health, free from disease, skin conditions and parasites.

☐ Don't put up with a large dog pulling on a leash when walking. Take the dog to obedience school or use a choke chain to keep the animal reined in.

☐ Know where your pets sleep at night so you won't trip over them in the dark, or use night lights so you can see where you're going.

☐ Be aware of pet behavior that annoys other household members, and consider how to modify that behavior to reduce the annoyance.

CHAPTER 6

HOLIDAY SAFETY

Please find a calendar and take a few moments to flip through the months. When you do, you'll probably recall how many of the dates hold important meanings for you. There's your birthday, your anniversary, and a lot of upcoming weekends. There's when your children's school holidays begin and end. Flipping backward, there's Super Bowl Sunday, Easter, the dates your golf and softball leagues start, the Fourth of July and Labor Day.

Certainly, we all like to get away from work or home once in a while, and enjoy a holiday or vacation. Why not? We work hard during the rest of the year, and the time off comes well earned.

Overall, it's safe to say that for most of us, holiday time is enjoyable time, time that's often kept alive a long while with the help of photo albums and pleasant memories. Unfortunately, for some individuals and their families, particular holidays or vacations bring depressing thoughts to mind instead. While *we* may take days off, accidents don't. In fact, holidays and vacations bring accidents out in full force: car crashes, drownings, heat strokes and home mishaps abound.

Holidays and vacation days are times we change our daily routines and do different things. Proper planning will prevent those special days from becoming bad memories. Holiday planning begins at home. This year, ask yourself a few questions before your holidays arrive.

• Do you know enough about what you'll be

doing (even though you may have done it before)?
• Do you know the risks involved?
• Do you know how to avoid those risks?
• Are you aware of hazards you can't control?

Here's a representative sampling of holidays celebrated by many, and how those and similar times can be made safer.

ST. PATRICK'S DAY

St. Patrick's Day is one of the earliest "informal" holidays celebrated during the year, where green is traditional and so are shamrocks, Irish folksongs, and plenty of beer drinking and partying. It comes after a long holiday drought of January, February, and part of March. The big dangers here, of course, are drinking and driving, slips on beer-soaked tavern floors and steps, and all of the accompanying hazards that go with socializing shoulder to shoulder with a bunch of unruly Irish and would-be-Irish patrons who spend the day and night celebrating St. Pat's. In fact, just walking along sidewalks and streets in the vicinity of an Irish tavern can put you in peril.

Celebrate if you must, but know your limits and arrange for transportation if you or your friends drink.

APRIL FOOL'S DAY

A gentle reminder to beware of pranksters. Every year it happens somewhere. Simple, innocuously planned jokes turn deadly. When someone pushed into a swimming pool hits his head and drowns. When someone locked in a car trunk suffocates by accident. When someone drinks a soda laced with something that turns out to be poisonous. The examples go on and on.

Think twice how someone could react to a "practical" joke, especially if you don't know the person that well. You're not sure of what lurks behind a person's expression; you could send someone over the edge with a poorly timed or devised joke. Without badmouthing the entire day, you're usually better off just letting others make fools of themselves.

EASTER

Easter is generally a joyous time. Spring weather, bright colors, religious ceremonies, visions of Easter bunnies, baskets with brightly colored straw, chocolate animals and egg hunts are all associated with this springtime holiday.

Many children and adults color hard-boiled eggs for display in Easter baskets. If the eggs are meant to be eaten later, watch how they're colored, handled and stored. Although most supermarket-variety egg dyes are made from nontoxic food colorings, some products are not. Certain marking pens or paints may be poisonous and not intended for use on food. When applied to delicate egg shells the color could leach into the egg and be eaten by unsuspecting children or adults.

Some recipes for egg coloring require the eggs to be warm so the color will dry correctly. Make sure the eggs have cooled enough so they won't burn tiny fingers eager to take the eggs out of a pan or bowl.

Because there's usually quite a bit of chocolate available in homes during Easter, pets have increased opportunities to grab a piece of it from a basket or tabletop, or to find bits of chocolate that children have misplaced or dropped onto the floor. Unfortunately, chocolate is particularly dangerous to pets. It contains a powerful stimulant called theobromine, which is toxic to pets. Enough chocolate ingestion could lead to pet heart irregularities and even death.

SUMMER VACATIONS

Summer is vacation time for millions of families. It's a time when people break out of their normal routines and do different things. They travel, pursue hobbies, socialize, plan remodeling projects, or just relax around the house.

Many vacations revolve around automobile trips. A few tips on defensive driving can help keep your vacation safe and sound. You've probably heard the saying "The best offense is a good defense." Well, in sports, that means that a strong, well-balanced offense is frequently not enough to win with. A good defense is needed to prevent the opposition from doing damage. No doubt you've also heard the term "defensive driving." And for good reason. Defensive driving means thinking and planning and driving in a way that will prevent accidents from happening. Defensive driving consists of training yourself and other household drivers to pay attention to a variety of important factors on the road.

Road Conditions

Poor visibility, blind spots on hills, ice, oil-slick concrete and huge potholes are all accident causers. The weather, the time of day or night, the shape of the road and the lay of the land can all conspire to make driving treacherous.

Equipment Conditions

Careless drivers don't bother to keep their tires properly inflated, their wipers working or their brakes adjusted. Regular inspection and maintenance will head off dangerous breakdowns in the field.

Traffic Conditions

Rush hours are just that—times of the day and night when people are in a hurry, coming and going. Many people don't give themselves enough time to get places, so they take chances on the road that can get themselves or other drivers in trouble.

Other Drivers

Just because *you* drive safely doesn't mean everyone else will. Be on guard against the dangerous driving habits of other people: the person who drives or slides through a stop sign, the trucker who falls asleep on the thruway, the teenager who abruptly turns without a turn signal, the drunk driver.

Your Own Driving Skills

Know your own limits and don't try anything fancy. Maintain a safe distance behind vehicles in front of you and don't go too fast for conditions.

Consider all of the above whenever you're on the road. Keep rolling them over in your mind, as if each of the points has a turn under a magnifying glass. Pay close attention to the driving conditions, the traffic and your own driving.

THE FOURTH OF JULY

Fireworks are fun and exciting to watch, but they're best left to experts who know how to handle them safely. Firecrackers and even sparklers in the wrong hands can bring about all kinds of hazardous situations, from fires through critical injuries.

Other Independence Day safety concerns include safe travel, drinking and driving hazards, picnics (safe food handling), overexertion at outdoor sporting events, and safe water sports.

HALLOWEEN

Maybe you could have gotten away with it years ago, but today, never let young children go trick-or-treating door-to-door without the presence of a responsible adult. Older children should stay together and let someone know the route they are taking and when they'll be home. For safety's sake, children should dress in light-colored costumes or darker costumes with strips of reflective tape applied to the front, back and sides. Masks are dangerous because even with large eye openings they block peripheral vision. Face paint is often a safer alternative. Children should also be encouraged to carry flashlights or glow sticks throughout the evening (see Figure 6-1).

All candy should be brought home so parents can look at it and weed out any pieces that don't look right. Look for candy wrappers that may have already been opened, or wrappers with holes or slits in them. Never eat homemade treats unless they were received from a trusted neighbor.

Figure. 6-1. Trick-or-treater with flashlight.

Consider having a Halloween party for children where they can get candy and play games. It's a lot safer. Each year, parents can take turns hosting and helping out. It will eliminate the potential hazards of night traffic, bad weather, and altercations between older children who may bully younger participants along the way.

THANKSGIVING

Improper handling of Thanksgiving turkeys can put a damper on family parties. Consider the following precautions when preparing your birds.

Store a frozen turkey in its original wrapper at 0 degrees Fahrenheit or below. Don't keep it in a vehicle trunk—even if the outside temperature is cold enough, the effect of sunlight beating down on the trunk can raise inside temperatures far above freezing levels.

Thaw a frozen turkey in a refrigerator. Allow two or three days for a bird eighteen pounds and over and one or two days for a smaller bird. Turkeys can also be thawed partially in a refrigerator and then placed under cool running water until completely thawed. Avoid thawing a bird at room temperature or in standing water.

After a turkey is thawed, remove the giblets and rinse them. Then rinse the turkey thoroughly inside and out. Cook the bird within 24 hours of its thawing, to an internal temperature of at least 165 degrees Fahrenheit before serving.

CHRISTMAS

Although holiday times can be some of the happiest times of the year, traditions that are unfulfilled, or certain obligations can become overwhelming and stressful for household members. The weeks including Christmas and New Year's can be especially difficult. A few pointers will help you avoid added stress and stay safe during those times.

Avoid seasonal tensions—shop early. The closer the holidays get, the more harried and impatient people in the crowd become. Avoid this contagious feeling through advance planning. You'll get better gift selections as well.

When you shop, park in well-lit locations as close to your destination as possible. If someone asks you for help while you're in a vehicle, do not become physically involved. Stay inside of your locked vehicle and, if you must, say that you'll call for help when you reach a phone. Be attentive to situations in which hazards to your personal security could develop.

Be conscious of where you carry your money or wallet. Holiday crowds are ideal workplaces for pickpockets and other thieves. Don't flash large rolls of money when making purchases. Keep track of credit cards; tear up carbon copies from credit card purchases so no one gets your card numbers or sees what your signature looks like, and save all of your receipts. Keep a list of your credit card numbers at home in a safe place.

Be wary of potential scams—hustlers and con artists work the streets and neighborhoods during the holidays, "collecting" for all kinds of legitimate-sounding causes when in reality they are collecting for their own pockets.

If you are a holiday drinker, drink responsibly. A good way to handle the question of drinking at holiday parties is to know your limit. That will help

you avoid the pressure to have that extra drink. And of course, if you drink, don't drive.

Christmas Trees

There are two options available for Christmas trees: cut trees and artificial trees. Each type is prone to particular hazards. In general, never leave Christmas tree lights on while you're out of the house or asleep. Use tinsel made of nonlead, nonflammable material. Make sure trees are well supported so small children or pets can't easily knock them down. Ornaments that resemble candy or other edibles, decorations that have sharp points, or ones that have small removable parts should never be hung low enough on the tree to tempt toddlers and other young children.

Cut Trees

If you prefer a cut tree, have one cut from a field or select a fresh one that's recently been harvested locally. The needles should bend without breaking and they should be difficult to pull off the branches. The trunk should be sticky with sap, not dry and smooth to the touch.

When you get the tree home, cut off about two inches from the end of the tree's trunk and set up the tree in a sturdy stand with a reservoir for water. Keep the reservoir filled so the tree can absorb as much moisture as possible. The more moisture within the tree, the more fire-resistant the trunk and branches will be (see Figure 6-2).

Keep the tree away from fireplaces, wood-

Figure. 6-2. A Christmas tree stand.

burning stoves, space heaters and other sources of heat. Don't place it where it will block stairways, hallways or doorways either.

When decorating your Christmas tree, use the right kind of light strings. Outdoor lights will burn too hot for use indoors. Even indoor lights can give off considerable heat, sometimes enough to dry a tree's needles. As the holidays go by, check the tree's branches for brown dried spots and move the lights around occasionally. Better yet, buy low-watt bulbs that will use less energy and burn cooler. Small twinkle lights are ideal. And use fewer lights instead of more. Never use more than three light sets on any extension cord. Place extension cords against walls; don't run them beneath carpets.

Examine the individual light bulbs closely before you put the string up. If you have colored bulbs, look for bare or clear spots—signs that a light string is getting old. A bare spot could indicate a scrape, or it could be a sign that the bulb burned too hot, causing the paint to peel. Look at the wires themselves, and the plugs. Are wires frayed or kinked? Are the plugs coming loose from the wires? Inspect each string of lights for an Underwriters Laboratories (UL) testing seal (see Figure 6-3).

Avoid keeping a cut tree past the point where the needles start dropping off en masse. And resist the urge to cut up and burn the tree in your fireplace—it will likely burn too hot and virtually explode into flames. Instead, safely dispose of your tree. Your town or city may have a recycling program for turning dead Christmas trees into chips for landscaping mulch.

Artificial Trees
When purchasing an artificial tree, make sure you know how fire resistant it is. And learn how long

it will remain fire resistant; many trees lose their resistance to fire over time. Models with built-in electrical systems should always carry an Underwriters Laboratories label.

Never string electric lights on a metal tree—the tree is too efficient a conductor to take a chance with. A malfunction in the lights could cause someone touching the tree to be electrocuted. Shine colored spotlights on the tree instead.

When you're hanging decorations, avoid standing on chairs or stacked-up boxes. Instead use a sturdy ladder tall enough for the job.

Other Decorations
Inside stairways should be kept clear, and handrails should be kept free of decorations.

Candles
Avoid using candles near evergreen trees or other combustibles such as curtains, wrapping paper or carpeting. Place candles where they won't be accidentally knocked over by children, pets, or people who pass by. Blow out all candles when you leave the room or house or go to sleep.

Plants
Be aware that some holiday plants, such as mistletoe and holly, are poisonous and can cause severe stomach problems if eaten. Poinsettias can also cause stomach irritation. Keep all of them out of the reach of children and pets.

Outdoor Lights
Outdoor lights and lights on outside trees and shrubs should be rated for outdoor use and should be plugged into sockets or outdoor-rated extension cords that are in good condition with no frayed spots. Indoor-rated lights don't have waterproof connections and could short-circuit and start a fire. Extension cords should be plugged into ground fault circuit interrupters (GFCI), the type of outlet that has test buttons. A GFCI will detect the release of ungrounded electricity and shut down the power.

When running extension cords, a good rule of thumb to follow is that the extension cord diameter should not be any smaller than diameter of the ap-

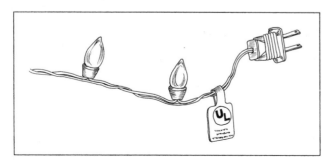

Figure. 6-3. UL seal on string of lights.

pliance cord or string of lights that's attached it.

While decorating the outside of the house, or installing a plastic Santa and his reindeer on your roof's ridge, use an appropriate ladder. Rent one if need be. Stake the bottom of the ladder for extra safety—especially if it's wet or icy out—and tie the top of the ladder to a window or other sturdy fixture. Avoid reaching too far to one or the other side—move the ladder instead. And watch out for overhead electrical wires while doing so.

Other Considerations

Don't burn gift wrappings in a fireplace or wood-burning stove. Some of the wrapping paper inks may contain lead or other toxic materials that give off fumes.

If you plan to hang stockings over the fireplace, don't do it while there's a fire in the hearth.

If you allow smoking in your house, make sure you provide wide, deep ashtrays. Empty them frequently after making certain the butts are dead out, and make a round through your party rooms before going to bed, checking for smoldering ashes and butts.

NEW YEAR'S EVE

There may be other holidays you traditionally celebrate, and for most of them—including birthdays, anniversaries, proms, graduations, and certain religious celebrations—many of these same party precautions apply.

Anyone who serves alcohol has some legal responsibility for the actions of guests who drink too much, even after they leave the party. But that's not your main reason for taking care of your guests. You simply don't want them to injure themselves or anyone else. A few pointers will help you throw a safe party, even when alcohol is served.

First, stay sober yourself. It's the only way you can act responsibly, and with clear mind. If you plan to drink at your own party, hire a professional bartender who has experience in recognizing inebriated individuals, and instruct the bartender to refuse to serve guests who are becoming intoxicated.

Offer plenty of alternatives to liquor: nonalcoholic punch, eggnog, fruit drinks, soda, and even nonalcoholic wine and beer (see Figure 6-4). Serve

lots of unsalted foods. Salted foods will cause people to want to drink more.

Figure. 6-4. Nonalcoholic drinks.

Don't let guests mix their own drinks so you won't lose control of alcohol quantities served. Stop serving alcohol at least an hour before the party ends to give guests enough time to regain full use of their faculties. Save an interesting activity, such as live entertainment or a gift exchange, for the end of the evening to keep guests from leaving early when they may be more intoxicated.

Do whatever is necessary to keep guests from driving drunk. Take their keys. Pull a spark plug wire. Call a cab for them. Offer them a couch to sleep on, or a room for the night.

One last precaution—wines and liquor can add special flavor to certain holiday party entrees. But even when cooking, alcohol should be handled carefully. Remember that all alcohol is a form of fuel that could, if improperly handled, cause an explosion or fire. Specifically, avoid doubling a recipe, even if only small amounts of alcohol are involved. Too much alcohol in a small, confined, heated space, such as an oven, could result in a holiday tragedy. Generally, dishes containing alcohol should be cooked uncovered. A lid or foil cover could cause pressure to build, which, when subject to heat, might cause an explosion.

IN GENERAL

The holidays are times to plan activities that will build good memories. Don't try to squeeze too many activities into a short span of time. Leave space in your schedule for simple pleasures. Avoid filling up every spare minute with social and other commitments. And give yourself plenty of time to get things done. Being rushed is a major cause of stress, so be sure to start holiday preparations early enough. Don't be afraid to say "No." Eliminate unnecessary activities and appointments.

Delegate holiday duties whenever you can. Buy cookies instead of baking them. Ask your family to pitch in. Have your grandmother prepare entrees for your family reunion dinner. Make the kids clean the house or wash the car. They can do some shopping, help write cards and wrap gifts. Enlist lots of help. You shouldn't have to do everything yourself.

Learn to relax. Do you eat on the run? Do you frequently feel rundown and ill? Are you too busy to exercise? Or too tired? Do you have a hard time sleeping? Do you eat or drink or smoke when you are nervous? Do you have difficulty saying "No"? Do you feel like your life is out of control?

If you answered yes to more than one or two of the above questions, you could be experiencing high levels of stress. Prolonged stress can lead to all kinds of ills, including accidental injury, insomnia, migraine headaches, and even serious illnesses such as high blood pressure, depression or alcoholism.

One of the most effective ways to relieve stress is to learn how to relax. Relaxing is a skill in itself. Listening to music, exercising, daydreaming, and even learning how to meditate can help quiet the mind and body down so you feel fresh and unencumbered by real or imaginary problems. Try taking a few deep breaths, closing your eyes and picturing a quiet scene — palm trees swaying in a gentle ocean breeze, the smell of salt water, the taste of a chilled lemonade, mid-morning sunlight warming your back, and the sounds of sea gulls and surf. Practicing that kind of imaging can help your mind reprogram itself to relax at will.

HOLIDAY SAFETY QUICK CHECKLIST

☐ Plan for safe holidays and vacations in advance. Give yourself enough time to prepare equipment, vehicles, parties or travel arrangements.

☐ Consider the risks involved with any new or old activities planned, and how to avoid those risks.

☐ If you drink, know your limit. Avoid drinking and driving. Prevent others from drinking too much at functions you host.

☐ Practice defensive driving skills.

☐ View fireworks from a distance; don't set them off yourself. Keep them away from children.

☐ Keep a close eye on children in crowded malls, at picnics, tourist attractions, and other places where strangers congregate.

☐ Follow safe food handling procedures; keep cold food cold, and hot food hot.

☐ Review chapter one on fire protection before each Christmas and New Year's season.

☐ Be careful with holiday plants that may be poisonous to children and pets.

☐ Learn how to relax during the holidays and during your vacations. These times should help relieve stress—not create it.

PART TWO

INDOOR SAFETY

Most people think of "home" as a safe place to be. But how safe is your home, really? Start with the things you take for granted: air and water. We've provided information for you to reevaluate how clean and safe these essentials are for you and your family. Then read on to discover the hazards unique to the rooms you probably spend a lot of your time in: the kitchen, bathroom and workshop. Accident *prevention* is the key here. A little extra effort in setting up a safe environment will reap tremendous rewards in averting trouble down the road.

CHAPTER 7

SAFE INDOOR AIR & WATER

Every home, no matter how simple or elaborate, needs a good supply of clean air and water. Anything less will result in an environment that's hazardous to the inhabitants.

SAFE AIR

How long can you go without air? A minute or two? Don't try to find out. Certainly, air has always been there for all of us from point of birth on. Fresh air, clean air, air that fills our lungs and supplies a steady supply of oxygen to our blood is something we take for granted.

But can we any longer? Is the air within your residence safe to breathe? Or could it be tainted with fumes or particles from harmful substances?

Major classes of indoor air pollutants include:

1. Biological contaminants such as bacteria, mold and pollen.
2. Combustion byproducts such as carbon monoxide, cigarette smoke, cooking smoke, and fuel particles and fumes.
3. Radon, a radioactive gas that is found in the ground and in groundwater.
4. Chemical products such as formaldehyde, benzene, and other harmful chemicals present in construction materials, cleaning supplies, paints and solvents, and a wide variety of other items.
5. House dust from many sources.

Together with industrial pollution that may be in the vicinity, and extremely high or low humidity levels, the above pollutants can be present in varying concentrations in any particular household.

Biological Contaminants

Bacteria, mold and fungi can thrive in areas of a residence that are frequently damp or wet. Problems usually develop more quickly during warm and humid weather conditions, but at any temperature, the most important step is moisture control.

Signs of trouble include stuffy odors, moisture condensation on walls and windows, water stains, and areas where books, papers, magazines, clothes, furniture or other items become damp or moldy.

Some individuals are allergic to mold. How can you tell? Physicians can diagnose conditions related to "biological pollutant" sickness. To help a doctor determine if a person's health problems may be related to biological pollution, make sure you know the answers to some of the following questions:

• Does anyone in the household have frequent headaches, fevers, itchy watery eyes, a stuffy nose, a dry throat, or a persistent cough?

• Does anyone complain of feeling tired or dizzy all the time, or having difficulties breathing?

• Did any of the symptoms above appear after you moved to a new residence?

• Do the symptoms disappear or become less intense when the affected person goes to school, work, or anywhere else away from home—only to return when the person comes back?

• Have you recently remodeled your home or performed any energy conservation projects such as installing storm windows or weather stripping? Did symptoms occur after the residence became more weather resistant?

• Does your home feel humid? Have you had any recent water damage? Can you see moisture on the windows or on other surfaces such as walls and ceilings?

• What is the usual temperature in your residence?

• Do you have any new pets?

• Do symptoms get worse from exposure to hay or fields, from raking dry leaves, from a lawn being mowed, when in a damp basement, or after consuming foods and drinks prepared by fermentation such as beer, wine, sharp cheese, sauerkraut, pickles or mushrooms?

• Are you allergic to penicillin, which is made from mold?

To reduce unwanted moisture, vent clothes dryers to the outdoors to minimize moisture buildups in basement or laundry rooms. If there aren't enough vents on your home's roof, install additional units to keep attics and crawl spaces dry and reasonably cool or warm. How can you tell if your ventilation is adequate? If your attic surfaces are damp or more than warm to the touch during hot summer temperatures, ventilation must be improved. For a second or third opinion, ask several reputable roofing contractors to take a look and supply you with suggestions or quotes.

Install fans that vent to the outdoors in kitchens and bathrooms. In the kitchen, make sure you run them when cooking soups and other liquids. Mold frequently develops where water pipes enter the space in a cupboard below a sink. Another potential problem is in surplus water trays on self-defrosting refrigerators. A small amount of borax—a natural mold fighter—when sprinkled over the area and wiped clean a few hours later will usually remove and prevent mold from forming. In the bathroom, run the exhaust fan when you take showers or baths. Clean shower stalls and other damp surfaces with mild disinfectants.

In bathrooms, mold often begins to grow in the grouting between tiles, and in the caulking seams between the tub and shower unit and wall. See if caulking and grouting is still intact. If not, repair damaged sections. Shower curtains are another common bathroom mold producer, especially if they are lined. The floor at the rear base of a toilet can also be a problem. The overall solution is air circulation. A built-in shower exhaust fan is usually a sufficient solution.

Empty water trays in air conditioners, dehumidifiers and refrigerators frequently. And pay special attention to your household humidifier. Humidifiers are used to add moisture to air that's too dry for comfort—a common problem in the low humidity conditions of winter. Humidifiers can become breeding grounds for biological contaminants because they contain standing water for long periods of time. An effective way to combat bacteria growth is to clean "cool mist" and ultrasonic humidifiers daily, and use only distilled water in them.

Damp or wet carpeting can be a persistent cause of moisture and provides an effective medium for the growth of mold, especially in basement or lower-level bathrooms, bedrooms or family rooms. Dry carpeting by using a dehumidifier and by setting up one or more large fans to constantly move air over the wet fabric.

In basements that tend to leak or collect moisture, take care of problems. Patch cracks in the walls and floor, renew the drainage tile system around the building's foundation, keep sump pumps in good operating condition, paint damp walls with a water-sealing basement paint, and periodically clean and disinfect floor drains with commercial drain cleaner. It's not enough to keep leaks at a standstill—the foundation must be sealed off from outside air as well. Air entering a home from the soil can contain considerable amounts of moisture.

Use basements as living areas only if they are leak proof and have adequate ventilation. Set up dehumidifiers, if necessary, to maintain comfortable humidity levels. In large basements, two dehumidifiers—one placed at each end of the basement—may be enough to rid the area of excessive moisture. Buy large-capacity models equipped with controls that automatically turn the units off when the collection tubs fill with water or when the room's humidity level drops to an acceptable level, a level that you can control by setting the unit from low to medium to highest moisture removal.

A number of biological villains are residents of household dust. Pollens and tiny dust mites cause allergies that result in itchy eyes or noses or even asthmatic attacks. Mold spores are also hidden in house dust. During winter, mold spores are usually not active, unless areas of your basement or other rooms are particularly damp. But during warm weather, when humidity rises, mold or fungi can grow or bloom on basement walls, in closets, on wallpaper glue, in drywall, and on leather and all sorts of clothing items. As the molds mature they'll send new spores floating throughout the house where they're breathed into the lungs of household members. It's a good idea to wash your bedding at least once a week with hot water, to kill dust mites and help keep pollen and other spores from close contact with yourself and other family members.

Combustion Byproducts

Apart from hazards brought about by uncontrolled house fires, so-called "controlled" burning can introduce undesirable combustion byproducts into a residence, including carbon monoxide, smoke, tiny particles of carbon, and other substances.

Combustion byproducts come from a variety of sources. Unvented kerosene and gasoline heaters and stoves do not burn with 100 percent efficiency; they send unburned particles and fumes into the air. Chimneys and flues can leak smoke and fumes into a house or garage. Downdrafts can hold combustion byproducts within wood stoves and fireplaces until they're eventually forced out of seams or other openings in the sides. Other hazards may come from tobacco smoke, or automobile, lawn mower or snowblower exhausts, and even smoke and fumes from cooking supper in the kitchen.

Carbon Monoxide

Carbon monoxide is produced when organic material such as coal, wood, paper, oil, gasoline, gas or related fuels are burned in a limited supply of air or oxygen. Or in other words, any process where incomplete burning of organic material may occur is a potential source of carbon monoxide. It's a color-less, tasteless and almost odorless gas that is lighter than air.

The International Labor Office states that carbon monoxide is thought to be by far the most common single cause of poisonings both in industry and in homes. One reason that's true is because there are so many ways for carbon monoxide to be produced.

The appearance of symptoms depends on the concentration of carbon monoxide in the air, the exposure time, how active the person is while exposed, and how susceptible the individual is. Loss of consciousness can occur almost instantaneously and can be fatal, with few signs or symptoms in advance, if concentrations are high enough. Lower concentrations can produce tell-tale symptoms of headache, dizziness and nausea. Those can be followed by weakness, vomiting and eventual coma. The victim may first appear pale in color, but will quickly turn cherry red because of the harmful chemical changes occurring to the blood.

Luckily, carbon monoxide does not accumulate in the body. It's ventilated from the blood and lungs if enough exposure to fresh air is allowed. This, though, does not minimize the possible effects of repeated mild or moderate exposures, which may result in the death of brain cells and damage to the central nervous system. Children and pregnant women are especially at risk.

At home, what are the signs of potentially dangerous levels of carbon monoxide?

- Persistently stuffy, stale or smelly air that never clears.
- The smell of exhaust fumes.
- Very high humidity, often showing up as moisture on the windows.
- Soot around the outside of a fireplace, furnace or chimney.
- Persistent severe headaches.
- Dizziness or blurred vision.
- Rapid heartbeat, pulse, or a tightening of the chest.
- Sleepiness, but never feeling rested.
- Chest pain or angina while exercising.
- Feeling sick and tired when at home, but fine once you leave the house.

There are steps you can take to reduce the possibility of carbon monoxide exposure. First, vent all furnaces to the outdoors, and make sure there is adequate ventilation with a healthy supply of fresh air when using unvented space heaters. Take special precautions when operating fuel-burning, unvented kerosene or gas space heaters. In fact, you're better off not to use them at all. But if you do, closely adhere to the manufacturer's guidelines, especially the instructions on the proper fuel to use, and on keeping the heater tuned and correctly adjusted for optimum burning efficiency and safety. A continuous or flickering yellow-tipped flame usually indicates something out of line that is polluting the surrounding air. And don't worry about keeping all of the heat in—open a door or a window slightly for ventilation.

If you heat with wood, choose a properly sized wood stove that is certified to meet pollution emission standards. Doors on wood stoves should fit tightly, and the installations should be done professionally. Too many carbon monoxide poisonings result from amateur wood stove setups. Use aged or cured wood only. Avoid tossing newspapers, magazines and miscellaneous trash into wood stoves. And follow the manufacturer's directions for starting, stoking and putting out the fires.

Have a trained heating technician inspect, clean and tune-up your central heating system (furnaces, boilers, flues and chimneys) annually. Repair any leaks promptly. Be especially wary of blocked, leaking or otherwise damaged chimneys, and of cracked furnace heat exchangers. Gas company representatives can be helpful when you have any questions or concerns with appliances that use natural gas or propane gas as fuel. They'll often agree to inspect gas burning appliances you have concerns about. They can check for carbon monoxide and other pollutants.

To further control household pollutants, consider installing sealed combustion heating equipment. With sealed-combustion equipment, outside air is drawn directly into the combustion chamber. Flue gases exhaust directly outside, too—usually through a wall in plastic pipe or stainless steel ducts instead of up a chimney. Such a system completely seals the combustion from household air.

Change filters on central heating and cooling systems and air cleaners according to the manufacturer's recommendations. Keep all gas appliances properly adjusted for optimal burning efficiency.

Install and use exhaust fans vented to the outdoors over gas cooking stoves and ranges. (*Never* use picnic charcoal grills or barbecues indoors.) Vents should not be located next to potential sources of outdoor air pollution, such as adjacent to a parking garage, loading dock or alley where vehicles may frequently park with their engines idling. (This is not likely in suburban or country settings, but can figure in with city and downtown apartment living.) If you have an attached garage avoid allowing vehicles to idle inside of your garage.

Tobacco Smoke
Say what, Surgeon General?

If you haven't noticed by now, cigarette, cigar and pipe smoke is not good for anyone's health. There is no controversy about the facts. To put things in perspective, hundreds of thousands of Americans die each year from the effects of cigarette smoking—more than the combined total of Americans who die from AIDS, drug abuse, car accidents and homicide. And what's more, secondary tobacco smoke—smoke inhaled by non-smokers who share the same air with smokers—contains the same harmful components. And these components are the main causes of emphysema, lung cancer and chronic bronchitis.

What's in tobacco smoke? Unbelievably, there are over 4,000 chemicals, almost 50 of which are suspected of causing cancer. Some of the pollutants in tobacco smoke include formaldehyde, urethane, ammonia, nitrites, carbon monoxide, hydrogen cyanide, vinyl chloride, volatile alcohols and various sulfur compounds. The most well-known hazardous ingredients are tar and nicotine. Tar refers to the combined chemical content in tobacco smoke (less nicotine and moisture)—the stuff that goes into the room or into the lungs of a smoker. Nicotine is an addictive drug in cigarettes, a powerful stimulant similar to caffeine or amphetamines. It increases your heart rate and raises your blood pressure. It's powerful, too. In fact, it's as habit-forming as heroin. People also become psychologically dependent on smoking, and they automatically reach for cigarettes whenever they're pressured, bored, or even when they just want to relax.

What's the solution here? How do you stop polluting your home with tobacco smoke? It's easy but difficult. Stop smoking and encourage others to do the same. That's the best solution. If smokers *must* smoke, let them smoke outdoors, so non-smokers needn't breathe polluted air in the house. If it's too cold or rainy outside for smokers to pursue their hazardous habit, at the very best, banish them to a remote room that's well ventilated. By all means, recognize the non-smoker's right to breathe clean, unaffected air.

Smoke From Burning Foods
Although this source of smoke causes nowhere near the problems that cigarette smoking causes, it can still be a source of air pollution in the home. Use common sense in the kitchen. Avoid leaving meats and other dishes cooking in the oven while you're gone from the house. Teach children not to adjust or turn on the stove or cooktop burners by themselves. Make sure a smoke alarm is installed in the kitchen, but not directly over the stove. See that the ovens and cooking surfaces are vented to the outdoors.

Radon
Radon is a radioactive gas that's produced by the gradual breakdown or decomposition of radium, an element that occurs naturally within ground and groundwater in varying (usually very small) concentrations. Air pressure within a home is usually lower than the pressure in the soil around the building's foundation. This difference in pressure acts like a vacuum that can draw radon in through foundation cracks and other openings.

That radon exposure is hazardous to humans was suspected years ago when high percentages of German and Czechoslovakian miners developed lung cancer while working in areas having high concentrations of radon.

How Radon Enters a House
Radon can enter a dwelling in a number of ways (see Figure 7-1):
- Through cracks and voids in basement side

walls, foundations and floors, or in openings around drains, sump pumps, joints and pipes.
- Through dirt-floor basements.
- Through areas left unfinished by the builder.
- Water drawn from a private well may contain radon that subsequently gets released into the house.
- Low air pressure can increase radon levels. Low air pressure can be caused by large appliances, such as a furnace or clothes dryer, that draw air into the house, by a warm indoor temperature during cold weather, through chimneys, and through kitchen and other exhaust fans.

Testing for Radon
Before you make any kind of decision about testing for radon, contact your local or state environmental agency or health department, and ask what they recommend. Some agencies offer free testing services. At the very least, they may be able to tell you, based on your location, if you're in a known radon area.

If a government agency will not perform the test, you can have a commercial testing service come to your residence and perform a radon test, or you can purchase a radon kit and complete the test yourself. Either method is acceptable. If you don't want to bother with learning how to use a test kit, and you don't mind paying a little more for the results, hire a reputable testing agency. If you'd like to save a few dollars and are interested in learning more about the testing process, then several types of inexpensive, simple-to-use radon-detecting kits are available at local hardware or building supply stores. Just make sure that the kit has passed the Environmental Protection Agency's testing program, or is state certified. If so, the kits will usually display the phrase "Meets EPA Requirements" on the package.

Two commonly used kits are the charcoal canister and the alpha track detector. The charcoal canister consists of activated charcoal that draws in radon. After a designated time period—usually a week or less—you simply reseal the canister and return it to the manufacturer for analysis. Use the charcoal canister as a preliminary screening tool. Its

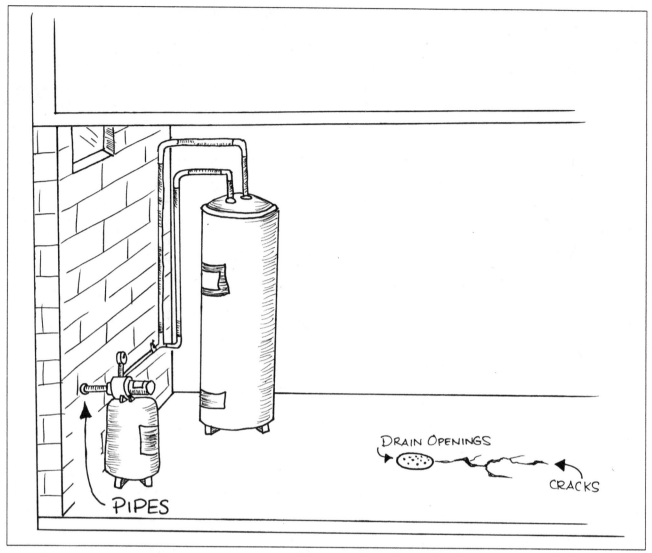

DRAIN OPENINGS

CRACKS

PIPES

Figure 7-1. Routes of radon intrusion.

results will tell you if there is nothing to worry about or if further tests are needed.

The alpha track detector consists of special plastic material in a filtered container. After a certain period of time which, depending on the model, could be from a few weeks to a year—the container is resealed and returned to the manufacturer for analysis.

Generally, radon tests should be conducted in the lowest levels of your residence, because radon is heavier than air. And the best time of year to test for radon is during winter. That's when your house is likely to be sealed against the elements, when doors and windows are kept closed and when radon concentrations tend to build up to higher levels. Always follow the instructions that come with

a test kit to the letter. That usually means, on a short-term test, closing windows and outside doors and keeping them closed as much as possible during the test. On short-term tests of only two or three days, it's best to close windows and outside doors at least twelve hours before the test begins, or else radon that may be entering will be too dispersed to measure accurately. Don't conduct short-term tests during severe storms or periods of unusually high winds for the same reason. Complete tests of longer-duration while the home is occupied. A weekend out won't ruin the results, but if the home will be sealed off from use for a month or two, abnormally high radon concentrations may give misleading results.

Again, the test kit should be placed in the lowest

lived-in level of the home: the basement, if it's frequently visited, or the first floor. Put the kit in a room that's used every day—such as a living room, family room, den or bedroom—but not in a kitchen or bathroom that's already vented to the outdoors. The kit collection container should be placed at least twenty inches above the floor in a location where it won't be bothered: away from drafts, sources of heat or high humidity, or exterior walls. Leave the kit alone for as long as the instructions say. Avoid moving it from one part of the house to another during the test.

Radon Test Results

Results from radon tests should be read and interpreted by health department officials. They will help you decide if additional tests should be performed, as well as what steps should be taken to try to reduce radon levels in your home, if necessary.

Radon Preventive Measures

Before you consider costly methods such as remodeling to reduce radon levels, consider taking simpler, less expensive steps. Often the most effective method of reducing radon infiltration is to make a dwelling more airtight in those areas radon has been entering.

Cover exposed earth in crawl spaces, storage areas, drainage areas, and the open part of a basement sump system. Seal cracks and voids where radon enters, such as in basement floors, openings around utility pipes, gaps between floors and walls, and holes at the top of concrete block walls and foundations. Sealing cracks and joints will result in several benefits. It limits the flow of radon into your home while reducing the loss of your conditioned air (warmed or cooled air), which then makes other radon reduction techniques more effective and cost-efficient.

Improve natural ventilation. Windows, doors and vents can be opened to allow radon concentrations to dilute and escape, so radon won't collect in a basement or lower-level living area. Use forced-air fans to blow air into the house, increasing the natural air exchange and reducing the amount of radon drawn in.

Other methods of reducing radon infiltration include providing alternative air supplies for furnaces and clothes dryers; ventilating foundations, block walls and drainage lines; and even supplying a pressurized atmosphere inside the house. Radon-contaminated well water can be treated with aeration or by filtering through granulated activated charcoal.

If You Need Help From a Contractor

If the preventive measures don't work, you have two options: Either move out of the house or make more extensive improvements or corrections to the dwelling. That will usually involve a contractor. The way to select a contractor to fix radon problems in a home is really the same way any contractor should be chosen. See which contractors have the best reputations, get three quotes, and make sure you're comparing apples with apples.

Here's a checklist you can use to compare services offered by three different contractors you may be considering:

• Will the contractor provide references or photographs, and test results "before" and "after," as evidence of successful past radon reduction work?

• Will the contractor inspect the entire home before giving an estimate? (Don't use anyone who doesn't plan to inspect your dwelling before providing a quote.)

• Did the contractor ask to see the results of earlier radon tests? Will a fee be charged for further testing on the contractor's part? If so, what is the cost?

• Can the contractor thoroughly explain in understandable language what he or she expects to do, how long it will take to complete, and how the radon reduction system will work?

• How will you know if the system *isn't* working? Will there be a warning device?

• What operating and maintenance costs can you expect after the system is installed? Weigh expectations and benefits carefully. An inexpensive system that's troublesome and expensive to run may not be the most cost efficient. A more expensive system may offer fewer headaches and less maintenance costs over the long term.

• Is there a written guarantee to reduce radon levels below a specific concentration? How long is that guarantee good for?

• Has the contractor shown proof of liability insurance coverage? Of state certification? Ask your environmental agency what certification, licenses and insurance contractors should have.

• Will the contractor provide you with a detailed written contract, spelling out everything that will be provided, how the work will be done, how long it will take, and exactly how much it will cost?

• Are any warranties or guarantees transferable if you sell your home?

Chemical Products

A number of common household products, when introduced to a household, can be considered harmful fume- or particle-generating substances. Formaldehyde is a rather common pollutant that can be found in varying, usually small, concentrations within households. It can be emitted by such everyday items as permanent press clothing, waxed paper, facial tissues, room deodorizers, plywood, and urea-foam insulation used in home construction. Other potentially harmful substances are benzene and trichloroethylene, found in products such as paints, thinners, strippers, solvents, synthetic fibers, rubber, plastics, detergents, wood preservatives, aerosol sprays, cleansers and disinfectants, moth repellents, air fresheners, stored fuel, printing inks and adhesives.

Pesticides, herbicides and even fertilizers can also be harmful. Although they may not actually be used within the home, products applied in the yard can still be blown inside by the wind, tracked into the house underfoot, or leached into the house in contaminated water that seeps through porous or cracked foundations. Warning labels on the cans or packages should explain the hazards involved with each product.

Steps You Can Take to Reduce Exposure

Whenever possible, use chemical products outdoors or in well-ventilated places. This especially goes for paints, solvents, waxes, glues and similar materials. Follow manufacturer's instructions exactly. Wear protective equipment such as a respirator, dust mask, goggles or gloves if specified. Only purchase as much product as you plan to use over the short term. Discard empty containers safely.

Store chemical products in an outside shed or well ventilated garage, since they can slowly leak fumes into the air. If need be, bring some products into a basement or other heated area during winter. Throw or give away products you don't plan on using in the near future so they won't clutter up your storage areas.

Use mothballs, crystals, and solid home deodorizers sparingly. As they "melt" or evaporate, some of these products release a nasty sounding chemical called paraperidichlorobenzene, a substance that's suspected of causing cancer. To mothproof woolen garments, instead of using mothballs, try dry-cleaning them to kill any moth larvae, air the clothes outside for a few hours, then seal the garments in airtight plastic containers, or place in a cedar-lined closet.

Remember that synthetic carpeting may give off fumes, especially when first installed. Consider having new carpeting installed during warm or cool weather when you can open the windows often after the carpet is laid.

Whether your carpet is old or new, it's a good practice to remove your shoes and leave them near whatever entrance you came in. After a morning walk or a day's activities, you could track in residues from powerful pesticides, fertilizers, or even lead contaminated soil or dirt. Those substances can dry and mix with the dust in your carpet, and when your children wrestle with their dog, the dust—along with the tracked-in substances—may become airborne. And since most vacuum cleaners can't possibly pick up all soil, dirt and dust in your carpeting, you're stuck with the stuff for quite a while.

How to reduce the amount of formaldehyde in a home

Whenever a choice is available, use exterior-grade pressed wood products such as plywood and fiberboard because they contain phenol resins, not formaldehyde-producing urea resins. If the home has urea-foam insulation, make sure the insulation is not damp and that there are no cracks in the walls. It's likely that formaldehyde emissions from the foam will decline with time. It's further likely that urea-foam insulation has not been installed since the 1970s. As time goes on, it will present less of a problem.

Air conditioning and dehumidifiers should be used to maintain moderate temperatures and lower humidity levels—which will slow down formaldehyde emissions. And increased ventilation will help, particularly after new sources of formaldehyde, such as furniture made of pressed wood, paneling and plywood, are introduced to the home. Increase the ventilation until the product's "new odor" is gone.

And don't overlook your wardrobe as a source of formaldehyde. Wash new permanent press clothes before you wear them because formaldehyde is commonly used as sizing to help keep permanent-press clothes crisp.

Keep a lot of houseplants. Plants are more than just items of decor. They do an effective job of cleaning the air we breathe by filtering out pollutants. It's nature's way of keeping the air clean. Tiny pores on the surface of plant leaves act as air filters. When air passes through the pores, carbon dioxide is removed to be used by the plant for its energy-providing photosynthesis. Dirt particles and pollutants the plant doesn't use react with the plant tissue. Some of them become part of the leaf.

To get rid of formaldehyde, keep philodendrons, spider plants, golden pathos, bamboo palms, corn plants and chrysanthemums. To keep benzene at bay, try English ivy, dracaenas, gerbera daisies, peace lilies and chrysanthemums. For tricloroethylene, go with gerbera daisies, peace lilies, dracaenas, marginates, and again, chrysanthemums.

The National Aeronautics and Space Administration estimates that plants can reduce concentrations of these three pollutants by up to 90 percent. Although no exact number has been established for how many plants it takes to purify the air in a typical home, here are some basic recommendations. In a home having rooms with eight-foot ceilings, keep two or three plants in eight-inch or ten-inch pots for every 100 square feet of floor space. Taller or larger plants, which usually come in twelve-inch or fourteen-inch pots, can reduce the required number of plants by half.

House Dust and Allergies

You may have seen "The Odd Couple" film with Jack Lemmon and Walter Matthau (it was later brought out as a television series starring Tony Randall and Jack Klugman). Jack Lemmon (and later, Tony Randall) played a character named Felix Unger, who was a hypochondriac of sorts—bothered by dusts and pollen, allergic to the most common ingredients of everyday life. In the movie it was funny, but in real life, there *are* unfortunate individuals who are hypersensitive to dust and other tiny particles commonly found in household air. Many people are allergic to cat hair, or rather, to the tiny dander or particles of animal skin found with the animal hair.

There are sometimes more insidious materials that become a part of house dust: lead and asbestos, for example. Either of these hazardous materials can become airborne if the right conditions exist. If lead-based paint is sanded, scraped or burned, the particles and fumes can be extremely hazardous, as can tiny bits of asbestos if sanded, scraped, broken or otherwise disturbed.

In short, house dust is composed of much more than simply dirt. It's a complex mixture of bits of lint; pieces of hair; particles of textiles from rugs, bedding, clothing, furniture, drapes, carpet padding and pillows; and substances tracked into the house on the feet and shoes of household pets and people.

Individuals who are allergic to house dust and many other tiny particles found in household air can have a difficult time keeping their home clean enough for comfort. They may not be able to use dusters, mops or brooms, or even commercial dusting oils or other fume-producing preparations. Glazed ceramic, brick, tile, marble and polyethylene-coated hardwood or wood plank floors offer a number of advantages over carpeting and plastic flooring in helping to keep down dust levels and maintaining improved air quality: They hold virtually no electric charges, they're inert (they generate neither airborne particles nor fumes), they require no waxing, and they can be easily cleaned of dust.

With carpeting, vacuum cleaners aren't always a good enough solution, because most vacuums cannot hold the tiniest particles of dust that pass directly through the cleaner's entrapment bag back into the air. The most effective vacuum system for dust is one built into the home, a system that pulls dust into a central unit that, in turn, blows the dust outside.

As mentioned in the discussion of biological pollutants, pollen can cause respiratory allergies in sensitive individuals who commonly refer to their condition as "hay fever" or "pollinosis." Hay fever often begins in childhood and may continue throughout a person's life. Pollen from trees in the springtime, grass during early summer, and ragweed during the fall can be practically anywhere outdoors, and may be tracked or blown into the house in surprisingly high concentrations.

To guard against pollen and similar allergy-causing agents, learn the safest times to be outside. Pollen counts are generally lowest for several hours after a hard rain. They're highest very early in the morning, around 6:00 A.M. on clear days with light winds. Limit your exposure to pollen by using air conditioners whenever possible and cleaning the filters often, keeping windows and doors closed, avoiding open fields when you're outside, and hiring someone else to do your landscaping work.

Consider installing a state-of-the art electrostatically charged furnace and room air conditioning filters. These units can, when properly installed and operated, remove up to 97 percent of airborne particles, including dust, mold, pollen and smoke. Contact several heating and cooling contractors in your area to compare what's available.

If your allergy is severe, you may want to build up your resistance with periodic "allergy shots" that contain small amounts of the pollens that affect you. Physicians call this "desensitization," and say it works for about 80 percent of the hay fever patients who try it.

Nonprescription antihistamines and decongestants can temporarily help dry and open up sinuses. Prescription nasal sprays can reduce irritation, but may not reach their full potential for several days.

Wash your hair often during the spring and summer months to remove pollen. Bathe pets often, too, especially if they spend time running outdoors through fields and forest.

Alcohol use generally causes an allergy sufferer to become more congested. Smoking can cause allergic reactions or make existing conditions worse.

So can stress. Indoor exercise, however, can open up nasal passages and make you feel better.

HUMIDITY

Everyone knows the importance of using a dehumidifier during those damp, hot conditions in which the air feels heavy, stifling and sticky. But what about the opposite conditions—during the winter months when unusually dry, cold conditions prevail?

At less than a comfortable 30 to 40 percent humidity, the air will have a drying effect on protective linings of the nose, throat and lungs. Medical researchers believe that dry linings are a major reason people are more susceptible to colds during the winter months. Dry nasal and other linings can't function as they're supposed to, so their ability to combat viruses is reduced.

Humidifiers are available as add-ons to any kind of furnace or heating/cooling system. But to work correctly, they've got to be maintained year-round. Far too many humidifiers are let go after the first or second season of their operation, when they're allowed to dry out, or are not properly disconnected and prepared for future use when the season comes to an end.

Obviously humidifiers add healthy moisture to the household environment. An additional benefit supplied by a humidifier is that a residence with a higher humidity level will feel warmer that one without. The drier the air, the faster perspiration evaporates from and cools the skin. In a less dry atmosphere, perspiration evaporates more slowly, so the skin feels warmer, and not as much heat is needed to keep conditions at comfortable levels.

KEEPING A HEALTHY OFFICE

Many home offices are located in basements or lower levels away from distracting main living areas. If possible, arrange for good ventilation. At the very least, use a small fan to keep air circulating, or consider purchasing a freestanding air filter that circulates and filters the air in your office.

Eliminate or avoid as many pollutants and contaminants as possible by purchasing nontoxic supplies. Consider using unbleached or oxygen-bleached paper that's free of residual dioxin and toxic fumes caused by the more common chlorine bleaching method. Buy nontoxic glues and colored markers, such as those sold for school supplies.

Be aware that radiation is emitted from many parts of electronic equipment. Computers, video monitors, and even other electronic appliances such as televisions, microwave ovens and radios can generate electrical fields that may cause headaches. Use glare-free screens or radiation filters on your computer monitor.

Laser printers and copy machines can emit ozone, a colorless, odorless gas that some people are sensitive to. Keep such units at a distance from your work area; make sure exhaust ports are directed away from your desk. And take frequent breaks.

Stress from inadequate or poorly designed lighting can produce eyestrain and headaches. Consider using full-spectrum compact fluorescent lights or bulbs made with neodymium—they not only produce gentle illumination that's more like natural light, they also save energy and cost less to use.

And finally, don't work yourself into an unhealthy level of fitness. A strong, healthy body will go a long way toward protecting you from both stress and from susceptibility to environmental contaminants.

SAFE WATER

The human body consists more of water than anything else; water makes up between 60 and 70 percent of the body's total weight. It helps regulate our internal temperature. It helps transport blood, chemicals, food and wastes. And it lubricates and protects our joints and organs. Water is a necessity of life. In fact, practically every comprehensive fitness and health program recommends drinking from six to eight twelve-ounce glasses of water per day.

Your water supply can be either a public or private water system, or a well on your property. No matter what your water source is, there are three major threats to its suitability for drinking:

- Microbes, including viruses, coliform and other bacteria, and even intestinal parasites.
- Chemicals such as lead, benzene, radium, nitrate, and dozens of other harmful contaminants.

- Disinfection byproducts—substances that chlorine produces when it reacts with residues from organic debris, such as decomposing leaves and other plant matter.

Public and Private Water Systems

In general, public water systems are the most worry free from a mechanical, operating point of view. But that doesn't mean *you're* completely worry free. The water supply may be plentiful, but what about the quality? For example, the Environmental Protection Agency has estimated that as high as 13 percent of the community water services in the United States do not meet the requirements of the Safe Drinking Water Act.

Water Wells

As anyone who has ever lived in the country knows, the location of a water well can be critical. A well should be located as close to the house as possible, yet as far from any septic disposal system as practical—preferably uphill from it. And well water that once tested safe may not always remain so. Neighbors may install sewage systems at the back or side of your property, or rivers, swamps, and other bodies of water may become polluted and affect your supply.

Well water may also be contaminated through the homeowner's mishandling of the following hazardous household materials:

- Automotive products, including brake fluid, antifreeze and motor oil
- Household cleaners, including bleaches, disinfectants, drain cleaners and oven cleaners
- Paints and solvents
- Pesticides and herbicides

Dispose of excess amounts of the above materials in the proper way. Avoid flushing hazardous products down a toilet or drain. Sewage treatment plants may not be able to break down all of the toxic ingredients, and some could enter the groundwater table from which your drinking water is drawn. They can also wreak havoc with the biological processes that septic tank systems need to work efficiently. And never dump household toxins in a ditch or low area of a backyard.

Water Quality—Is It Safe?

How can you verify the quality of your water? By having it analyzed at a reputable testing laboratory. Signs of trouble include cloudy water, strong tastes and odors, or hard-to-clean stains on sinks, bathtubs and laundry. Contact your local water or health department for the names of qualified independent testing labs.

What will the labs test for? The labs will already have a good idea of what may be found and what to test for because water quality generally varies by locale, not by individual households. Impurities tested for will include toxic metals such as lead, biological contaminants, minerals, pesticides, chlorine, chloroform, and even radiological contaminants, such as radon.

Lead is one of the most well-known water contaminants. Too much lead in a human body can cause serious damage to the brain, kidneys, nervous system and red blood cells. Children and pregnant women have the greatest risk of elevated lead levels. Sources of lead in drinking water can also come from within the home itself. Brass faucets or fittings contain lead. Copper pipes that have been jointed with lead solder can contribute to the problem, especially if water sits in the piping for hours, and sometimes days, at a time.

When securing a water sample, make sure your method agrees with what the testing lab recommends. Many labs will want you to turn on your cold water and let it run until it reaches the coldest temperature it will get. The lab may also want a separate sample of water that *has* been sitting in the pipes, to see if the piping is contributing to the problem.

There are actions you can take to reduce the lead content in your water. Use only cold water for consumption. Hot water dissolves lead more easily than does cold water so it's more likely to contain lead washed from the tap or pipes. Make sure you use the cold water tap for drinking, cooking and preparing baby formulas.

Whenever the water from a cold water faucet has not been used for six hours or longer, flush the cold water pipe by running the water until it gets as cold as it will.

You can treat the water with a variety of mechanical purifying equipment and systems, or replace lead-producing plumbing pipes and fittings.

If you are very concerned with the quality of your water supply, drink bottled water.

Water Filters and Purifiers

There are a variety of water filters and purifiers on the market. Activated carbon filters can improve the look, taste and odor of water. Carbon filters can remove impurities such as chloroform, chlorine, pesticides and other chemicals.

Ion exchange filters can remove toxic metals and minerals. Distillers also can remove toxic metals and minerals and even biological contaminants. Reverse osmosis filters can remove toxic metals and radiological contaminants.

INDOOR AIR AND WATER SAFETY QUICK CHECKLIST

☐ Don't allow high levels of moisture to build up within your residence.

☐ Be aware of environmental air pollution symptoms, and conditions that may cause them.

☐ At home, make sure there's adequate means of ventilation to the outdoors.

☐ Prevent combustion processes from producing dangerous levels of carbon monoxide and other harmful gases, fumes and particles.

☐ Carefully inspect and maintain all wood stoves, space heaters and other heating equipment, including their exhaust systems. Avoid the use of kerosene and gasoline space heaters.

☐ Cut down on or eliminate tobacco smoke from within your residence.

☐ Find out if your home is in an area where radon levels are relatively high. If so, or if you are unsure, perform an inexpensive carbon canister radon test.

☐ If radon concentrations are above or near safe tolerance levels, take action to reduce them.

☐ Store chemical products in an "outside" utility area such as a garage, shed or outbuilding, or store chemicals indoors during freezing weather conditions in a well-ventilated area outside of children's reach.

☐ Use chemical products outdoors whenever possible, and wear personal protective equipment such as dust masks, respirators, goggles and gloves when necessary.

☐ Follow chemical product manufacturer safety procedures to the letter. Be aware of the hazards before starting to use the product.

☐ Purchase only as much product as you intend to use at a time. Give away or safely discard portions that cannot be used immediately.

☐ Be aware of lead-based paint or asbestos building materials, such as siding shingles or insulation, and make sure they are either removed or treated to prevent particles from working their way into the home's air supply.

INDOOR AIR AND WATER SAFETY QUICK CHECKLIST
(continued)

☐ Make it a habit not to wear shoes throughout the house—they can track in harmful substances that may end up as airborne particles.

☐ Purchase environmental- and people-friendly products whenever you have the opportunity.

☐ Use a number of air-filtering houseplants in your home's decor.

☐ Try to keep house dust to a minimum. Consider installing a central vacuum system.

☐ If there are pollen- and dust-sensitive members of your household, limit pollen exposures within the home by using air conditioners and central air systems often, keeping filters changed, and doors and windows closed. Consider the installation of an electrostatically charged furnace or room air conditioner.

☐ Consider installing a humidifier if your winters cause extremely dry air in the home.

☐ Maintain a healthy home office by limiting exposure to electronic equipment, dust and other contaminants; by arranging for plentiful ventilation; and by installing proper lighting.

☐ Test your water supply for quality.

☐ If anything changes with the neighborhood land surrounding a water well—such as new construction of homes, businesses or roads—have the water supply retested.

☐ If a water supply is contaminated, research your options. Consult local health authorities before attempting to remedy the situation.

CHAPTER 8

KITCHEN SAFETY

People spend a lot of time in kitchens. And because they do, and because of the nature of the work they do there, opportunities for injury are present. Think of what's found in the typical kitchen: sharp blades, hot cooking surfaces, boiling liquids, spattering cooking oil, wet and greasy surfaces, slippery floors, and a multitude of electrical appliances.

FOOD SHOPPING, HANDLING AND PREPARATION

If possible, make the supermarket your last stop before going home. This is particularly important during warm weather when food left in a locked car can spoil quickly. Take food straight home to the refrigerator and freezer. Or if you know you need to perform an errand that could take several hours, consider taking a large, ice-packed cooler along to store frozen and refrigerated food.

Don't buy anything you won't consume before the use-by date. Some people assume that buying in bulk is the right thing to do because it's less expensive per ounce, pound or package. Many foods actually should be purchased in *smaller* portions, to be eaten without waste and before the food spoils or loses nutrients to storage. Even though the smaller portions may be more expensive per ounce or unit, if they promote safer, healthier eating, that's a more desirable trade-off.

Avoid purchasing food that's in poor condition, even at "bargain" prices. Make sure refrigerated food is cold to the touch. Frozen food should be rock solid. Canned goods should be free of large dents. Cans with bulging lids or sides usually indicate spoilage inside, and are a serious food poisoning threat.

Foods that spoil quickly should be inspected carefully. Seafood, for instance, should not smell "fishy." Fresh fish steaks and fillets should be moist, with no drying or browning around the edges. The eyes of fresh, whole fish should be bright and clear, not cloudy or sunken. Scales shouldn't be slimy or loose. Gills should be red or bright pink.

When purchasing frozen foods, try to select items that are stored below display case "frost" or "load" lines—lines marked on commercial freezer chests and cabinets that indicate the safety level for package storage.

Select cold foods last, and ask cashiers to bag all refrigerated and frozen foods together, so those items can help keep each other cold during the trip home, and so they can be quickly identified and put away when you arrive.

Storing Food

Keep frozen foods frozen, cold foods cold, and dry foods dry.

Most non-dried foods keep longest when they're frozen. (See chapter fourteen, in the section on hot weather food handling.) If they're not, the next best thing is usually refrigeration. Both freezing and refrigeration prevent bacteria in food from multiplying and rendering poultry, fish, meat and other food inedible or poisonous. Check the temperature of your refrigerator with an inexpensive appliance thermometer available at hardware or appliance stores. To keep bacteria under control, the refrigerator should operate at or just below 40 degrees Fahrenheit, and the freezer portion at or below 0 degrees Fahrenheit. In non-numerical terms, safe refrigeration means keeping the temperature in the refrigerator compartment as cold as possible without freezing your milk or lettuce.

If foodstuffs were mishandled before freezing, large numbers of micro-organisms may be present and freezing won't correct the situation. That's why cleanliness is so important.

Freeze fresh meat, poultry or fish immediately if you can't use it within a few days. More specifically, red meat can be refrigerated at home for three or four days, then it must be either cooked or frozen. Freeze any refrigerated poultry and seafood that won't be cooked within two days.

If your freezer gets knocked out of service by a power outage or general failure, find out when the electricity will be back on. A full freezer will keep frozen food frozen for two days without power, and a half-full freezer, for one day—if you don't frequently open the freezer door in the meantime. Food in the refrigerator section will last four to six hours under similar no-power conditions. If your freezer is almost empty when it shuts down, or will be out of service for more than two days in a row, either place dry ice in it or store your frozen foods in a neighbor's or friend's freezer. In the refrigerated section, use block ice.

When the power comes back on, food that is still refrigerator cold can be safely refrozen; it may, however, suffer a change in texture. If the food reaches temperatures above 40 degrees Fahrenheit it should be cooked before being refrozen. If food has been stored above 40 degrees Fahrenheit for more than two hours, it should be discarded.

If you refrigerate raw meat, poultry or fish, place them on a plate so their juices cannot leak from the packages and drip on other foods. Raw juices can contain harmful bacteria that could contaminate other foods, such as leftovers that will be eaten without being heated again.

Food Preparation

To make sure that food makes a safe transition between storage and the serving table, a few basic procedures should be followed. (For more on this topic, see chapter fourteen on hot weather safety.) Before handling foods, wash your hands in hot, soapy water, and see that others do the same. Remind children to wash their hands after using the bathroom or playing with pets.

Keep raw meat, poultry, fish and their juices away from ingredients. Don't cross-contaminate ingredients by preparing different foods on the same cutting board, kitchen countertop or tabletop surfaces without washing those surfaces in between. For example, wash your hands, cutting board and sharp knife in hot, soapy water after cutting up raw chicken or fish—*before* you place a head of lettuce on the same surface to be chopped for salad with the same knife.

Consider wearing surgical gloves (thin plastic gloves) when working with ingredients like onions, chili peppers or jalapeño peppers. Volatile oils in these foods can cause severe pain if they come into contact with your eyes.

Thaw food in the refrigerator, inside a sealed plastic freezer bag held beneath cold running water, in a microwave oven, or as part of a continuous cooking process—*not* on a counter or stove top. Bacteria can thrive within the warmer outer parts of a turkey, for example, while the inside remains frozen. That also means a certain amount of planning must be done, because a twenty-pound frozen turkey can take as long as four days to thaw. Follow recommended thawing methods and times given on the manufacturer's packaging. Always make sure the item has completely thawed. All foods contain water that forms ice crystals during the freezing process. If foods such as meat, poultry and fish are incompletely thawed before cooking—and you don't realize it—layers or pockets of ice may still surround some bacteria within the meat, and standard cooking times may fail to destroy them.

Never leave perishable food unrefrigerated for more than two hours, or less if the food will be exposed to high temperatures. Bacteria that can cause food poisoning grow quickly in warm environments.

Cooking Food

The big worry here is bacteria. It takes thorough cooking to kill harmful bacteria. Although many people enjoy items such as raw fish and rare beef, an element of danger exists whenever those dishes are consumed. It's the same for poultry, hamburger and other meats, fish, and eggs that are only partially cooked. And never marinate at room temperature. It's best to marinate foods in the refrigerator to prevent harmful bacteria from taking hold.

There should be a food "pecking order" within the refrigerator. Place cooked foods *above* raw items in the refrigerator, even though you use plates to store the raw foods on. The reason? Any accidental tip-overs, or a few drops of raw meat juices dripped onto already cooked foods, can contaminate a lunch or supper entree.

If foods are still partly frozen when you start cooking them, increase cooking times so internal temperatures of meats and poultry get high enough to kill any bacteria present. Cook red meat to at least 160 degrees Fahrenheit, and poultry to at least 180 degrees Fahrenheit. Use a meat thermometer to check that a roast or bird is cooked all the way through. To check visually, red meat is done when it's brown or gray inside. Poultry juices should run clear. Cooked fish should flake with a fork.

When you cook ahead, divide large portions of food into small, shallow containers for quick refrigeration or freezing. Heat leftover food to a temperature of at least 165 degrees Fahrenheit to eliminate bacteria growth. Use a meat thermometer inserted into the center of the food to check temperatures.

Keep food preparation surfaces clean to prevent bacteria growth and transfer. Counters should be washed, rinsed and sanitized: Clean surfaces with a mixture of hot, soapy water, rinse thoroughly, then sanitize with commercially available cleansers, or create your own solution with one capful of chlorine bleach mixed with one gallon of lukewarm water. You can even put some homemade solution into a well-marked spray bottle for quick use. Cutting boards should also be kept clean. Maple is the hardwood of choice for restaurant wood cutting boards, but no matter what a cutting board is made of, the board should be refinished if possible, or discarded, when it gets full of deep scratches, cuts and gouges that bacteria can thrive in.

Cooks who usually follow all of the rules of cleanliness may still sometimes forget this one: Never use the same plate you used to take uncooked meats to the stove, for transporting the cooked meats back to the table. Why not? Because raw meat juices and bacteria can be transferred to the cooked product. Instead, use a different plate or platter. Remember to do the same for meats grilled outdoors.

Whether gas or electric, range tops and ovens are not designed for storage. Keep the tops clear of all combustibles, and the oven empty when you're not cooking. Pots, pans and other items left in ovens can be either ruined or heated to high temperatures by accident if the oven is preheated by a household cook who forgets what's inside. Some unsuspecting kitchen helper could then burn himself while attempting to remove the heated contents.

Use the back burners whenever possible (see Figure 8-1), especially for frying and boiling. When the front burners or cooktop surfaces are used, turn pot handles toward the back of the stove, but not over another hot burner. That applies whether you have children in the house or not; it will eliminate a child's temptation to grab pan handles and will also prevent pan handles from getting caught on clothing as someone walks past the stove.

Electric range top metal burners and ceramic cooking surfaces can look deceptively cool. Always look at the heating controls to see what position they're in before wiping or otherwise touching the cooking surface. Instruct children that the oven and range top are strictly off limits. Special stove guards are available to help keep tiny hands away from cooktops (see Figure 8-2). They resemble small fences that wrap around the top of the stove at the outside edges, and fasten to the cooktop with rubber suction cups.

Don't hold children or allow others to hold children while standing near a hot stove or cooking appliance. And when cooking foods that have a tendency to spatter or pop, use a cover or spatter screen, and keep children away.

Burns are common injuries in kitchens when several people are preparing food and cooking at

Figure 8-1. Using a back burner.

Figure 8-2. Cooktop guards.

the same time. A hot pan from the stove could be placed in a sink by one cook, then another person could reach for it without knowing that the pan is still hot. If possible, let hot pans and other containers cool at the back of the cooktop, instead of placing them in the sink—where most of the action is. At the very least, announce to others that a hot pan or dish is present if it must be put elsewhere than on the cooktop.

While cooking, remember to place utensils such as meat forks, knives, hand mixers, and even glass measuring cups and bowls toward the back of the counter or middle of the table. Keep bowls, utensils and ingredients away from countertop and table

KITCHEN SAFETY ■ 87

edges. Watch where you put hot pans and casserole dishes.

The cleaning mode of self-cleaning ovens heats the inside of the oven to extremely high temperatures, sometimes hot enough to cause a flash fire if the door is opened. To avoid flare-ups, keep the oven latched while it's self-cleaning, and avoid using any chemical oven cleaners in either self-cleaning or continuous-cleaning ovens. Use ammonia solutions and scrubbing pads instead.

Accumulated grease and food particles on and in ovens can catch fire. Keep all oven and range tops clean. It's easiest to wipe the surfaces immediately after spills.

If possible, avoid placing an oven and cooktop unit beneath a window. A breeze could extinguish a gas burner, allowing unburned gas to seep into the room; nearby curtains could ignite; or a stove fire could spread out of the window to the exterior walls. If you already have a stove beneath a window, and you plan to keep it there, at least consider the use of nonflammable fiberglass curtains on the window.

Natural gas generally contains a foul-smelling additive so leaks can be detected as soon as they occur. If you smell gas in the kitchen but you can't stop the smell by turning off all of the stove's burners, extinguish any other flames in the area and open all nearby windows and doors to ventilate the area. Don't operate any electrical switches (a spark could possibly ignite fugitive gas). Call your gas supplier immediately, preferably from a neighbor's home.

Uncover hot containers away from your face. And be careful when opening a hot oven. Some people have injured themselves by bending down and placing their face directly above the oven door when opening the door—only to be blasted by hot air and steam.

Cooking in a Microwave Oven

A primary safety rule with a microwave unit is that it shouldn't be operated if its door does not shut properly and create a tight seal. A microwave oven should not continue to operate when its door is open.

Remember to use microwave-safe containers for cooking. Some plastic containers that products are packaged in cannot stand the heat: Margarine tubs, for instance, and some plastic storage bags may melt and even catch fire when subjected to higher microwave settings. It's best to use lightweight, unbreakable plastic containers that are equipped with handles and covers.

If a fire starts in a microwave oven, shut the door and press the stop button. Don't open the door—that will feed the fire by supplying it with additional oxygen.

With containers of food that are covered during microwave cooking, open the lid slightly or peel back a corner of plastic wrap to let built-up steam escape in a direction away from your face (see Figure 8-3). And remember to use pot holders while transferring cooked foods from microwave to table. A microwave oven stays cool inside, but the cookware or dish can get extremely hot from the heated food or drink.

Figure 8-3. Releasing steam.

Microwave ovens may not heat foods evenly. Some ovens have turntables that slowly rotate foods for more even heating, but others do not. Always test temperatures of foods you microwave for babies and children, especially drinks or soups. Microwaves can heat a bowl's contents without heating the bowl. Even the contents can be heated unevenly, so be sure to stir liquids or thick soups before serving them. Unevenly heated foods can burn mouths; the outer surfaces of the foods can be warm while the insides are scalding hot.

Be especially careful with cheese-, jelly-, or fruit-filled items such as pastries, and ravioli. After microwaving, break filled items open before biting into them to make sure the fillings are not too hot. Unless the unit has a rotating turntable, get into the habit of turning the foods several times on your own before the cooking is completed. Stir soups and stews several times. Rearrange foods like potatoes or waffles. This results in evenly cooked food and prevents cold spots—and bacteria growth—that could otherwise result.

Never microwave raw eggs in their shells. Pressure can build up and the eggs may explode. And before cooking, prick foods that have thick skins or membrane coverings, such as whole potatoes (see Figure 8-4), apples, hot dogs or sausages, so those foods will not explode.

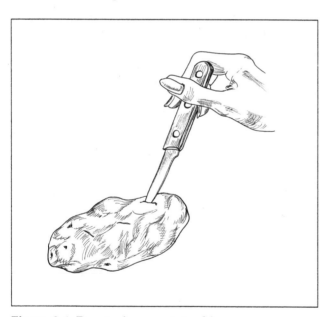

Figure 8-4. Puncturing a potato skin.

Use cookware designed for microwave ovens to prepare specialty items such as bacon and popcorn. Paper plates and towels will work for bacon, but they're often not sturdy enough for the job. Cooks have been burned by hot grease when paper towels or plates have ripped apart while the cooked bacon was being carried to the table, or when hot bacon grease dripped through the paper. Popcorn generates enough energy when it pops, that it may break some glass bowls or burn paper bags.

Serving Food

Keep hot foods hot and cold foods cold when they're out of the oven or refrigerator. Never leave perishable food unrefrigerated for longer than two hours. Bacteria that can cause food poisoning grow quickly, especially at warm temperatures. This goes for party foods, too. Keep cold party food on ice or serve it on platters directly from the refrigerator. Consider placing hot party food onto smaller platters or dishes that can be refrigerated until it's time to warm them up. Bring sauces, soups and gravies to a boil before serving.

Leftovers should be refrigerated as soon as possible. It's a mistake to let serving bowls full of mashed potatoes, stuffing, green beans and turkey sit on counters for hours while the family members play cards or watch television. Make it a habit to put leftovers away as quickly as possible. Divide large quantities of warm food into smaller portions for quicker cooling in the fridge. With poultry and other stuffed meats, remove the stuffing and refrigerate it in separate containers so both the meat and the stuffing will cool faster.

Before frying chicken, fish or other meats, carefully pat each piece dry with a paper towel to prevent excess water from splattering when it hits hot oil in the pan. Be extra careful when deep frying. Take care not to overheat cooking oil or grease. Use kitchen tongs to turn fast-frying food (see Figure 8-5). Otherwise the pieces can slip off a fork and splatter hot cooking oil and juices. Turn burners off when you leave the room to answer a phone or doorbell—if you're distracted by the caller or visitor you may forget what's on the stove until it's too late.

Avoid wearing long, floppy sleeves while cook-

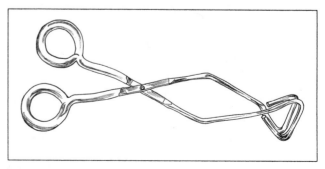

Figure 8-5. Kitchen tongs.

ing, or garments with scarves, fringe or other dangling accessories that could brush a heated burner and quickly ignite.

Make sure potholders are dry when you use them. Wet potholders will transfer heat almost immediately, and will not prevent burns when hot cookware is handled. Also refrain from using dish towels as potholders—loose ends of a towel may come into contact with a hot cooktop burner and catch fire. Keep plenty of potholders on hand so you won't be tempted to use dangerous substitutes, such as the bottom of your sweatshirt.

Avoid tasting food that looks or smells strange to see if you can still use it. Whatever the ingredient, toss it out and replace it with new.

APPLIANCE AND UTENSIL SAFETY

There are lots of ways to get cut in a kitchen. Numerous sharp instruments include knives, forks, shears, can openers and sharp can lids, glass containers that drop and shatter on tile floors, food processor blades, plastic wrap packages, fruit and vegetable peelers, and graters. It's best to clean knives and other sharp utensils as soon as you're done using them. Avoid letting them sit on counters and tables. Heavy knives can be shoved off the end of a table or counter onto someone's foot, and other sharp utensils could be stepped on.

A classic way to get cut is to reach into a sink full of dirty dishwater and slice a finger on a chef's knife that someone has tossed into the water, or on a dirty food processor blade in the same place. Another way is to get cut on a blade while reaching into a dishwasher, past the utensils to grab a glass or bowl. For those reasons, consider washing sharp knives and other implements by themselves. Small steak knives and old paring knives will fit nicely, sharp points and edges pointing down into a silverware rack on a dishwasher, but it's best to keep the quality boning, butcher and chef's knives out of the hot washing cycles of dishwashers. Instead, carefully clean sharp blades one by one in soapy water prepared with dishwashing liquid, then rinse, wipe dry and put away.

When unloading a dishwasher immediately after the washing or drying cycle has ended, avoid reaching down to grab a utensil or other item that's fallen to the bottom of the washer. You could accidentally touch the heating element and get burned. Wait until later, after the heating element cools.

Store blades in either a special knife drawer, in slim boxes the knives were purchased in, or in butcher-block or wall holders that keep the blades covered and out of children's reach. Remember that knives should be kept sharp and ready to use. Dull knives cause more cuts than sharp ones because dull knives require more force to use.

Be especially careful with food processors. Children are naturally inquisitive and have been known to reach into the see-through processing bowls to try to play with the cutting blades.

When purchasing microwave ovens, trash compactors, dishwashers, blenders, food processors or small broiler ovens, favor models that won't operate unless their doors or tops are fully closed. Trash compactors should be operated by key, then household or visiting children cannot just flip a switch and turn the unit on. Some compactors have control knobs that can be easily removed and stored in a safe place between uses. Garbage disposals operated by a wall switch should have a safety lock for the same reason. Freezers, too, should be kept locked, with the keys well hidden.

The safest garbage disposals use bidirectional vibrators instead of whirring blades. Added safety features include fitted drain covers that keep silverware and other items from falling in. The drain cover can also function as the on-off mechanism.

Consult your owner's manual if something such as a child's spoon becomes wedged in a disposal. Make sure you achieve zero energy—that the disposal cannot be turned on—while you attempt to dislodge the item.

Most instruction booklets included with small kitchen appliances say to unplug the appliances while the appliances are not in use. That's because if an appliance is plugged in, there's always a possibility of shock. Thermostat controls on appliances such as irons, electric saute pans and electric ovens don't always provide a complete "off" setting. They can be accidentally turned on, too. A removable thermostat cord that's plugged into an outlet—but not into the appliance—can cause shocks if someone touches the end. It may also short-circuit if water or another liquid spills on it.

When using equipment with detachable electrical cords, plug the cord into the appliance first, and then into the wall, with dry hands. Keep electrical appliances such as clocks, radios, toasters and similar units away from sinks, where the appliances could fall into water or be touched by wet hands. GFCIs should be included with all receptacles that are within six feet of a water source. And remember that all major appliances used for cooktop or surface cooking must have adequate ventilation systems.

OTHER KITCHEN SAFETY CONCERNS

Tile flooring in kitchens may look good, but it can be tough on families. Tile can be slippery, especially when wet. It's also very unforgiving (more so than wood) when glass, ceramic or even plastic is dropped on it. Carpeting, while soft on cookware and serving dishes, can be difficult to keep clean. Grape juice and grease spilled or spattered onto carpet can be impossible to clean completely. A textured vinyl tile or linoleum flooring is the best choice.

Avoid the natural urge to pick up broken glass with your fingers. Use a dustpan and broom instead, then vacuum the swept areas. Before placing broken glass in the garbage, wrap it in newspaper then in several paper grocery bags. Consider purchasing glasses, cups, dishes, and serving bowls and trays that are manufactured of relatively inexpensive "tempered" glass or similar materials that are difficult to break.

If you need to store potentially harmful items, such as knives, in drawers, inexpensive drawer latches are available at hardware and builder's supply stores. The latches are easy to install. Household members must remember to push the drawers all the way closed though, so the latching mechanisms will engage properly. If you have toddlers or young children, or if children visit your kitchen, have safety latches on cabinets and drawers that contain cleaning supplies, medicine and vitamins, alcohol, serrated packages of plastic wrap and aluminum foil, matches and lighters, knives and other sharp objects, and glassware.

Post emergency phone numbers near the kitchen phone, including the numbers for ambulance service, fire and police departments, the family doctor and nearby trusted neighbors.

Keep a multipurpose ABC fire extinguisher in or near the kitchen, and make sure all family members know where it is and how to use it. The best location for the fire extinguisher is across from the cooktop.

Don't work in the dark. Overhead lighting in the kitchen is critical to comfortable food preparation, cooking and clean up. Don't settle for less than lots of task lighting—spotlights focused on kitchen work and dining areas. Working in your own shadow, as many household chefs tend to do, can cause accidental injury.

Avoid storing cookies, candies, gum, and other children's favorites in cupboards positioned over or near an oven or cooktop. Children may try to climb onto the stove when you're not around.

Due to the risk of suffocation, plastic trash bags and grocery bags should be either stored out of sight and reach, or tied into knots and thrown away. That goes for other large plastic bags, too, such as dry cleaning bags. Discard used plastic food wrap immediately, too. It only takes a small piece to completely block the breathing airways of a young child.

If an infant or toddler is in the kitchen while the family chef is cooking, make sure the child is in a safety seat, high chair or playpen far out of reach of the oven, cooktop and other hazards. Children who have outgrown high chairs and playpens should not be allowed to play in a kitchen while someone is cooking. It only takes seconds for a child to pull a pan of boiling water onto himself.

All children, at one time or another, are exactly the right height to stand next to and peer into wastebaskets and kitchen trash containers. Eliminate a youngster's access to your trash by making sure the container has a lid that cannot be removed by the child. And don't forget the safety of whomever takes the trash outside and whomever picks it up at the curb line: Avoid putting sharp "surprises" such as broken glass, razor blades, syringes, sharp bamboo cake testers, can lids, and other dangerous items loose in your trash. Instead, wrap sharp objects in newspaper and place the wrapped items in paper grocery bags or inside a small cardboard box before putting those containers into a trash bag.

KITCHEN SAFETY
QUICK CHECKLIST

- ☐ If possible, plan grocery shopping so it's the last stop before you return home.

- ☐ While shopping, frozen and refrigerated foods should be the last items you place in your shopping cart, and they should be packed together at the checkout counter.

- ☐ Avoid purchasing foods in bulk if you may not be able to consume them before their use-by dates.

- ☐ Buy only foods that are in top condition.

- ☐ Be especially careful with quick-spoiling items such as seafood, poultry and frozen foods that are less-than-frozen at the time you're selecting them.

- ☐ While storing foods, keep frozen foods frozen, refrigerated foods refrigerated, and dry foods dry.

- ☐ A refrigerator should operate between 35 and 40 degrees Fahrenheit, and a freezer at or below 0 degrees Fahrenheit.

- ☐ Freeze red meat, poultry or seafood immediately if you can't use it within a few days.

- ☐ Prevent juices from stored raw meats from dripping on or coming in contact with cooked foods.

- ☐ Avoid contaminating ingredients by washing knives, cutting boards, plates and counter surfaces that were used to prepare raw meats before reusing them.

- ☐ Wear thin plastic gloves when working with hot peppers and onions.

- ☐ Avoid thawing frozen foods on a counter or stove top at room temperature.

- ☐ Never leave perishable food unrefrigerated for more than two hours, or less during hot weather.

- ☐ Leftover cooked foods that are reheated should be brought to a temperature of at least 165 degrees Fahrenheit to eliminate bacterial growth.

- ☐ Use cooktop back burners whenever possible, and keep pan handles turned toward the rear or sides of the stove (but not over another hot burner).

- ☐ Make sure controls are turned off and burners have cooled before cleaning, touching or temporarily placing items on those cooking surfaces.

**KITCHEN SAFETY
QUICK CHECKLIST**
(continued)

☐ While cooking, keep children out of the immediate area.

☐ Avoid putting hot pans, dishes and implements where someone could accidentally get burned by touching them.

☐ Keep all ovens and rangetops clean of grease and food particles.

☐ Uncover hot foods and containers so escaping steam will be released away from your hands and face.

☐ Because microwave ovens sometimes heat unevenly, test temperatures of microwaved foods before you eat them or give them to children.

☐ Use microwave-safe containers in microwave ovens.

☐ When cooking in advance, divide large portions of food into small, shallow containers for quick refrigeration or freezing.

☐ When serving, keep hot foods hot and cold foods cold.

☐ Refrigerate leftovers as soon as possible.

☐ Avoid keeping sharp knives and other implements loose in drawers. Clean and store sharp utensils when you're finished with them, and keep them out of automatic dishwashers.

☐ Restrict children's access to kitchen appliances such as trash compactors, garbage disposals, blenders and food processors.

☐ Most portable appliances should be unplugged when not in use. Keep electric radios and clocks away from sinks and other water sources.

☐ GFCIs should be installed on all receptacles near sources of water in the kitchen.

☐ A kitchen should be adequately ventilated above all cooking surfaces.

☐ If young children visit the kitchen, have safety latches on cabinets and drawers that contain potentially dangerous materials.

☐ Post emergency phone numbers near the kitchen phone.

☐ Keep a multipurpose ABC fire extinguisher across from the cooktop.

☐ Good lighting is a must wherever food is prepared or cooked.

☐ Safely dispose of "sharp" waste such as broken glass and can lids, and keep kitchen and other trash in containers that have childproof covers.

CHAPTER 9
BATHROOM SAFETY

You've heard the story before. A world-famous mountain climber, legendary in his twenty-eight years of scaling vertical heights from the Himalayas to the Alps with hardly a scratch, slips at home in his bathtub and is crippled for life. Per square foot of space, the typical bathroom contains more hazards than any other room in the home. It's likely to feature a virtual smorgasbord of chemical products, from medicines and cosmetics to cleaning products and alcohols. It can also house razor blades, aerosol cans, sprays and tonics, glass doors and mirrors, sharp cabinet edges, slippery floor and tub surfaces, electrical outlets, scalding water, hair dryers and curlers, and even sun lamps.

CHILD SAFETY IN THE BATHROOM

You may be a bit overwhelmed by the number of potential hazards the typical bathroom holds for children. Unfortunately, they're all real, and have caused real-life accidental injuries ranging from bumps, cuts and burns, all the way up to fatalities. Let's look at the most frequently encountered dangers and how to minimize them.

First rule: Never leave a child alone in a bathroom. For our purposes, a child means a youngster at or younger than the potty-training stage—and the level of maturity needs to be evaluated in addition to age. This rule goes double for never leaving a child alone in a bathtub. Not for even a minute.

Use a rubber bath mat to protect children against slips and falls in a tub or shower. Nonskid strips and rough-tread appliques may not work for children because the strips can leave unprotected slippery spaces large enough for tiny feet to slip on.

Some slip-resistant mats contain built-in thermometers that provide instant readouts of water temperatures to prevent unpleasant scalding experiences for children. A thermometer-mat can also come in handy for adults. The comfort zone for hot water is between 95 to 105 degrees Fahrenheit. Water at or beyond 115 degrees can damage skin.

Turn tub and sink hot water faucet handles off tightly so children cannot turn them on easily. Devices are available to restrict how far a handle can be pushed to the hot side, called "hot stop limits."

Faucet spouts in tubs can pose particular dangers to children, who can slip and bump against the hard chrome or brass. Protective padding is available to prevent injury. Some padding units are cleverly designed as animals: The rubber head of an elephant, for instance, complete with a spout-like trunk the water flows from can be placed over conventional bathtub spouts (see Figure 9-1).

If your tub or shower has glass doors, see if they are made of safety glass. While safety glass is commonly used now, in older homes it may not have been selected or even available at the time the home was constructed. Regular glass, if shattered, can have terrible consequences for both children or adults. That goes for mirrors, too. Safety mirrors are the only kind to use in or near the tub or shower.

Figure 9-1. Protective spout cover.

Sliding doors on a tub or shower can be secured against children's exploration through the installation of safety latches. A variety of latch styles are available, including Velcro units that can be positioned high enough on the door(s) so children can't reach them.

Step stools (see Figure 9-2) used by children at bathroom sinks should have trip-resistant, nonskid rubber treads. And because young children always seem to be stepping up on their tiptoes, reaching here and there, the base of a step stool should also have nonslip rubber feet.

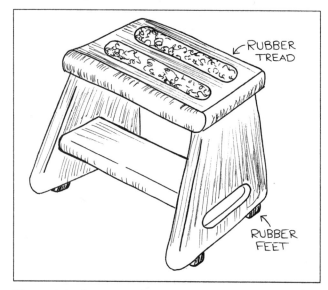

Figure 9-2. A stepstool.

Sharp cabinet tops and edges should be covered and protected with edge cushions (see Figure 9-3) and corner cushions (see Figure 9-4).

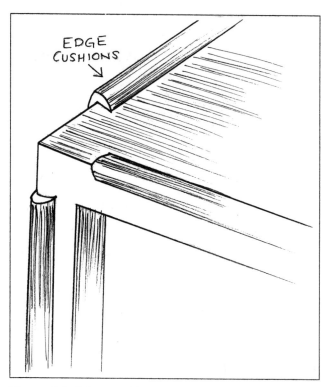

Figure 9-3. Edge cushions.

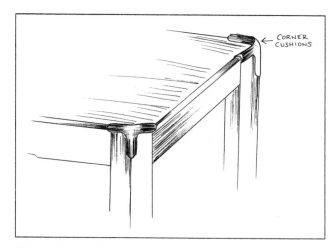

Figure 9-4. Corner cushions.

Wet, slippery floors can cause trouble. To help prevent falls, keep a rubber-backed bath rug on the floor next to the tub.

Consider installing a toilet lock on the toilet (see Figure 9-5) to lock the lid down so a child can't lift it. Several designs are available, but the ones featuring positive mechanical latches are the safest.

Make sure that children cannot lock themselves inside of a bathroom. Many bathroom doors have push-button locks. These locks should have a small

cups for drinking (see Figure 9-6). They're sanitary because they're discarded after use, and family members won't be tempted to drink from the same plastic or glass cup and possibly toss cold and flu germs back and forth.

Figure 9-5. Toilet locks.

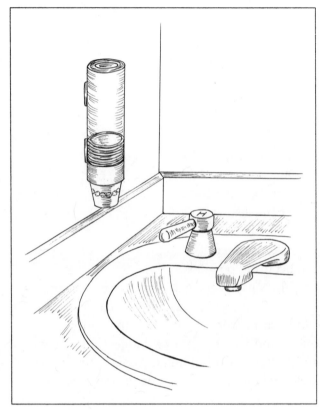

Figure 9-6. Paper drinking cup holder.

hole drilled on the outside knob so a piece of wire or a long nail inserted through the knob can unlock the door.

Avoid using colorful or clear automatic chemical bowl cleaners in toilets until all children in the house are old enough to know they shouldn't be playing in toilet bowls.

Try to keep glass out of the bathroom. That goes for drinking glasses, plates, decorative crystal or porcelain, and even perfumes and colognes. Purchase products with shatterproof containers, and, if possible, childproof caps. Consider using paper

Medicine cabinets should be kept locked. Since these units are usually above a sink or vanity top, they can often be reached by adventurous children who love to climb.

Cosmetics, medicines, cleaning products, alcohols, razors, and all other chemical or hazardous products should either be locked in a cabinet or stored out of reach in a different room. Here's a list of products to be concerned with:

All medicines (prescription and
    nonprescription)
Vitamins and minerals
Mouthwashes
Laxatives
Epsom salts
Petroleum jelly
Shaving cream
Denture cleaners

Deodorant

Perfume, colognes and aftershaves

Cosmetics

Hair tonics

Hair shampoo and rinse

Hair spray

Hair treatments (colorings, permanents)

Bath salts and oils

Antiseptics

Ointments and salves

Disinfectants

Rubbing alcohol

Nail polish and remover

Deodorizers and air fresheners

Aerosol cans

Razors and blades

Drain cleaners

Toilet bowl cleaners

Tile cleaners

Scouring powders

Electric shavers, hair dryers or other appliances

Electrical appliances should not be plugged in while children have access to the bathroom. Electricity and water present a dangerous combination to children and adults alike. Avoid letting teenagers operate radios, hair dryers or curling irons near uncovered toilets or water-filled tubs and sinks. Even when electrical appliances are turned off, they shouldn't be left plugged in, lying on a countertop near a sink, tub or toilet bowl.

An electric hair dryer gets extremely hot. It can cause burns, even at a medium heat range, when used by a child or on an infant who may not be able to tell you it's getting too hot. It's best to simply avoid using hair dryers on children.

Bathroom electrical outlets should be of the GFCI style. These devices will instantly shut off power to a faulty or shorted circuit, providing some protection against electrocution. All outlets should be protected with safety covers or inserts, and located well out of reach of shower, tub and lavatory water.

Bathroom wastebaskets can be a source of hazards to children. Disposable razors and blades can cause cuts, and "empty" medicine and cleaning product containers can still contain harmful residues. Either dispose of items like these somewhere else, or consider acquiring a lid-locking diaper pail to use as a wastebasket in the bathroom.

SAFEGUARDS FOR SENIORS AND THE DISABLED

As the huge class of baby boomers matures, coupled with increasing longevity and declining birthrates in the U.S., more and more of our population will reach an age of 65 years and older. By the year 2020, in fact, approximately one out of every six individuals living in the United States will be in their late sixties.

That's going to have an effect on home design and construction—especially in regards to kitchens and bathrooms. The government has already included "universal design factors" in public government and other buildings, where wheelchair access is mandatory. That means bathrooms should be spacious enough to maneuver in. Wheelchairs are generally 42- to 45-inches long, and 22½- to 26½-inches wide, and require a 4½- to 5½-feet turning radius. Doorways for wheelchairs should be at least 32-inches wide, excluding the width of the door. Wheelchair footrests make floor-mounted base cabinet doors an obstacle, so vanities should have no floor, no toekicks or bottom rails, that way wheelchairs can pull right up to the countertop and water basin.

Bathrooms may also feature safety rails in showers, tub and toilet areas. Various manufacturers offer lines of support rails, grab handles, backrests and shower seats that can be installed in existing bathrooms; some models may be raised or lowered, and most can be wall-mounted, free-standing or floor mounted. Hanging-ladder grab bars—nylon bars hung on ropes that are suspended from a wall or ceiling—are designed to make getting out of a tub easier for a handicapped person.

For elderly and disabled household members, faucets should be easy to operate. Faucets and showers should be equipped with pressure balanced temperature-controlled thermostatic faucets, to reduce the dangers of scalding. Hand-held showers can provide more flexibility and an easier reach. Tubs should have aprons at convenient heights, wide enough to make entry and exit easy. Showers should have seats. Some units offer special entries for wheelchair access, where entry lips are flush with the floor. Walk-in tubs are available that feature a door in the side wall to allow the user to walk into the tub rather than stepping over an edge. Some models include a molded seat at wheelchair height, with special options such as left or right seating, water temperature controls and grab bars.

Older adults also have different lighting requirements. They need more light than younger individuals to distinguish between slight color contrasts.

GENERAL BATHROOM SAFETY

In addition to the points discussed in the previous section, there are other tips that will make your bathroom a safer place. For instance, bathroom doors traditionally swing inward. Where possible, they should be re-hung so they open outward to prevent an accident victim from being trapped inside. Along the same lines, it's best if shower and tub enclosure doors open outward or slide sideways.

You should be able to open your bathroom doors from the outside, after they've been locked from the inside, to free accident victims or individuals who may be unable to unlock a door by themselves.

Any rugs used in a bathroom should have nonskid rubber backs. When you have a choice, select thin rugs that are not as likely to cause tripping.

Use night-lights in bathrooms. They're useful for late-night visits. Automatic models are available at reasonable cost; they turn on when light levels fall below a certain intensity.

All bathroom lighting, especially lighting in bathrooms without windows, has to be well thought out. You need good general lighting, plus very good task lighting, for shaving and applying make-up. And don't forget lighting to read by in the bathtub. Some of the most successful lighting for bathrooms is created by indirect rather than direct light sources. Light can be bounced off a white ceiling, concealed behind battens, and doubled off of mirrors. When ceilings are low, flush recessed fittings are handy because you won't strike them while toweling off.

Consider installing safety railings and support handles in the bathroom, especially around the tub, shower, toilet and whirlpool if you have one. Don't

consider these accessories "only for the elderly and disabled." You may rarely lose your balance now, but who can tell what the future may hold, and beyond that, visitors who are not so spry will appreciate the extra support that railings and handles provide.

If a shower curtain is used, the shower rod should be securely fastened in case a bather slips and grabs the curtain or rod to prevent a fall.

Don't take risks with a slippery tub or shower unit. Hospital emergency rooms frequently receive patients who thought they'd never slip and fall in their own bathtubs. Use a good rubber mat with suction cups that firmly grasp the tub surface when stepped on (see Figure 9-7). Place the mat in the tub when the tub is dry to assure good suction.

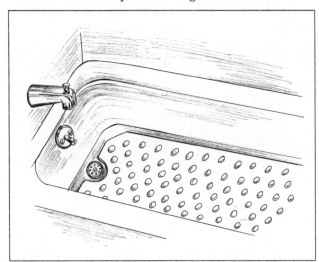

Figure 9-7. A rubber bath mat.

As baths have begun to receive more attention during recent years, and have had to make room for more elaborate whirlpool designs, some of them are becoming more dangerous—especially the ones containing elaborate steps and platforms surrounding the whirlpool units.

Entering and exiting a tub is one of the most dangerous acts the typical household member does day-in and day-out. If you have to climb slippery tile steps before you step down into a whirlpool or tub—and there's no grab bar present—then that's a serious accident just waiting to happen.

Sun or heat lamps should operate only on short-term timers so people who fall asleep in the bathroom can't get burned, and so the fixtures won't overheat if someone leaves and forgets to turn a lamp off.

Make sure your hands and feet are dry before you reach for any plugged-in appliance. It's best to keep radios, televisions, and other non-bathroom-related appliances out of bathrooms. And again, never leave a plugged-in appliance near a water-filled basin or tub. Unplug and remove the items when they're not being used or attended.

Keep floor, wall and fixture surfaces clean of soap and other residues that could encourage the growth of mildew and bacteria.

If you keep medical and first-aid supplies in the bathroom, consider placing them all in a kit that can be easily taken wherever it's needed.

Design Considerations

Ceramic tile flooring is durable and easy to maintain, but should have a nonskid glaze surface. Floor tiles should have a Coefficient of Friction (COF) rating of .5 or higher—a rating recognized by the tile industry for expressing slipping resistance.

Elevated tubs should have steps with risers (the vertical parts of the steps) no higher than seven inches, and treads at least ten inches deep. Again, floor and step tile should be slip resistant, and marble should be honed for traction. A handrail should also be installed—attached to wall studs only, for strength and stability.

Locate a whirlpool's switch far enough away from the tub to eliminate the possibility of someone trying to turn it on while in the water. Keep towels, however, within easy reach.

A good ventilation or exhaust fan is important for removing odors and excess humidity in the air. Such humidity can be harmful to the walls, paint, paper and insulation. Plus it encourages mold to grow, which is bad for your health.

Tub faucets should be no more than fifteen to eighteen inches away from the tub edge to prevent lengthy reaches. Tub and sink faucets that are easy to grab include various blade-style or single-lever models. Buy anti-scald shower valves and position shower controls away from the water flow.

Vanities should be thirty-four to thirty-six inches high to prevent back strain, and a recessed "kick" or bottom helps prevent stubbed toes. Rounded edges on all countertops and cabinets are less dangerous in case of slips and falls.

Windows that are operable should be in positions and of types that can be reached and opened easily. Would a sliding unit or a casement model work better than a double hung window?

Carpeting is not generally recommended for bathrooms because it attracts moisture that encourages the growth of fungi and bacteria.

Special no-fog mirrors are available for bathrooms. Shaving mirrors for the shower can be hooked up to the hot water line, which heats them while the water is running. A waterproof light in the shower will help prevent nicks and cuts for those who shave there. Be careful with lighting fixtures located above tubs. Can such fixtures be safely and easily reached to change bulbs? If you need a step stool or ladder in the tub to change bulbs, then change to a safer lighting arrangement.

BATHROOM SAFETY QUICK CHECKLIST

☐ Never leave young children alone in a bathroom.

☐ Make sure bathtub and shower units have nonslip surfaces. Use rubber bath mats or rough-tread strips applied closely together.

☐ Tub and shower glass doors should be made of safety glass. So should all mirrors used in the tub and shower.

☐ If a bathroom floor is made of tile that gets slippery when wet, place a thin rubber-backed bath carpet next to the tub/shower.

☐ You should be able to unlock a bathroom from the outside in case someone locks himself in.

☐ Try to keep glass drinking cups and containers out of bathrooms. Use paper cups for drinking.

☐ Avoid operating electrical appliances near water-filled sinks, tubs and toilet bowls. Unplug appliances when you're not using the bathroom or the appliances.

☐ Bathroom electrical outlets should be GFCI style.

☐ Ideally, bathroom, tub and shower doors should swing outward or slide sideways to prevent accident victims from becoming trapped inside.

☐ Use night-lights in bathrooms.

☐ Consider installing safety railings and support handles near tubs, showers and toilets.

☐ Sunlamps or heat lamps should operate only on short-term timers.

☐ Whirlpool off and on switches should be located far enough away from the tub that no one in the tub can turn on the unit.

☐ Make sure your hands and feet are dry before you reach for any plugged-in appliances.

☐ Keep floor, wall and fixture surfaces clean of soap and other residues.

CHAPTER 10

WORKSHOP SAFETY

A workshop can mean a tiny bench in the corner of a basement, with a pegboard on the wall behind it, and a handful of tools. Or it could mean an elaborate woodworking center, complete with table saws, routers, drill presses, planers, and related equipment and machinery. Small or large, most have similar safety needs.

PERSONAL PROTECTION EQUIPMENT (PPE)

Did you know that far more accidents happen in the home than in the workplace? That's partly because manufacturing and other companies must follow strict regulations and rules enforced by OSHA and other regulatory agencies, so safe equipment, conditions and processes are maintained to ensure the safety of their employees. Modern management operates as safely as possible, because injuries are expensive both in terms of accident insurance and medical costs, and costs incurred in replacing injured workers, plus it's the morally right thing to do. But when was the last time OSHA inspected your residence? While companies have comprehensive safety management programs, households usually do not. The following PPE items should be available in most workshops to prevent accidental injuries.

Eye Protection

Wear safety glasses, goggles or other protection whenever your work may endanger your eyes. That means when cutting, sawing, sanding, drilling, planing, routing, chiseling, hammering—in fact, you might well consider forming a habit of putting on safety glasses with side shields, or safety goggles, the minute you enter the workshop, and keeping them on until you leave. Naturally, the heavier the hazard, the sturdier the eyewear protection should be. Different lenses are needed for welding or cutting and burning. But always go for a little more protection than you think you will need.

Most serious eye injuries are from foreign bodies that enter the eyes: bits or pieces of metal, wood, plastic, stone, or whatever material is being worked with. Corneal foreign bodies are very painful and potentially damaging in a number of ways—the cornea heals extremely slowly because of its limited blood supply, and once the integrity of the cornea is "run through," bacteria can cause severe infection and damage to the inner eye.

Certainly, every workshop should have several pairs of safety glasses with side shields, goggles and face shields (see Figure 10-1). These are inexpensive investments when you consider what could be lost without them. Too often safety glasses or goggles are not worn because they get misplaced or are not handy. A good solution is to keep pairs in several places in the shop, so a pair is always just a short reach away. Hang a pair on each end of the workbench and have a pair near each piece of power equipment, so there's never an excuse not to wear them.

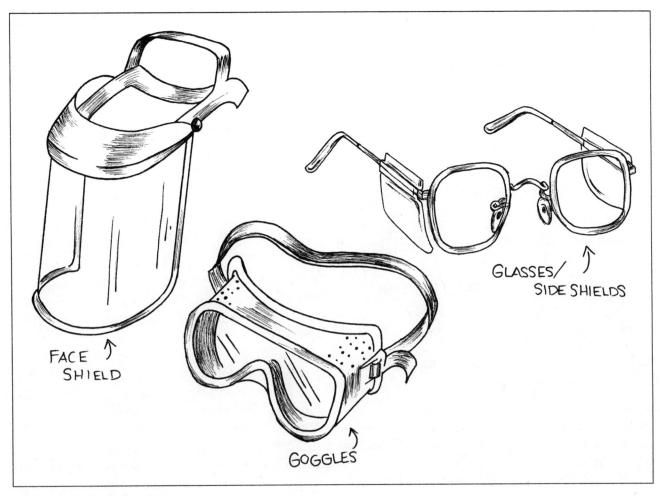

FACE SHIELD

GOGGLES

GLASSES/ SIDE SHIELDS

Figure 10-1. Protective eyewear.

Safety glasses with side shields offer adequate protection when hammering or when using hand tools or slow-moving power tools. If you take prescription lenses, safety glasses made of durable impact-resistant polycarbonate lenses are available in your prescription. Make sure they come with permanently attached side shields to block particles or pieces of metal or wood from striking your eyes from the side, or purchase sturdy individual side shields that slide easily on and off your eyewear frame. The frames of most safety glasses are more rugged than those of ordinary dress glasses. Inexpensive safety glasses are made to go over regular prescription glasses, so visitors with prescription eyewear can be protected when visiting your shop.

Goggles can also be worn over regular prescription glasses and safety glasses when the hazard of dust, particles or splashing liquid is present.

Clear plastic face shields can give full facial pro-

tection. They're held on your head by an adjustable band that allows the shield to be conveniently flipped up and down. A face shield is a must when working with power equipment such as a grinder or a lathe—if a chisel or other working tool should snag or break and be thrown in the air, a full shield would protect your face and neck. Although they're fine for blocking chips and shavings, they don't offer enough protection against heavy impact or from objects that may fly up around the shield, so it's a good practice to always wear either safety glasses or goggles beneath a shield. Full shields should be kept near the equipment they will be used with.

Tinted safety eyewear should be used when welding, torch-cutting or brazing. Tinted safety lenses will protect eyes from the brightness of the flame or arc, and from infrared rays given off by the processes. Make sure also to wear protective safety glasses to guard against flying particles and sparks.

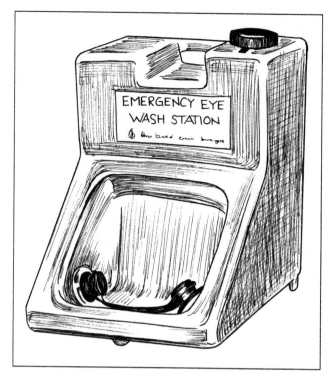

Figure 10-2. Eyewash station.

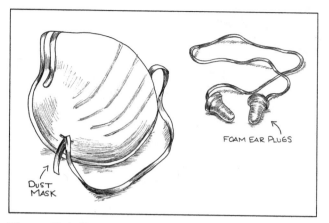

Figure 10-3. Dust mask and earplugs.

Some eye protection, such as that offered by a welding hood, combine tinted protection with a safety-glass lens.

If you're working with materials that may splash, consider installing an eyewash station. Many manufacturers of chemical products such as paints, cleaners, and other caustic liquids recommend flushing the eyes thoroughly as first aid. There are several main types of eyewash stations available: ones tied into a home's main water supply, and units that are self-contained—full of an eye-rinsing liquid (see Figure 10-2). With either model, make sure you test it at least once a month, and instruct other household members who may be exposed to chemical hazards in your workshop how to use it.

Respiratory Protection

Even though you may have a good ventilation or vacuum system, wear an appropriately rated dust mask or respirator whenever particles are airborne or chemical fumes are present.

Most people would be surprised at how much sawdust is produced in the few seconds it takes to power-saw through a board. Have someone shine a flashlight through the air around the working saw and see for yourself. The air will be literally filled with tiny wood particles and dust. Without some kind of respiratory protection, some of this dust will end up in your lungs, which is a definite health hazard—it's a lot easier for dust and other tiny particles to get into your lungs, than it is for them to get back out. Minimize the amount of dust you breathe in by using a dust mask or respirator. The simplest dust masks are paper throw-away ones that cover your nose and mouth and are held against your face with rubber bands or straps (see Figure 10-3). Others have plastic frames with replaceable sponge-rubber inserts. Both types cut down on the sawdust and other dust particles you'd otherwise breathe. Make it a habit to wear respiratory protection whenever you saw, sand, plane, grind, weld, burn, or when you use power tools that produce noxious fumes, sprays or clouds of dust. When you see how discolored or clogged the filters get, you'll be glad the materials you are filtering out did not get into your lungs.

Hearing Protection

Prolonged exposure to loud noise can destroy or greatly impair your hearing. Noise from power saws, sanders, drills and similar workshop machinery needs to be "softened" or partially blocked out by earplugs or full ear protectors. Otherwise the long-term effect of such high decibel noise is a slow loss of hearing, which you may not notice until it's too late. While full ear protection offers the most comprehensive noise damage prevention, throw-away foam or other earplugs (see Figure 10-3) are also acceptable, and are inexpensive enough for you to keep a whole box full on hand for yourself and visitors alike.

Hand Protection

There are few tasks you perform that don't involve your hands in one way or another. Your hands are incredible tools, able to grasp and twist, pinch and manipulate. Unfortunately, because they're always where the action is—where the work or play is getting done—they're subject to numerous safety hazards.

Depending on what you do in your workshop, you may need several kinds of gloves to protect your hands. Cloth gloves—lightweight and heavyweight models—will protect hands from dirt, dry chemical products, chafing, abrasions, some wood and other slivers, and low heat. Leather gloves will protect against thicker slivers, metal chips, rough materials, sparks and moderate heat. Rubber or plastic gloves protect against caustic and other liquid chemicals, and can help act as an electrical insulator. Metal mesh gloves will protect against cuts, rough materials, and blows from sharp-edged tools. Various skin creams can also function as "invisible" gloves to protect against excessive water contact and substances that could otherwise harm the skin.

Make sure your gloves fit properly. If they're too large, they'll restrict your ability to handle small items. If they're too small, they'll be uncomfortable and can lead to hand fatigue.

Foot Protection

If you work with heavy materials, parts or machinery where there is a possibility of items dropping on your feet, it's a good idea to wear hard-toe or safety steel-toe shoes in the workshop (see Figure 10-4). Certainly, avoid wearing dress shoes, sneakers or sandals.

THE WORKSHOP ENVIRONMENT

Take control of your surroundings by paying particular attention to lighting, electrical service, ventilation, fire protection, housekeeping and waste disposal.

Figure 10-4. Safety shoes.

Workshop Lighting

Lighting is vital to a safe shop, especially when you're operating power tools for fine work. Inadequate lighting will tire your eyes and could cause you to misjudge cutting, drilling, or other power-tool operations. Good shop lighting consists of bright illumination that doesn't result in a lot of shadows. This means you can see your work area without bending over, squinting or angling your head.

It's relatively simple and inexpensive to upgrade inadequate overhead lighting by installing fluorescent fixtures spaced six or eight feet apart. If that's not good enough, place the fixtures every four feet. Gooseneck lamps placed at tools are also helpful for close work. Make sure all areas where blades or drill bits or other power tool attachments contact the material are well illuminated.

Use available windows during daylight hours, and keep windows and all light bulbs clean, since accumulations of dust and grime will block out light. It's also a good idea to place protective sleeves over exposed fluorescent bulbs to control shattering glass in case a bulb is accidentally broken. If such breakage occurs with unprotected bulbs, turn off power to the fixture before attempting to remove the metal bulb base. If your shop area is illuminated with incandescent bulbs, protect them with metal or plastic wire cages manufactured for this purpose. They're available at hardware stores and electrical supply houses.

Workshop Electricity

Underpowered workshops and homeowners who carelessly use extension cords cause a lot of fires and other accidents. Power lines that run every which way cause tripping hazards and overloaded electrical circuits. To eliminate such an unhealthy mess, install additional permanent outlets. Another solution is to purchase several overhead reel extension cords—drum-type containers with spring-loaded reels that store the cords when they're not in use (see Figure 10-5). Each is simply hung from a hook on the shop ceiling and plugged into a nearby outlet. When you need power you just pull out the amount of cord required.

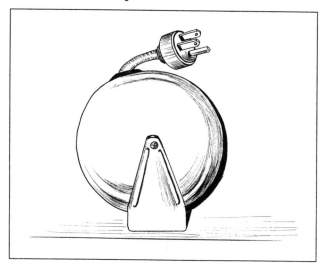

Figure 10-5. A reel extension cord.

Use power or extension cords only occasionally, if no other outlets are available. Sometimes extension cords remain part of the workshop. Soon several "temporary" lightweight cords are in use. If you ever use an undersized cord, feel the cord with your fingertips the next time you work with it. If it feels warm, the line is overloaded. This means the insulation or covering is baking and will eventually crack or flake off to expose bare wires. If such a cord is in service and you or a metal tool or part comes in contact with the bare wire, a shock may result that could be fatal.

One of the most effective means of protecting against shocks and possible electrocution is to use GFCIs. A GFCI senses any changes in current, such as the fluctuation caused by a short, and immediately shuts down the power in response. At least several electric outlets in a workshop should be of the GFCI style. And GFCIs also come as "plug-in add-ons" to be inserted in regular outlets, and are available built into special extension cord power strips.

Workshop Ventilation

Air quality in a workshop goes a long way toward making the environment a pleasant and healthy place in which to work. The best way to minimize airborne dust particles is with a dust collection system. There are plenty of commercial systems available, but they can cost thousands of dollars. Thanks to the market that home workshops have recently opened up, adequate dust collection systems are available at lower prices for the home hobbyist or workshop owner.

Another effective alternative is to purchase shop vacuum attachments that can be hooked up to or near power tools that generate dust. A homemade solution is to tape a new furnace filter to the exhaust side of the grid or cage on a portable fan, then place the fan on a table about waist high—aimed away from the work. When the fan pulls the dusty air through itself, most of the dust is removed as the air passes through the filter.

You can remove most of the dust that escapes the vacuum attachments by installing a window-mounted or through-the-wall exhaust fan. The window exhaust fan will also exhaust fumes, and if you can cross-ventilate by opening a window on the opposite wall, you'll have a constant supply of fresh air. The exhaust fan you select should be rated to draw between one-hundred and two-hundred cubic feet of air per minute (cfm). To determine the recommended fan capacity needed to ventilate your workshop, simply multiply its square footage by eight. For example, to ventilate a three-hundred-square-foot workshop, a fan with a 240 cfm rating should be adequate. But an exhaust fan must pull fresh air in from somewhere. If you can't supply it with a window, you might have to remove an inch or two from the bottom of your shop door so fresh air can be drawn in and toward the exhaust fan.

Workshop Fire Extinguishers

For most workshops you should purchase at least two UL-approved ABC multipurpose extinguishers.

They can extinguish oil, grease, gasoline, electrical, wood, cloth, paper, and most plastic and other fires. Stand back about six feet or so from the flame, pull the safety ring, aim the nozzle at the base of the flames, and make smooth sweeping motions while squeezing the trigger. Inspect fire extinguisher gauges at least once per month and remember to recharge units in the event of an incident when they're used on a fire.

Workshop Housekeeping

Good housekeeping will go a long way toward improving the enjoyment, efficiency and safety of any activity, and especially so with a workshop. Even a serious "shopsmith" or workshop owner who wants to, or is forced to, earn a living from his or her shop, eventually will come to the conclusion that proper housekeeping has a direct effect on the efficiency, productivity and safety of the business. Those who never learn this will never prosper as they could otherwise. Why spend hour after hour wondering where you put that tool, or sifting through sawdust on the floor for your car keys? Most workshops need all the available space they can get. A shop littered with raw materials, piles of waste, and equipment haphazardly strewn about will be neither a safe nor an enjoyable place to work.

Avoid overfilling racks, bins and other storage containers. Keep bench tops neat and free from clutter. This is one of the most important things you can do. Cluttered workbenches invite injuries, spills and other accidents. Give yourself some working space on your benches. Keep all drawers closed. Don't overfill them so they can't be closed all the way. Stack and store materials and other items neatly, keeping heavy objects on bottom shelves.

A workshop floor can sometimes become so cluttered with parts, supplies, equipment, tools, wastes, extension cords and other items that the floor itself becomes a hazard. Sweep the workshop floor frequently to keep it clean of wood scraps, metal chips, sawdust and other debris. Clean oil and grease spills immediately. If the floor is slippery even when clean and dry, apply peel-and-stick anti-skid strips, or paint it with anti-slip abrasive floor paint, to improve traction. Hard floors, especially concrete, can cause foot and leg fatigue. Anti-fatigue mats are available to provide cushioning, and may solve several ergonomic problems such as foot and leg fatigue and back strain at the same time, while providing a slip-resistant surface.

Oil, Grease and Solvent Disposal

Used motor oil and grease should be disposed of in approved recycling centers in your community.

Solvents, paints, oil and other chemical spills need to be cleaned as soon as possible so no one slips on them or accidentally ignites them with a wayward cigarette butt or the flame from a burning torch or propane heater. The rags or absorbent material used to clean up a spill should be either removed from the shop and stored outside until the next trash pickup, or placed in an approved metal can with a tight-fitting lid. That way if they ignite, the flames will go out quickly once the limited supply of oxygen in the can is used up. If the spill is on a wooden floor, neutralize the area by pouring water onto it, drying the floor immediately afterward.

TOOL SAFETY

If you have young children, store all tools in locked cabinets or drawers. As the children grow, introduce them gradually to locked-up tools. But continue to lock up power tools until the children are old enough and mature enough to be trained correctly in tool use and safety.

Pointed or sharp tools can be stored by inserting their blades into a block of plastic foam cut from the lining material found in appliance cartons.

If your tool drawers pull out and spill their contents, screw a small rectangular piece of wood to the inside of the drawer's back panel to act as a stop (see Figure 10-6). Turning the stop to a vertical position will keep the drawer in place. To remove the drawer, turn the stop to a horizontal position.

Avoid cutting toward your hand or body. Aim the business end or edge of a tool to miss your body, should the tool slip.

Work only with tools that are in good condition. If a tool is broken or worn, fix it or throw it away. Avoid working with dull tools, blades and bits. Take time to have them sharpened first. And don't force tools in order to get the job done faster, because

Figure 10-6. A tool drawer with safety stop.

hurrying will make for poor work and will increase the likelihood of accidental injury.

Plastic handles on pliers or screwdrivers are provided more for comfort than for safety. The plastic won't ensure adequate protection against electrical shock unless the tools are specified as having insulated handles.

Injuries often result when tools are used for jobs they weren't designed to handle. Pliers grip and cut and are not recommended as substitutes for wrenches. Screwdrivers should not be used as chisels—their metal won't take the impact. Claw hammers should not be used to strike concrete just as sledge hammers should not be used to drive nails. Use the tool designed for the job at hand. Never try to improvise or take short cuts by attempting to use tools in "creative" ways.

Power Tools

Avoid working directly overhead with power tools. Stand on a bench or ladder, so the work is more in front of you instead of directly above you.

Keep hand tools and loose objects off an operating power tool's work surface and away from the power tool or blade.

Avoid wearing loose or unbuttoned, dangling clothing when using power tools. Keep long sleeves, ties, scarves, bandannas, long hair, necklaces and work apron strings away from turning or spinning machinery. Roll up your sleeves or wear a short sleeve shirt. Put your hair up in a bun or tuck it beneath a cap. Remove or tuck out of sight anything that could dangle or catch in moving equipment parts. Rings, watches, bracelets and other hand jewelry should be removed before you begin working with powered shop machinery, because those decorative items can easily be snagged or caught by a moving tool, causing serious injury to the wearer.

Don't wear loose or bulky gloves for tasks requiring fine manipulation skills, or if there's a chance they could get caught in moving machinery.

If possible, remove start/stop keys to large pieces of power equipment so only you can start the machinery. Another option is to shut down the electrical power at a circuit box, so children or others who may not be qualified to operate the machinery cannot start it.

Inspect power cords for frayed or cut sections and damaged plugs that can short out and cause fires or and shock someone who happens to touch a bare wire (see Figure 10-7).

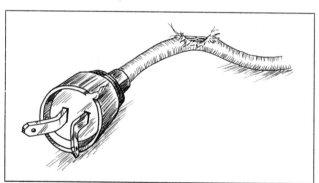

Figure 10-7. Damaged plug and cord.

With power saws, try to cut straight across the wood surface whenever possible, and don't apply sideways leverage, prying or twisting while you cut.

Safety guards on saws, grinders, or other power tools must be present and in good condition for safe operation. Tools with removed or altered guards should not be used until they're repaired.

Avoid distractions. Refrain from speaking to anyone while operating power equipment. Delay activities if you are tired or ill or otherwise unable to concentrate.

Alcohol has no place in the workshop. Instead, quench your thirst with fruit juices, sodas or water.

CONTROL HAZARDOUS ENERGY

This is a simple yet often violated concept. While working on, adjusting, storing, or otherwise handling tools that are not in active use, make sure the item or piece of equipment cannot be accidentally energized. Unplug any tools on which you must change blades or bits. Don't leave machinery and equipment that can be started up by a mere flick of an on/off switch, especially if children have access to the workshop. See chapter twelve, on lawn safety, for more discussions on hazardous energy and zero-energy control procedures.

IN GENERAL

Do things the right way, even if it means taking more time than you want to. Concentrate while working. If a friend or neighbor stops to talk with you, postpone using that power saw or drill until he or she leaves. Always think about what you're doing at that very moment, not about the next step in a project or what you'll be having for dinner.

Consider installing a phone jack or extension in your workshop so you can make and take calls in between (not during) work tasks, or for use in emergencies. Keep a well-stocked first-aid kit handy.

WORKSHOP SAFETY QUICK CHECKLIST

☐ Maintain and use personal safety equipment for eyes, lungs, ears, hands and feet when your work involves hazards related to them.

☐ Keep a well-stocked first-aid kit handy.

☐ Consider installing a telephone extension for convenience and emergencies.

☐ Establish and maintain proper lighting levels for overall and task use.

☐ Install enough electrical outlets so extension cords are not needed all over the place. At least several outlets should be GFCIs.

☐ If extension cords are needed on a temporary basis, use only heavy-duty cords or install appropriate overhead reel extension cords.

☐ Maintain an adequate dust collection system when working with equipment and materials that generate large quantities of dust.

☐ Make sure the workshop has good ventilation.

☐ Keep at least two fully charged UL-approved ABC multipurpose fire extinguishers handy, and know how to use them.

☐ Maintain good housekeeping at all times. Keep tools, equipment, and supplies neatly stored away between uses.

WORKSHOP SAFETY QUICK CHECKLIST
(continued)

☐ Keep items off the floor as much as possible. Workbench surfaces should also be uncluttered. Put tools back after each use.

☐ Repair broken tools or get rid of them.

☐ Regularly refer to power tool and equipment maintenance and operating manuals.

☐ Avoid working directly overhead with power or other tools.

☐ Wear snug-fitting clothing, pull long hair up, and remove jewelry when working with power tools.

☐ Achieve a zero-energy state before working on or adjusting a piece of power equipment.

☐ Collect oily or solvent-soiled rags and other clean-up materials in metal containers with lids, not in regular wastebaskets. Dispose of these materials according to your local regulations.

☐ Recycle waste and scraps whenever possible.

☐ Avoid distractions. Postpone work if you're tired, ill or unable to concentrate.

PART THREE

OUT-DOOR SAFETY

The great outdoors. Tinkering in the garage, working in the garden, going for a swim or a picnic, or taking a walk in the first glistening snow. What could be healthier than fresh air and a little exercise? But along with the benefits come many hazardous situations you can learn to prevent. We'll share guidelines for safe procedures that will help you make the most of your time outdoors, whether it's working on household chores, pursuing a hobby or recreation, or just getting from here to there in ice and snow.

CHAPTER 11

GARAGE SAFETY

G arages. Some homes have them and others don't. If you don't have a garage, but if you have young children or if you live someplace where you could be visited by youngsters, please read this chapter anyway, because it's likely that either your kids will be playing in other people's garages or that other children will eventually visit your garage. It's best to be aware of the most common garage hazards.

The main function of a garage is to provide secure shelter for vehicles, "outdoor" and seasonal items such as lawn mowers and landscaping equipment, sporting goods, bicycles and other toys, barbecues, lawn furniture, ladders and other tools, snow tires and Christmas decorations. Depending on the household, garages can also serve as places to pursue a favorite hobby such as woodworking, photography or ceramics. Too, they can be convenient gathering places for children and pets on rainy Saturday afternoons. They can be part-time auto mechanic shops or hair styling salons. They have even been turned into mother-in-law apartments. It all depends.

For safety's sake, this chapter will consider the traditional garage use: storage for vehicles and other outdoor and seasonal possessions.

ELECTRIC GARAGE DOOR OPENERS

Years ago, when electric garage door openers first became available, many of them were dangerous for children to be around. Why? Because the openers didn't have auto-reverse features that would prevent heavy bay doors from continuing to lower against whatever they struck on the way down. The doors injured children, adults and even pets who happened to be in the way. Nowadays, all electric garage door openers carrying the UL (Underwriters Laboratories) label *must* reverse their closing motion within two seconds if the door comes in contact with almost any object higher than an inch off the ground. The one-inch margin allows for a buildup of dirt, stones, snow or ice on the ground.

If you don't know if your electric garage door opener has auto-reverse, get a piece of wood thicker than one inch and put it on the garage floor, across the plane of the door track. Activate the opener. When the door hits the wood it should reverse and reopen within two seconds. If it doesn't, disconnect the opener right then and there, and operate the door manually until the opener is either repaired (if it is indeed an auto-reverse model) or replaced (if it doesn't have an auto-reverse feature).

It's important to have a copy of the operating manuals for both the garage door and the door opener. Request copies from the manufacturers if the manuals are missing. Then read and follow all of the recommended safety procedures.

To operate an electric garage door opener by hand or manually, there should be an emergency release handle (see Figure 11-1) on the inside. Try the emergency release at least once a month to make sure it's working and hasn't "frozen up" from lack of use. If there's ever a power outage or a problem with the opener, you need to know that the emergency release will operate and let your car out of the garage, especially in response to an emergency.

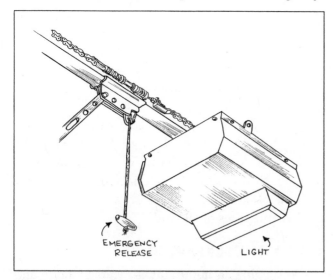

Figure 11-1. Garage door opener with light.

Electric garage door openers are not toys. Locate stationary controls and portable units out of children's reach. Keep young children away from the controls. Teach older, responsible children how to safely operate door openers. Although you may be able to push the close button from inside the garage, and then hurry outside beneath the closing door, it's not a good habit to develop. In fact, to do so sets a bad example for children who might try to imitate such dangerous behavior. It's best never to walk or drive beneath a closing garage door.

Make sure the opener's automatic light (see Figure 11-1) is in working order. When the bulb burns out, replace it as soon as possible.

Garage Door Springs and Hardware

Check the torsion springs and cables (see Figure 11-2) that provide the mechanical power assistance to open or close the door. Unless you are thoroughly familiar with garage doors, never try to repair or adjust torsion springs. The springs are under tension and could cause serious injury if accidentally released at the wrong time. Visually inspect the springs, cables, rollers (see Figure 11-2) and other door hardware for signs of wear. Examine cables for fraying or kinks. Inspect the condition of the rollers:

Metal rollers will rarely fail, but nylon ones can be damaged easily. See if the hinges are fastened securely to the door panels (see Figure 11-2). The same hinges will also be attached to the door's rollers. Call a qualified door technician for a second look or to make needed repairs. Consider installing a restraining cable on the extension spring to help contain the spring in case it breaks. It's important that the door's hardware is in good shape because a failure could damage the electric opener—and someone's back if a broken door has to be opened manually.

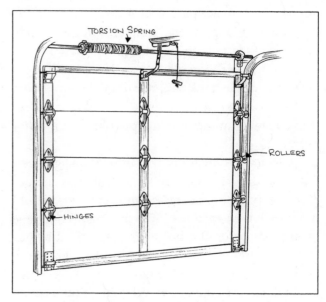

Figure 11-2. Garage door, inside view.

GARAGE FLOORS

The chief hazards with garage floors are slips, trips and falls. From a maintenance and safety perspective, it's best not to paint a concrete garage floor. Several coats of a good sealer are a better option.

When garages are used to house vehicles, concrete floors can become stained with oil, antifreeze, brake and transmission fluids, and grease. Clean up these stains as quickly as possible.

Small floor cracks can develop into larger ones. Repair them before they do. Resurface flaking or crumbling floor areas, and repair raised or sunken sections of concrete that pose tripping hazards.

Water should not be permitted to collect or stand on a garage floor. If floor drains are present in the garage, keep them open throughout the year, occasionally running water from a hose into them. If water tends to run in from the outside or from a driveway that slopes downward to the garage, install a strip drain or catch basin outside, or take other measures of prevention.

HEATING APPLIANCES

Home heating furnaces or boilers located in a garage should be partitioned off from the rest of the garage area to prevent accidental ignition of gasoline fumes from a leaky automobile tank or line. If a water heater must be placed in a garage, and cannot be placed in a separate enclosure of the garage, it should be mounted on a concrete or other sturdy platform at least eighteen inches high. Gasoline vapors are heavier than air. If a car has a leaking gas tank, line or gas tank cap, it will take many hours for the gasoline fumes to rise over eighteen inches to the level of an open flame pilot light in a water heater.

Adequate ventilation is necessary in all garages. Fumes and dusts from fuels and materials such as gasoline, propane, fiberglass and fertilizers should not be allowed to collect. On one hand, a garage should not be drafty, but neither should it be airtight. Be careful when warming up a vehicle in a closed garage (idling the engine) or working with a running engine (such as when doing a tune-up on a car or pickup truck). Every year fatalities result from carbon monoxide fumes produced under those same circumstances.

ELECTRICITY

GFCIs belong in a garage. They can help prevent shocks when people are using hedge trimmers, electric lawn mowers, drills or other tools.

If you have to use an extension cord with a power tool, be sure that the cord's current rating equals or is greater than the rating of the equipment. Never operate power tools while your feet are bare or while you are wearing wet or damp shoes. And don't enter a flooded garage if you suspect that any electrical wiring has contacted water.

Most garages are not equipped with good lighting. There's probably one or two bare bulbs from simple fixtures attached to the ceiling above the car bays, and another light that's part of the electric garage door opener. If you're going to do any work in the garage—especially on overcast days or at night, you'll need to arrange for task lighting that's either portable (such as a commercial extension lamp with a heavy-duty outdoor-rated cord) or permanent (fluorescent fixtures installed over workbenches, tables or wherever needed). Don't suffer in the dark. Good lighting is especially critical when you're working with cutting and drilling tools at close quarters.

Be careful, as well, with space heaters and wood stoves that are operated during the colder months of the year. Keep these burning and heating units away from combustible materials, especially from curtains, clothing, newspapers, rags, and flammable liquids and gases of all kinds.

GOOD HOUSEKEEPING

Housekeeping is important for garage floor and storage space safety. It's best not to consider your garage a catch-all for everything. Some families fill their garages so full that their cars no longer fit and it's difficult to walk inside. Once this happens, it's hard to clean the floor or to reach the things stored there. Some items get stored out of place because the correct shelves or cabinets can't be approached easily. The garage becomes an obstacle course—a fire hazard and danger zone for household members who periodically must try to retrieve items from its far reaches.

Keep tools, equipment and accessories elevated off the floor on racks, pegboards, wall "grabber" strips, shelves, hooks or other fixtures (see Figure 11-3). In short, hang everything you can to keep the floor free for large items such as lawn mowers, snow blowers and bicycles. During the off-season, bicycles can be hung from the same garage wall hooks that held a sled, toboggan or ice-fishing hut during the summer.

To allow for safe movement within a garage, things have to be organized. The first step to organizing a garage is to get rid of what you don't need. Recycle what can be recycled, such as newspapers, magazines, old metal items, dead plants, and toys your children have outgrown. Sell what can be sold, or donate items to charitable organizations. Then throw out the stuff you can't get rid of any other

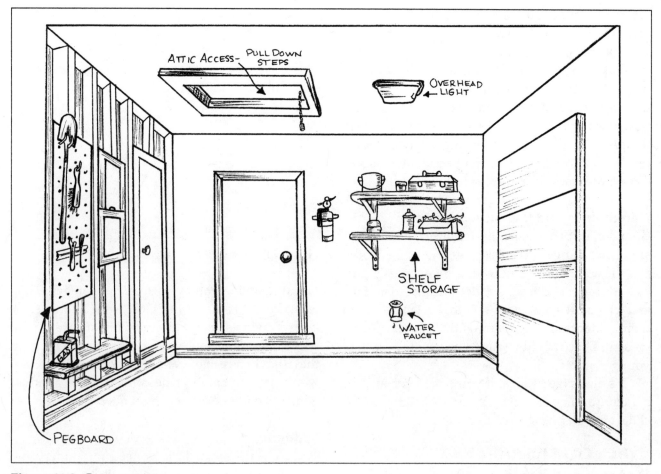

Figure 11-3. Garage storage.

way. Many localities offer a free trash pickup day in April to make spring cleaning easy on their residents.

After you weed out the unneeded items and do some cleaning, divide the garage into "use" areas. Naturally, the most important area will likely be the space for your vehicles and vehicle accessories. The accessories can be located on a heavy-duty rack system that's placed against one wall of the garage. Some rack systems are large enough to accommodate a spare set of tires. Automotive tools, extra motor oil, gasoline and other fuels in approved containers, windshield washer fluid, leftover antifreeze, car cleaning supplies, and even a child's safety seat when it's removed from your vehicle can be stored on the shelves.

In another part of the garage, make room for lawn and garden supplies, and home maintenance equipment and materials.

In a third part of the garage, keep sporting goods, toys and bicycles.

Of course, there are many variations of storage setups you can subscribe to. Custom tailor your storage scheme to your belongings. Try installing shelving on your garage walls (see Figure 11-3). One or more shelves twenty-four to thirty inches deep can be installed around the two sides and the back of the garage (wherever rack systems are not already standing), attached by brackets fixed to the walls. Remember that the more items you keep elevated, the easier and faster you'll be able to clean the garage floor.

Keep heavy-duty, rust-proof containers in one location to hold leaf clippings, garbage and recyclable materials. A large-wheeled refuse cart will make it easy to move things to the curb on pick-up day.

Containers of heavy see-through plastic with tight snap-on lids can hold paint cans, small accessories, and other supplies to help neaten the garage's appearance. Smaller containers can hold car wax, cleaners and rags.

Make it a habit to return tools to their proper place. It's a lot easier to put things back when you have a specific place or container to put them in. Use labels if you find yourself questioning where things go. Time spent organizing today can save time tomorrow, and can prevent accidental injuries caused by a lack of housekeeping.

Flammables and Chemical Storage

Gasoline, turpentine, paints, fertilizers, insecticides and other dangerous substances should be stored in their original containers or in commercially purchased containers designed for those materials. Fuel and chemical containers should be labeled with their contents and the hazards that those contents present. They should be stored beyond the reach of young children.

It's also a good idea, if you store beer in your garage, to keep it locked away so neighborhood children won't have easy access to it.

OTHER CONSIDERATIONS

Freezers and Refrigerators

Garages, during the spring, summer and fall months, are not the most secure places in many homes. Freezers—both the chest and upright types—and refrigerators placed in garages should be kept locked so no one can steal their contents and so no small children can lock themselves inside of the units.

Attic Access

An attic over a garage should have a safe, approachable access. That doesn't mean placing a stepladder beneath a small rectangular hole in the garage ceiling. The most efficient access is usually a pull-down, folding step unit (see Figure 11-4) that's installed with springs and hinges so the unit disappears into

Figure 11-4. Garage attic access.

the attic and becomes part of the garage ceiling when lifted back out of service. These folding staircases provide safe and secure climbing. Be careful when lifting items into and retrieving objects from the attic. If possible, get someone to help so you won't have to climb or descend steps or a ladder while carrying boxes or other bulky containers.

Ladders

There always seems to be a need for ladders in a garage, either to change a light bulb, to access a garage door opener, or to place some item high in storage. Before climbing a ladder, place it on a solid, level surface so the legs won't slip. Avoid leaning to either side, or standing on the top two rungs of a ladder. Wear dry shoes with good soles. Aluminum ladders found in many households will conduct electricity; wooden and fiberglass ladders will not.

Communications

To keep in touch with household members inside of the house, why not install a home intercom and phone line in a corner of the garage? How many times have you been working in the garage, only to have to race inside to try to catch a phone call in time?

GARAGE SAFETY QUICK CHECKLIST

☐ Manually operated garage bay doors should be kept in good working order so minimal effort is required to open and close them.

☐ Electric garage door openers should have an auto-reverse feature.

☐ Obtain, read and follow garage door and garage door opener operating manuals.

☐ With garage doors equipped with electric openers, test the inside emergency release handle at least once a month.

☐ Keep stationary and portable garage door opener control units out of young children's reach.

☐ Teach older, responsible children how to safely operate electric door openers.

☐ Avoid getting into the habit of running beneath a closing garage door.

☐ An opener's automatic light should be in working order.

☐ Garage floors should be kept clean, dry, and free of clutter and tripping hazards.

☐ Home heating appliances with pilot lights should be partitioned off from the rest of the garage or mounted on a concrete or other sturdy platform at least eighteen inches high.

☐ All garages should have adequate ventilation.

☐ Beware of gasoline, propane, fiberglass, carbon monoxide, fertilizer, paint, and other fumes and dusts when working or performing any activity within the confined space of a closed garage.

☐ Electrical outlets should be of GFCI design.

☐ Provide adequate lighting for tasks requiring close, fine work such as sawing, drilling, sanding or repairing cars.

☐ Keep space heaters and wood stoves away from combustible materials. Make sure young children cannot accidentally touch them.

**GARAGE SAFETY
QUICK CHECKLIST**
(continued)

☐ Inventory the belongings you keep in the garage and get rid of everything you don't want or need.

☐ Organize garage storage and work spaces, using as much wall and ceiling space as you can for shelving racks, hangers, pegboards, hooks and brackets to keep the floor uncluttered.

☐ Always return tools and other items to their proper place; insist that children do the same.

☐ Store flammable liquids, chemical products and all dangerous substances in their original containers or in approved commercially purchased containers. Keep these items out of the sight and reach of children.

☐ Lock garage freezers and refrigerators so no small children can play in them.

☐ Garage attics should have safe, accessible entrances, such as fold-down staircase units.

☐ Consider installing a home intercom and phone line in the garage

CHAPTER 12

LAWN AND GARDEN SAFETY

Landscaping and gardening are favorite pastimes to millions of homeowners. These activities can be very rewarding, but only if they're done safely. Main lawn and garden hazards include the improper use of lawn mowers and other power tools, heat stress and illness, lifting and bending problems, and careless use and care of hand tools, and chemical products. (See chapter fourteen for information on hot weather safety.)

MOWING THE LAWN

How to Dress

Heavy-duty nonslip shoes provide traction and guard against sharp or hard objects hidden in the lawn; never mow a lawn or operate a garden tractor in your bare feet. Avoid loose clothing or dangling jewelry that could snag on mower or tractor controls. Wear close-fitting long pants, substantial socks, and preferably a long-sleeved shirt to protect yourself from small objects thrown by the mower's blades. If you feel that the weather is too hot for full-length pants and shirt sleeves, mow early in the morning or near the end of the day when temperatures are cooler.

Hearing protection is a good idea when operating noisy mowers for any length of time, but avoid listening to music through earphones while you work—it will hinder your ability to hear other sounds while you're mowing.

Although many people may think this is over-kill, wearing safety goggles while mowing grass is a smart move. How many times have bits of grass, weeds, leaves, dust, dirt or other materials been propelled out of the mower discharge chute, only to bounce off the side of a house, a tree, fence or other obstruction and into your face? The same thing happens when you cut grass on a windy day. Tiny bits of vegetation and dirt can whirl through the air and end up in your eyes.

Carry a pair of tight-fitting cloth or leather gloves in your back pocket in case you need to remove plugged grass or perform minor adjustments or maintenance on the mower.

Preparing to Mow

Plan to mow during daylight hours, when the grass is dry. If grass is wet enough to cause your feet to slip when you walk across it, a mower or lawn tractor could also slip. The chance of *you* slipping and coming in contact with mower blades greatly increases on wet grass. Soggy turf also clogs the blades, underside and discharge chutes, and the compacted wet trimmings may have to be removed. That can be dangerous because manually turning the blades during the cleaning process may start the motor even after the motor has been turned off. It's important not only to turn off the motor, but also to disconnect the spark plug before reaching into the blade housing to clean out trimmings. Another hazard of mowing a wet lawn is the possibility of shock or electrocution if you use an electric mower.

The best options are either to wait a few hours for the grass to dry or mow another day.

Before you take the mower out of your garage, walk the yard. Clear the lawn of sticks, rocks, bottles, pieces of old wire, dog bones, toys, and all items and debris that could otherwise be struck and thrown by the mower. The simplest item can become a deadly missile when propelled by the mower at speeds up to two hundred miles per hour. Also, be aware of "unmovable" objects at or below grass height level, such as a tree stump, pipe or rock that's sticking slightly out of the ground.

Make sure that children and pets are somewhere else—not in the areas you are planning to mow. In fact, it's best to send the children to another yard or keep them indoors. Even if you're confident that they know enough not to dart in front of a moving tractor or lawn mower, they could be struck by an object the mower kicks up. It simply isn't worth the risk.

Inspect the mower before every use. Many old lawn mowers—even though they may still be in good running condition—have no safety features engineered into their design. A modern mower has safety features such as a discharge chute guard and a rear skirt (see Figure 12-1) to prevent objects from being thrown from the blades, a retaining post to hold the spark plug wire when the mower is not in use, and a bail bar on the handle that will stop the engine when released. Certainly, make sure that safety shields and deflectors are in place.

Never disconnect lawn mower safety features. They may cause you the inconvenience of turning off the engine when you need to answer a phone or move some lawn furniture, or they may prevent you from cutting as close as you'd like to a fence, but they could easily save you a trip to the hospital.

See that all nuts and bolts are tight. A lawn mower puts out heavy vibrations that can easily loosen fasteners. Add fuel and oil outdoors while the motor is still cold. Wipe up any spills and let the mower air-dry a few minutes before starting the motor.

Adjust the mowing height, inspect the grass chute and remove or install the grass-catcher bag before you start. If you're using an electric mower, be sure the cord is in good condition and is plugged

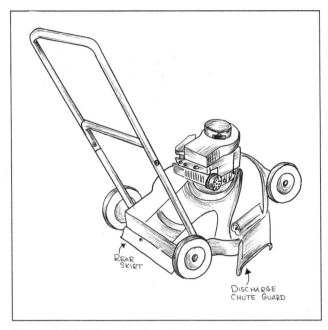

Figure 12-1. Mower safety features.

into a grounded outlet. Again, never mow wet grass or when it's raining.

Mowing

Make sure you know how the mower works and what the controls do. Read the operator's manual and pay particular attention to the safety tips.

Before starting the engine, make any necessary adjustments, especially to the lower blade. Never reach beneath the mower while the blade is still rotating. We know someone who cut off the tips of his fingers not once, but twice, this way. Both times he thought the blade had stopped rotating. The few minutes you save (by failing to achieve a zero-energy state with the piece of equipment) aren't worth losing part of your fingers or hand. Naturally, whenever you're around mowing equipment, protect your hands and feet by keeping them away from the blades and discharge chutes.

Gas fumes can be ignited by a hot engine. Never refuel a mower while it is running, or while the engine is hot. Before refueling, turn off the mower, disconnect the spark plug, and let the engine cool for at least ten minutes. Fill the tank only three-quarters full to allow the gas to expand in response to the hot engine and the sun's heat.

Never leave a mower unattended with the engine running—even if you intend to come right back in a matter of moments. Turn it off instead. Take extra precaution with a riding lawn mower by lowering the mowing deck then removing the key.

If you must remove grass clumps or clear a discharge chute, stop the engine, wait until the blades stop revolving, and disconnect the spark-plug wire. Do the same before checking any problem with the lower unit. Never, never place your hands under the machine while it's still running. Avoid making contact with hot parts of the engine or exhaust system. Muffler temperatures can reach as high as 1,200 degrees Fahrenheit.

Lawn mowers are neither toys nor pleasure vehicles. Never give children rides on equipment. Once a child has had a ride, he or she could run up unseen behind the mower to ask for just one more turn. Also avoid giving children rides on small gardening carts or utility trailers pulled behind garden tractor mowers. A child could fall from the cart into the path of the mower.

Try to mow in a forward direction at all times. If you must go backward, stop the riding mower or lawn tractor before shifting into reverse, and keep checking behind you. Push, don't pull hand mowers. There's less chance of accidentally falling and pulling the mower over your feet. And when you're pulling the mower, you're usually fighting the mower's rear skirt along the way.

With hand mowers, mow across slopes for better footing, not up and down them. With riding mowers it's just the opposite: Mow slopes up and down so the tractor won't slip or fall over sideways. In either case, if hills are very steep, consider planting a decorative ground cover to completely eliminate the need to mow.

Keep all four wheels on the ground when turning a walk-behind mower. If you tip the mower while turning you'll expose the blades. This could easily send debris flying through the air.

Storing Lawn Mowers

Allow the engine to cool before storing a mower inside. Lawn equipment should be stored safely away from curious youngsters. A lawn tractor with keys in the ignition can be mighty tempting to a child with time on her hands. Remember to keep gasoline in tightly capped safety cans in a well-ventilated place, out of children's reach, away from the living quarters and any flame or heat source.

OTHER LANDSCAPING AND GARDENING TOOLS

Many landscaping and gardening tools are either gasoline or electric powered.

When refueling gas-powered equipment, make sure the unit has been allowed to cool first. After filling, clean spills, both on the equipment and on the floor or ground, and securely refasten all gas caps. When attempting to restart the unit, move away from the gas can, and make sure there is adequate ventilation to prevent gas and carbon monoxide fumes from accumulating to a dangerous point.

With electric-powered equipment, use only extension cords designed for outdoor use. Use a three-wire grounded type if the electrical tool has a three-pronged grounded plug (see Figure 12-2). If the tool draws a great deal of power, the extension cord must be a heavy-duty model. Using a cord designed for low amperages could result in an electrical overload, which can cause overheating and possibly fire. The cord should be inspected before each use to ensure that it isn't frayed or worn, and wasn't cut during the last use. Avoid cords that have been cut and taped or spliced together—such a weak link could lead to overheating and injury. Loose or worn plugs could cause similar problems. As a general precaution, cords and electrical devices should not be used on damp or wet ground.

Concentrate when using any kind of tool, powered or not. Don't allow yourself to be distracted. If someone wants something from you while you're working with tools, shut the tool down, put it out of harm's reach, and take care of the other business before returning to your landscaping or gardening task.

Naturally, refrain from operating landscaping and gardening tools when you are tired, ill, or under the influence of alcohol or drugs.

Hedge Trimmers

Hedge trimmers are one of the most commonly used landscaping tools. There are a variety of models, but most noncommercial units are powered by

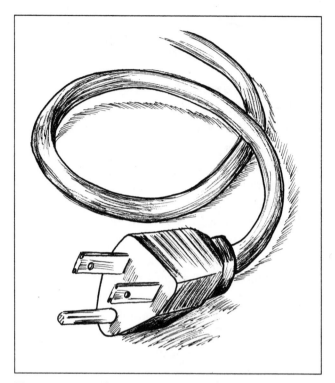

Figure 12-2. A three-pronged, grounded plug.

electricity. As with any electric power tool used outdoors, a hedge trimmer should be plugged into a GFCI outlet; if there aren't any GFCIs permanently installed on the outside of your house or in your garage, you can purchase portable units at electrical supply stores (see Figure 12-3).

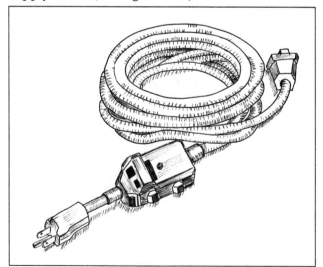

Figure 12-3. A ground fault circuit interrupter (GFCI).

While a lawn mower operates with its blades near the ground and covered by the mower deck, hedge clippers and weed trimmers have their cut-ting parts right out in the open, sometimes at face level. Because of this there are a wide variety of hazards to consider.

One problem that all too many homeowners are familiar with is the possibility of cutting the electrical cord while using the trimmers. To avoid this, take your time, or have a helper whose only duty is to manage the cord and let you go from one side of a hedgerow to the other, and end to end, without worrying about the position of the cord.

No matter where you cut with a set of trimmers, position yourself so you have maximum stability, always use two hands to grip the trimmer, and organize the work so you don't have to overreach or stretch—hedge trimming is hard on the arms. Be particularly careful when you must use a ladder to reach part of your work. It is often better to get what you can from the ground and then resort to hand clippers with an extension to complete uppermost work. Or simply hire a landscaper to do hard-to-reach trimming. Take frequent breaks, but never let the trimmers go unwatched. Keep children out of the area while you're working.

It's possible for a trimmer to contact an object that could be thrown back at you, or to encounter a solid object, such as a metal pole or cable hidden within a shrub or hedge, that could cause the trimmer to kick backward; know what you're cutting at all times. If something blocks or jams the blades, disconnect the trimmer before you attempt to remove the cause of the obstruction. Also, don't force a cutting tool. It will do a better job with less risk of injury when used at the speed and manner for which it was designed.

Avoid accidental starting. Keep your hands and fingers off the trigger switch while handling the tool between cutting tasks. Even if the tool has a neutral gear—which many gas models do—it's a good idea to turn off the engine for other than a brief pause in the cutting. Unplug electric trimmers when they are not in use.

Gasoline models are generally heavier and more powerful. They're also a lot louder, and create high-intensity vibrations.

While trimming, always wear snug-fitting, durable clothing. Avoid wearing loose clothing that could become entangled if contact is made with the trimmer. Wear long hair tied up or in a bun. Keep your sneakers and sandals for the beach—wear work shoes with nonskid soles to ensure proper footing, and wear nonslip, heavy-duty work gloves to improve your grip on trimmer handles. The gloves also help reduce the transmission of machine vibrations to your hands.

Spectators, children and animals should be kept at least sixty feet away from where the trimmer is being used.

Chain Saws

If you've seen or heard about any of the "Texas Chain Saw Murder" movies, you know (or can imagine) what goes on in them. No doubt, chain saws are dangerous instruments to use, even in the best of circumstances. The cutting blades or edges are right there in front of you, whirring through wood and other vegetation, spitting slivers and sawdust into the air. To use chain saws as safely as possible frequently review and refer to the chain saw's operating manual. Use protective clothing and equipment, including a hard hat, eye and ear protection, chain saw chaps or pants, and sturdy work boots.

Make sure the saw, and especially the chain brake, is in good condition. The saw should not have loose or broken parts, and the chain should be correctly tightened.

Be aware of the reactive forces involved with the bar and chain. For example, a kickback can be caused by any type of pinch to the top of the bar, while a pull-in can occur with a pinch to the bottom part of the bar. If possible, learn cutting techniques from a structured training program or from an experienced forester.

When felling a tree, plan the job by first considering what could go wrong, and then take steps to prevent those possibilities. Could anything fall or fly back and hit you? Which way is the tree leaning? Are you positioning yourself on a safe side while cutting? Is there an escape path for you to follow once the tree is falling? Where should the initial cut be made, and which cuts should come next? If you don't feel comfortable with some of these questions, you should get help from someone who's more experienced.

Brush Cutters and Weed Whips

Wear long pants, shirts with sleeves, gloves, hearing protection and safety goggles when cutting or trimming brush and weeds. Make sure that cutting blades and line spools are the correct models and are properly secured before starting work. Avoid cutting close to fences, sides of buildings and other obstacles that could cause the machine to ricochet. Keep children, bystanders and pets away from where you're cutting. Never allow the machine to idle; always shut it down if you must leave it alone.

Garden Tillers

One question you might want to ask yourself is if you really need a tiller. If you're only going to use it once or twice per year, you might be better off contracting the job out to someone who goes around from house to house, tilling gardens as a part-time job.

To operate your own tiller, begin every season by rereading the operator's manual so you're familiar with how to shut the machine off and how to disengage the traction drive. Know how to work all the controls. Before starting the unit, make sure the tilling arms and the traction drive to the wheels are in neutral positions.

Inspect the ground before you till. All foreign objects should be removed, and children and bystanders should be kept far to the side, out of the way.

Hand Tools

It's not only power tools that cause accidents and injuries; hand-operated tools can be just as dangerous if misused or used unwisely. Rakes, hoes, brooms and similar garden tools can be extremely dangerous if left lying around instead of being properly hung up or stored out of the way. They can cause anyone to trip and fall, or can seriously injure someone who steps on them.

TREES

Regular tree pruning is essential to keep trees healthy and free of dead wood. And that could help keep you healthy, too. Don't allow branches to hang over your home or your neighbor's dwelling. Next to lightning, trees are the second leading cause of electrical service outages. Most such interruptions occur during wind, rain, ice or snowstorms, when branches split and crash onto roofs and yards. Tree trimming should remove branches that are at risk of falling and causing electrical or other damage. Qualified experts should prune, top or remove offending trees.

If you attempt to prune large trees yourself, beware of electrical lines. You don't want to accidentally touch a pole pruner to a power line, nor do you want a falling limb to knock down a live wire. Contact your utility company if you notice a potential problem in your area—there may be no charge for the utility to take care of pruning and trimming that safeguards their wires.

GARDENING

Gardening can mean different things to different people. It can mean purchasing small plants in the middle of spring, sinking them into a small plot in a backyard, and leaving them to fend for themselves until fall—when they are harvested along with bundles after bundle of pesky weeds. Or it can mean day after day of devoted attention by the homeowner who digs, rakes, fertilizes, mulches, weeds, lifts, carries, bends, and baby-sits his or her plants throughout the growing season, and then, like a doting parent, practically cries when the produce is ready to be picked, cleaned, prepared and eaten. Even with the smallest outdoor garden, considerable effort is required for good results. Gardening, in short, can be a strenuous activity in which muscles rarely used for anything else are put through their paces pulling weeds or hoeing rows. After the infrequent tilling, most of the efforts are manual. A few pointers can keep you safe in the garden from season to season. First, dress properly. A quick look in a specialty gardener's catalog will tell you what's important. Devotees make sure they're equipped with knee pads (see Figure 12-4), comfortable footwear, tool aprons, vests, pouches, pail tool caddies, or other clothing or portable containers in which they can store small digging tools, shears, weeders, mulch plastic, fertilizers, sprays, and odds and ends associated with caring for the kinds of plants they are growing.

Figure 12-4. A kneepad for gardening.

It's a good idea to wear safety glasses with side shields while gardening. Injuries can occur to a gardener who stoops to tend a flower or plant, and pierces his eye with a twig or thorn.

Do stretching exercises before starting. Although gardening is not a recognized sport in the Olympics, it taxes many large and small muscles that should be warmed up in advance. Overall, intensive gardening activities can promote fitness, helping you to burn up to two-hundred calories per half hour while toning arm, leg, back and stomach muscles.

In the spring, start out slow. Increase the intensity and duration of activities as you go through the season. Don't overdo it. Avoid the hottest times of the day, midmorning to late afternoon. Better to garden early in the morning or just before dusk. Pay particular attention to your body, noting aches and pains. Stop when the work seems to be getting too hard. Even two hours in the garden should be interrupted by frequent stretching or a lemonade break at least every half hour.

Avoid bending your back or twisting at the waist. Use your feet to move where you need to work, don't lean out this way and that. Most people plant themselves in one position and then work in every direction as far as they can reach. Instead, try moving and turning toward the work. Long-handled shovels, rakes and hoes can minimize bending, twisting and reaching movements.

Let the equipment and tools make your work easier. Gardening gloves, knee pads, stools, and kneeling mats or pads should be employed for comfort's sake. Hand tools should have grips or shapes that reduce stress on your hands. Try the tools out for size and comfort before you buy them. When you grip a small hand rake, notice how comfortable it feels in those places where blisters or callouses might form. Use a wheelbarrow or cart to transport heavy items such as large bags of mulch.

Fertilizers, Pesticides and Other Chemical Products

A wide variety of chemical products are available for the home gardener. Some are packaged in relatively childproof containers; others are not. All chemical products should be handled as if they are hazardous and poisonous, with no exceptions. Some chemicals can kill even if they aren't swallowed—just inhaling them or absorbing them through the skin can cause fatal injuries to children. Whenever possible, use the least toxic chemicals for the job. For example, insecticidal soap can kill aphids, fleas, and other lawn and garden pests.

Store all chemical products in their original containers out of reach of children, preferably in a locked cabinet. If you pour a product into a smaller, unmarked container, you may forget what's inside of it. Children have been poisoned by drinking harmful liquids that had been poured into old apple juice jars, because the appearance of the product

stored in the glass containers did indeed resemble the clear golden color of true apple juice.

Read and follow all product safety directions. Don't take shortcuts or use more of or a higher concentration than is recommended. Don't hold a chemical product high when pouring it; it could splash or blow onto your skin or eyes. When using sprays, make sure the opening is pointed away from your body. And never use such products in a closed garage, shed or other area without proper ventilation. Powdered products should not be applied when it is extremely dry or windy outside. And keep off areas that have been treated until the treatment is absorbed into the grass, trees or plants, and cannot be seen or felt.

Always put pesticides and fertilizers away immediately when finished using them. Rinse out empty containers and secure their tops before disposing of them. Disposing of unused pesticides and other chemicals can be dangerous and even illegal. Try to mix only the amount of chemicals you need for a given task. If you have some left over, follow your local laws for its disposal.

Use extreme caution whenever you use chemicals in a garden or on fruit or nut trees. Read labels carefully, clear the area of children and pets when spraying, and wear protective clothing.

If the chemicals that we put on our yards and gardens aren't enough, the actual soil in our yards can contain dangerous organisms. If children accidentally swallow soil, or place soiled fingers in their mouths, they might ingest organisms that cause tetanus or other maladies. Some organisms can enter the body through a jab from a garden fork, a prick from a thorn, or a bite or scratch from an animal. Tell children about these dangers, and ask them to tell a responsible baby-sitter or adult if they cut or poke themselves so wounds will get immediate first aid. Along the same lines, it's wise for adults to use barrier creams and effective gloves when working in the garden.

LAWN AND GARDEN SAFETY QUICK CHECKLIST

☐ Dress for safety when using lawn mowers and other power tools.

☐ Avoid mowing wet lawns.

☐ Before mowing, inspect the grounds for items that may be partially hidden in the grass.

☐ Don't let children in or near areas you will be mowing.

☐ Inspect lawn mowers and other tools for loose parts and defects before each use.

☐ Make sure safety features on lawn mowers and other tools such as guards and automatic shutoffs, are present and in good working order.

☐ Fuel up when an engine is cold. Refuel after letting a hot engine cool for at least ten minutes.

☐ Refresh your memory on a particular tool's operating procedures by frequently reviewing the unit's owner's manual.

☐ When making blade or other adjustments, make sure the piece of equipment is shut off and cannot be accidentally started. Never leave a mower or other power tool running, or even plugged in, while you're not attending it.

☐ Never, ever let children ride on garden tractor mowers or on carts pulled behind or pushed ahead of mowing machines.

☐ Avoid pulling hand mowers backward or operating riding mowers in reverse.

☐ Mow across slopes with hand mowers, and up and down slopes with riding mowers and garden tractors. On very steep hills consider decorative ground cover instead of grass.

☐ When turning corners with push mowers, keep all four wheels on the ground.

☐ With electric power equipment use only heavy-duty outdoor cords and inspect them for defects before each use. Plug the cords into GFCI outlets—or use portable GFCIs.

LAWN AND GARDEN SAFETY QUICK CHECKLIST
(continued)

☐ Concentration while working is important; don't operate tools when you're tired, ill, or under the influence of alcohol or drugs.

☐ Don't use electric trimmers in wet conditions.

☐ Manage electrical cords so you don't cut them while trimming. Avoid accidental startings.

☐ Whenever possible, use two hands to grip power tools while cutting or trimming, and maintain good balance.

☐ Don't operate chain saws without safety equipment or without formal instruction in cutting techniques.

☐ Put all tools away immediately after use.

☐ Prune, top or remove tree branches or entire trees that threaten dwellings or electrical lines.

☐ Plan gardening tasks for early in the morning or late in the afternoon. Take frequent breaks and drink plenty of liquids.

☐ Dress properly and use the right hand tools, knee pads, safety equipment and other accessories.

☐ Warm up with some stretching exercises before beginning any intensive gardening that includes lifting, bending and reaching.

☐ Avoid bending your back or twisting at the waist. Instead of reaching, move yourself closer to the work at hand.

☐ Keep children and pets away from areas being treated with pesticides or fertilizers.

☐ All chemical products should be handled as if they were hazardous. Store them in locked cabinets or out of children's reach, using the product's original containers.

CHAPTER 13

SWIMMING POOL SAFETY

A swimming pool can be an asset to one household and a liability to another. On one hand, a handsome in-ground pool can be a social focal point or a place to relax in the sun in the privacy of an enclosed backyard. It can be a healthy place where children learn to swim and adults carry out regular exercise programs. However, the same pool can be a dangerous attraction to young, unsupervised children.

Keep your pool clean and full of healthy water, and insist on safe behaviors around and in the pool.

SWIMMING POOL WATER

Four main factors contribute to healthy pool water: free available chlorine, pH, total alkalinity, and calcium hardness.

Free Available Chlorine

Free available chlorine fights bacteria and algae in the pool. Inadequate levels of chlorine have a direct effect on pool cleanliness. Free available chlorine levels are expressed in parts per million. Ideal levels of free available chlorine are generally accepted as 1 to 3 parts per million (ppm). Simple test kits are available to check concentration levels on the spot.

pH

The measure of water acidity and basicity is called pH. A correct range for pH is between 7.2 and 7.6 on the pH scale. The proper pH is important to maintain healthy water. Levels of pH outside the desired parameters may cause eye and skin irritation, cloudy water, and chemical buildups on pool equipment.

Total Alkalinity

Total alkalinity is a measurement of the elements that help stabilize the water's pH. It is measured in parts per million, with between 60 and 100 ppm as a desired range. A hard to maintain pH balance, cloudy water and scaling (unsightly mineral deposits) may indicate that the total alkalinity of your pool's water is not within acceptable limits.

Calcium Hardness

Calcium hardness measures the amount of dissolved calcium in water. Insufficient levels can corrode pool equipment, which can, in turn, malfunction and result in unhealthy water. A desirable range is between 200 and 1,000 ppm.

Routine Water Maintenance

Free available chlorine and pH should be checked daily, total alkalinity monthly, and calcium hardness two or three times per swimming season. Pool water is much easier to maintain if you keep on top of changing conditions. During the swimming season, the water can be significantly affected by a number of common conditions. Unusually heavy rains, above-average temperatures and frequent pool use can all cause increases in chlorine demand. Peak demand conditions require special maintenance measures called superchlorination and shock treatment.

Both superchlorination and shock treatment involve the addition of chlorine in amounts required to elevate temporarily free available chlorine levels. Superchlorination is the addition of chlorine to achieve 5 ppm available chlorine to remove organic contaminants and prevent most common pool water problems. Shock treatment is the remedial addition of chlorine to achieve a 10 ppm available chlorine to kill visible algae. Pool experts recommend you superchlorinate or shock treat once every two weeks during an active swimming season.

Pool Water Cleaning

Again, a clean pool is a healthy pool. To keep the water clean, the pool itself must be attended to weekly. A number of components are required to keep the water clean. They include circulation systems, filters and skimmers (see Figure 13-1). Some pool owners believe if they don't use their pool, they don't have to monitor its condition. Nothing could be further from the truth.

Figure 13-1. Using a skimmer.

Solving Pool Water Problems

Eye Irritations

The two common causes of red and irritated eyes are improper pH and chloramine. Chloramine is a substance produced when chlorine in the water reacts with body wastes such as perspiration, saliva and miscellaneous other compounds. Pre-swim showers for pool users will reduce the amount of bacteria and other contaminants introduced to the

pool. If chloramine has developed in your pool, the free available chlorine concentrations are reduced to ineffective levels. Check the pH level. If it is too high, add an adjuster chemical. Check the free available chlorine level. If it is below 1 ppm, shock treat.

Strong "Chlorine" Odors

Ironically, the cause of strong "chlorine" odors is usually too *little* free available chlorine. It's likely the chloramine you actually smell, not the chlorine. First, adjust the pH. Next, shock treat the water.

Too Much Chlorine

If you have dark brown hair when you jump in, and blonde hair when you climb out, there is too much chlorine in the water. People have mistakenly added enough chlorine to bleach swimsuits and irritate eyes. Simply stop adding chlorine when the free available chlorine concentration is between 1 and 3 ppm. Commercial products are available that will immediately reduce chlorine levels, but they must be used exactly according to the manufacturer's instructions.

POOL SAFETY

Having a swimming pool is a big responsibility—to yourself, your family, friends and relatives, your neighbors, and even to total strangers. Here are a number of suggestions for minimizing the hazards that go along with owning a pool.

Locate and maintain lifesaving equipment at poolside such as a ring buoy with an attached line or a long-handled hook (see Figure 13-2). Never rely on inner tubes or water wings to keep children afloat. Such items can too easily slip off.

Figure 13-2. Ring buoy with rope.

Maintain a climb-proof fence to separate the pool from the rest of the yard. It may, indeed, be a law or requirement in your community or in your homeowner's insurance policy. A fence is especially important for families (or neighbors) with children under twelve years old. The fence, however, should not block views of the pool from the house. Always use gates with self-closing, self-latching spring locks. Latches should be at least fifty-four inches above ground to prevent tampering by youngsters. The fence should keep unsupervised children from using the pool. It will also prevent neighborhood pets from literally dropping in.

Watch nearby children at all times. Never assume a child is water safe, even if he or she has had swimming lessons. If a lone adult must leave the pool area, he should take the children along. *Never* leave children unsupervised at poolside. And never rely on your ears alone to assure that a child is safe.

It makes sense to establish safety practices that anyone using your pool must follow. Stress the list to visitors, especially at the beginning of each swimming season. A sample list might include:

1. No running or horseplay around or in the pool.
2. No eating or carrying food into the pool.
3. No pets in the pool.
4. No swimming alone.
5. No diving in the shallow end.
6. Children must have at least one adult swimmer present to supervise them.
7. No swimming when it is thundering (lightning can strike several miles ahead of a storm).

Keep toys away from the pool so children are not tempted to reach for toys that fall in the water. If extension cords are used near the pool, make sure they are properly insulated and protected. Keep glass and other breakables away from poolside, and keep a well-stocked first-aid kit nearby, out of children's reach. Encourage all members of your family to become proficient at CPR and artificial respiration. Keep an artificial respiration guide with the first-aid kit. Contact the Red Cross for related lifesaving information.

Establish a ten-minute rest period every hour or so for younger children using the pool. Mark the pool depths so visitors know what to expect. Most important, identify shallow areas where it is safe for small children to play. For lap swimming, serious swimmers need a depth of at least three and one-half feet so they won't touch bottom while swimming. Monitor the water depth to make sure it hasn't gradually become too shallow.

POOL CHEMICAL SAFETY

Keep all chemicals out of children's reach. Use the exact quantities of chemicals specified; never overuse. Add chemicals to the pool water, not vice versa. Carefully seal containers after use. Be sure to store them in a cool, dry place.

If chemicals come in contact with your skin, brush them off and flush with cold water for at least fifteen minutes. If irritation persists, get medical attention. Never smoke while handling pool chemicals. Keep pool chemicals away from lawns, shrubs and trees. Carefully dispose of any spillage as directed on each chemical container's label.

SWIMMING POOL SAFETY QUICK CHECKLIST

- [ ] Keep levels of free available chlorine in the water between 1 and 3 ppm.

- [ ] Maintain a pH level between 7.2 and 7.6.

- [ ] Maintain calcium levels between 200 and 1,000 ppm.

- [ ] Check free available chlorine and pH levels daily.

- [ ] Check total alkalinity at least monthly, more frequently during periods of hot weather or heavy pool usage.

- [ ] Check calcium hardness at least two or three times per season.

- [ ] Superchlorinate when needed.

- [ ] Shock treat when needed.

- [ ] Maintain and operate water circulation systems on a regular basis, even if the pool is not used during inclement weather.

- [ ] Keep lifesaving and first-aid equipment on hand.

- [ ] Maintain a childproof fence around the pool area.

- [ ] Never allow children in a pool to go unsupervised.

- [ ] Keep electrical extension cords and plugged-in appliances away from poolside.

- [ ] Use plastic and other nonbreakable food and drink containers in the pool area.

CHAPTER 14

HOT WEATHER SAFETY

The sun. It's a gigantic, middle-aged (4.6 billion years old) star, a ball of super-heated gas kept unbelievably hot by repeated atomic reactions at its center. Such reactions are expected to continue for another five billion years or so, until old "Sol" swells to a red giant and vaporizes the earth in the process. At that time, no amount of sunscreen is going to help. Until then, from ninety-three million miles away, the sun showers us with warmth and radiant energy.

RADIATION

It wasn't that many years ago when a deep, dark tan was a sign of affluence, acquired by vacationing in exotic locales, mainly at beach resorts from Acapulco to the Riviera. Today, however, the consensus is that skin should be protected from the sun, and the tanned look has fallen out of favor.

What changed? Just as the Surgeon General warns us against smoking, now physicians speak out against the sun's ultraviolet rays as harmful to our skin and eyes. Prompted both by disturbing changes in the earth's atmosphere—more ultraviolet rays are presently reaching the earth's surface—and by studies that associate ultraviolet light rays with skin damage, ranging in severity from sunburn and wrinkling to skin cancer, scientists and physicians are recommending that our skin and eyes be protected from several kinds of ultraviolet rays.

The sun emits three kinds of ultraviolet or UV rays: UVA, UVB and UVC. Only the first two, UVA and UVB, penetrate the ozone layer and reach the earth's atmosphere. Both of these can do serious damage. Exposure to UVB rays is associated with damage to the surface of the skin, and can result in sunburn, premature aging of the skin and skin cancer. If that's not harmful enough, UVA rays—which are more deeply penetrating—can damage the underlying tissues that help keep skin firm and wrinkle free. Together, these ultraviolet rays can really do a number on a person's skin, especially if the individual frequently participates in outdoor activities without wearing a sunscreen.

While UVB rays are most concentrated in the summertime, especially between 10:00 A.M. and 3:00 P.M., UVA rays are present year-round, even on cloudy days. They can reach down into at least three feet of water. And beware of high altitudes, where there's less atmosphere to filter out ultraviolet rays, and where harmful rays reflect from snow or ice. That's why skiers and mountain climbers always seem to sport shiny red faces, or why you see many of them with sunscreen all over their noses and foreheads.

Protecting Your Skin

The Sun Protection Factor (SPF) indicates about how much time you can expect to stay in the sun without burning. For example, if it normally takes your skin twenty minutes to turn red in the sun, then a sunscreen with a SPF of ten will theoretically allow you to stay ten times longer in the sun (or two-hundred minutes) without burning. These are estimates, of course, order-of-magnitude numbers to give you an idea of the amount of protection afforded by a particular sunscreen product.

Sun Protection Factors range from minimal SPFs of two to fifteen or more for maximum protection from UVB rays. The low SPF products are often used by people who tan quickly and never burn, and the high SPF sunscreens can protect fair-skinned people and others who burn easily. At one time, recommendations suggested a SPF of eight to fourteen for those who burn easily, but who tan gradually. Now, more often than not, advice from physicians and sunscreen manufacturers says that a SPF lotion or product of at least fifteen, with ingredients to block out a broad spectrum of UVA rays, should be used by everyone. Even dark skin that contains more melanin—a pigment that is part of the body's natural defense against the sun—should be protected by a sunscreen with a SPF of fifteen.

Individuals who have studied the long-term effects of sunlight on skin believe that a significant amount of damage is the result of cumulative incidental exposure, or routine, everyday contact with sunlight. Because younger skin is more delicate and sensitive than older skin, it burns easier. Studies indicate that much of the sun damage the typical person experiences over a lifetime happens before he or she is eighteen years old. It's thought that early exposure may play a crucial role in the development of skin cancer later in life.

All of this points to the importance of protecting our bodies from the sun. This can be done in a number of ways. Be sure to stay out of the sun by staying indoors or in full-shaded areas as much as possible. Wide-brimmed hats (see Figure 14-1) and other clothing items can be effective sunscreens. White or light-colored long-sleeved shirts and pants will effectively block most harmful rays. A bandanna loosely tied around your neck will also help. Remember that a good deal of ultraviolet radiation can penetrate a wet T-shirt, gauzy or net clothing and some nylon stockings.

A natural suntan helps protect you from sunburn, but is by itself one of the least desirable means of sun protection. Considering the long-term damage and cancer risks associated with repeated tan-

Figure 14-1. A wide-brimmed hat.

nings, individual bouts with sunburn will not be your only problems. And remember that the kind of tan you get "straight from the bottle" will not protect you from the sun's wrath.

Sunscreens are the most practical products to prevent ultraviolet ray damage. Go for a SPF of fifteen or higher. Women can get a little added protection by using tinted opaque cosmetic foundation along with a sunscreen—especially on places that are always exposed, such as the nose and forehead. Apply sunscreen at least a half hour before going into the sun, on cool, dry skin, and again after swimming or perspiring. In general, one application will not be enough for an entire day's activities. When applying sunscreen, remember to cover all the exposed areas of your body, including hard-to-reach places such as your lower back and the back of your legs. Don't forget to protect the tops of the ears, the back of the knees and the instep.

Opaque sunscreens such as zinc oxide or titanium oxide may be used on the nose or lips by people who need to be in the sun for long periods, like lifeguards or tennis players.

Babies should be protected all over, mainly with clothing such as bonnets with wide brims and light-colored, lightweight clothing and covered strollers. A baby should never be directly exposed to midday sun, and at other times should have no more exposure than five to ten minutes per encounter. If incidental exposure will be unavoidable, use a sunscreen.

What to look for in a sunscreen
- SPF levels
- Amount of broad UVA range protection
- A moisturizing formula that has a nice fragrance or no fragrance at all
- A formula that won't clog pores, which otherwise could promote acne (may be referred to as "non-comedogenic")
- Includes or is free from PABA, an ingredient found in a variety of waterproof sun protection products. You may be sensitive to PABA or any of its products—if so, choose a sunscreen without it.

Keep all sunscreens in cool, dry storage whenever possible. A sunscreen that gets too hot—if stored in a car glove compartment on a hot day, for example—can be rendered ineffective.

Even if you never burn at home, keep the sun in mind when you travel. In tropical regions, the sunlight is intense enough to burn almost anyone. And remember that the possibility of burning also increases at higher altitudes.

Some medicines can make you more susceptible to the sun's ultraviolet rays, and more likely to get sunburned. Your doctor or pharmacist can tell you if a prescription drug you're taking is likely to cause such a problem.

Avoid the use of indoor sunlamps, tanning parlors and tanning pills.

In short, even though overexposure to ultraviolet sun rays is a leading cause of skin afflictions, you don't have to give up the outdoors to stay healthy. Use good sense and simple measures whenever you work or play in the sun. Keep yourself screened.

And know your skin. Do a monthly self-exam of your skin and note the appearance of any moles, birthmarks or blemishes. If you ever notice any changes in their size, shape or color—or if a sore does not heal—see a physician as soon as possible.

Protecting Your Eyes

Although your eyes have built-in natural protection against the sun's brightness, glare and radiation,

you should take additional precautions. Recent research suggests that long-term exposure to the sun's ultraviolet radiation may cause cataracts or other sight-threatening conditions. Concrete, asphalt, chrome and glass can create unnatural glare situations you may have to cope with. Or your eyes may be more sensitive to the sun's brightness because you work indoors all day, and are accustomed to lower light levels at night.

Cataract surgery can reduce the eye's natural protection against ultraviolet radiation.

Wearing a good pair of sunglasses during the day will help protect your eyes and will allow them to adapt more easily to darkness later on.

HEAT ILLNESS

Heat illness is not contagious, but one or all of its versions can be "caught" by almost anyone if the conditions are right. In a nutshell, heat illness is what happens when the body can no longer maintain its normal temperature and is overcome by abnormally high temperatures. There are numerous forms of heat illness to be aware of: fainting, heat cramps, heat exhaustion and heat stroke. They can happen one at a time, or in any combination.

General preventive measures include wearing light-colored, loose clothing that allows air to circulate around your body. Again, a lightweight, wide-brimmed, light-colored hat keeps sun rays off the face, neck and eyes. Not only will a hat act as a visor, its shading effect helps keep the rest of your body cool as well.

Fainting

Fainting can be caused by an inadequate blood supply to the brain. It may be a minor heat-related disorder, but indicates that the body is having difficulty adjusting to the heat. A fall caused by fainting can easily injure someone. When in hot temperatures, move around and stretch to improve circulation to reduce the risk of fainting. When someone faints, have the person lie down in a cool place, out of the sun. Consult a physician.

Heat Cramps

Heat cramps are painful muscle spasms that can occur in the legs, arms, back or abdomen—the muscles that do the hardest work. They affect people who sweat profusely and drink large quantities of water, but who fail to replace the salt lost through sweating.

If there is no medical reason you shouldn't, then drink water with 0.1 percent salt concentration—that's only one level teaspoon dissolved in fifteen quarts of water. Or drink plenty of water and increase the salt you use with your meals. Keep in mind that salt can affect medical conditions such as high blood pressure, so consult your physician before increasing your salt intake. Salt tablets are not recommended, but products such as Gatorade and similar electrolyte drinks can provide enough additional salts to prevent heat cramps. If you get a cramp, massage the affected muscles.

Prickly Heat

Prickly heat is a skin rash caused by heat and humidity. When sweat doesn't evaporate, sweat ducts may become clogged and inflammation can result. Severe and prolonged rashes can cause complications such as infection, which should be treated by a physician. To prevent prickly heat, keep the skin as dry as possible. Shower often, and wear fast-drying cotton clothing. If you get a mild rash, apply soothing lotions or powder.

Heat Exhaustion

Heat exhaustion is a more serious disorder. It's caused by a failure to replenish fluids lost through perspiration. Symptoms may include sweating, clammy skin, a pale or flushed complexion, weakness, dizziness and nausea. To prevent heat exhaustion, drink plenty of water throughout the day. Consume enough salt to replace what's lost—always keeping in mind that salt intake can affect other medical conditions.

If someone is overwhelmed by heat exhaustion, have him rest in a place cooled by fans or mild air conditioning, or cover him with wet cloths. Give him a cool drink, not hot or ice cold fluids—water is fine. Get the victim to an emergency room or physician as soon as possible.

Heat Stroke

The most serious heat affliction, heat stroke is caused by a combination of prolonged exposure to high temperatures, inadequate water intake and ventilation, and usually strenuous physical activity. A heat stroke victim can't wait long for help. It's a life threatening situation that occurs when the body can't cool itself because its temperature regulating system is overloaded. Symptoms may include no sweating or profuse sweating, a high body temperature (105 degrees Fahrenheit or more), hot, dry, flushed skin, confused, delirious behavior, and a loss of consciousness or coma.

To prevent heat stroke, maintain a healthy level of cardiovascular fitness through proper exercise and diet. Work or play in shady areas, if possible, with plenty of ventilation. Rest often in cool areas. Drink fluids at regular intervals when active in hot temperatures—every twenty minutes is ideal.

If someone suffers heat stroke, she must be hospitalized without delay. Until an ambulance arrives, move the patient to a cool place. Place an ice bag against the victim's head. Soak her clothing in cool water and fan the body to promote additional cooling. Another method is to remove the victim's clothing and give a cool sponge bath, lightly rubbing the skin to increase circulation. Do not give the victim stimulants.

General Heat Illness Considerations

Thirst is not a reliable indicator as to how much liquid the body needs during hot weather. A typical person can lose up to 3 gallons of liquid per day. That's got to be replenished. One way is to drink a small glass of water, fruit juice, vegetable juice or other liquid about every half hour during hot-weather. That's more comfortable than drinking large amounts of water or other liquids at longer intervals.

Rest often in the shade or in well-ventilated or air-conditioned areas. If your residence isn't air conditioned, go to a library, movie theater or shopping mall during the day's hottest hours. Give your body a chance to cool off. Short, frequent breaks are more effective than long, infrequent ones.

Avoid alcohol. It causes dehydration, which further taxes your body during hot weather conditions.

Eat light, nutritious meals, preferably cold. Fatty gravies, sauces and solid foods are more difficult to digest in hot weather.

Never leave children, pets, or any passenger in a closed-up vehicle on a hot, sunny day.

Take the heat seriously. Never ignore danger signs such as nausea, dizziness, fatigue, long headaches, and an inability to hold liquids. Instead, get medical help at once.

ANIMALS AND HOT WEATHER

You've heard of the dog days of summer. There's a reason for that term—high temperatures can be tough on animals that are often better equipped for cold weather. To prevent animal bites and other nasty encounters, keep your distance from all animals during times of hot weather. This goes for tame or wild animals. Teach children and other family members to do the same. Leave animals alone when they're eating and drinking. Avoid teasing or scaring them. Don't pet animals when they have babies. Remember that most animals tend to guard their own territory, owners and property.

Leave injured, sick and dead animals alone. Never approach or capture a wild animal—even if you think it needs help and especially if you encounter it during the day. Avoid keeping wild animals as pets.

What To Do in a Threatening Situation

Stay calm if you come face to face with an aggressive animal. Stand still; don't turn and run. Turning or making any rapid movement may trigger an attack. Talk softly to the animal. Back away slowly, while looking at the animal.

If Bitten by a Wild Animal

Many small animal bites are reported each year. Opossums, skunks, foxes, raccoons, muskrats , rats, squirrels and chipmunks are common offenders. If you are bitten by a wild animal it should be captured and killed, if possible, so it can be tested for disease. Immediately wash the wound with lots of soap and running water. Get medical attention right away, from an emergency room or your family doctor.

If Bitten by a Pet Dog or Cat

Immediately wash the wound with soap and running water. Obtain the pet owner's name, address and phone number. Find out if the animal has a current rabies vaccination, and write down the rabies tag number. Get medical attention right away.

HOT WEATHER FOOD SAFETY

Warm weather brings about conditions that are just right for the growth of bacteria in formerly refrigerated food. Outbreaks of gastrointestinal illness or poisonings caused by bacteria consequently occur more frequently during hot summer months when foods are left out in the home or outdoors at picnics and other gatherings. To prevent bacterial food poisoning, keep hot foods hot and cold foods cold.

Most non-dried foods keep the longest when frozen. If they can't be frozen, the next best thing is refrigeration. Freezing or refrigeration are important storage methods, because they prevent bacteria in food from multiplying and rendering poultry, fish, meat or other food poisonous or inedible.

A general guideline for cold food storage is that refrigeration should run no warmer than 40 degrees Fahrenheit, and freezing should be at least 0 degrees Fahrenheit to effectively keep up the quality of perishables and to keep bacterial growth under control. At the opposite end of the spectrum, internal cooking temperatures can begin at about 140 degrees Fahrenheit for most foods. These temperatures are usually achieved from external cooking temperatures between 300 to 450 degrees Fahrenheit. The most dangerous temperatures to keep poultry, fish, meats and other perishable foods are between 45 and 140 degrees Fahrenheit—that range provides temperatures that bacteria thrive in.

Food Storage—Portable Coolers

Although many camping and recreational vehicles come equipped with icebox or refrigerator units, most people use coolers, ice chests (see Figure 14-2), or freezer cans (reusable gel-filled containers that are frozen before use). Ice chests or coolers make it possible to keep foods cold and fresh while enroute to a picnic or campsite. How long the food will remain chilled depends on the quality of the cooler, how often it's opened, how much ice or coolant it will hold, and even how it's packed. A good cooler is well-insulated, forms a tight seal when closed,

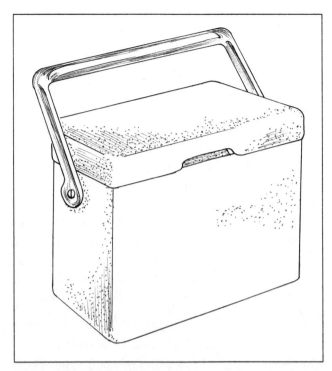

Figure 14-2. An ice chest.

and has an easy to clean stain- and rust-proof interior.

When packing a cooler, remember that cold settles and heat rises. For that reason, putting ice or coolant on top of the food makes the most sense. Place the most perishable foods on the bottom of the cooler, and the less perishable ones toward the top. One option is to put ice or freezer packs (self-contained plastic containers full of refreezable gel) in the middle of a cooler below less perishable items if the items are of a delicate nature—such as eggs.

The foods that go into a cooler can also become part of the refrigeration. If you're going to be away from home and regular refrigeration for a long time—on a long camping trip, for instance—it's best to freeze as many of the foods and drinks you can before packing them. And chill the rest of the items that will be going into the cooler. Wait until the last possible moment to transfer the foods from the home refrigerator/freezer to the cooler.

Pack a cooler with some idea as to the order in which things will be consumed, so time isn't wasted reshuffling items while selecting individual foods or drinks. If possible, the most perishable supplies should be used first. One way is to place all frozen foods in the center of the cooler, and putting the perishables that will be used last around them. The least perishable products would go on top, and the other spaces could be filled with small bags of sliced vegetables such as carrots, and chilled canned or bottled drinks.

Individual items in a cooler should be separately packed in plastic bags or wrap. Fresh milk and cream should be used up in the first few meals, and fresh vegetables should be eaten before they start to wilt and lose their nutritional value. Bacon, smoked meats, salted butter and margarine will generally keep for a week if kept cool. Other cooked and un-cooked meat, and poultry and fish should be transported frozen and cooked while still cold after being thawed. Ground meat is more perishable than solid cuts of meat, so it should be cooked first on a camping trip. Most canned goods need no refrigeration, and will keep for a long time.

Pack individual lunches in insulated carriers with a cold pack (plastic container in which refrigeration gel is frozen). Warn children never to leave lunches in direct sunlight or on a warm radiator.

Avoid putting coolers and picnic baskets in a hot vehicle trunk. And keep them in the shade at the camp or cooking site. If you're preparing for a backyard picnic, or a picnic a short driving distance from home, whether you pack sandwiches or pick up fried chicken along the way, keep the food in an iced cooler, or eat it within two hours—or one hour if the temperature is above 85 degrees Fahrenheit.

Food cooked at home should be thoroughly chilled (several hours or overnight) before being packed in a cooler. Avoid partially cooking foods at home, and then transporting them to be finished later because incomplete cooking encourages bacterial growth if there's much time delay between the first and second stages. When you're talking about a backyard cookout, however, it's okay to get a jump on the cooking with your oven broiler or cooktop before transferring chicken or steaks to the outdoor gas or barbecue grill.

Food Preparation, Cooking and Reheating

Keep cold party or picnic foods on ice, or serve them throughout the gathering on platters directly from the cooler or refrigerator.

Keep preparation and serving times to a minimum during hot weather picnics, barbecues and other celebrations. Cook and serve hot foods immediately; bring cooled dishes out only when it's time to eat them.

Because it can be difficult to keep hot foods hot while on the way to a picnic site, precooked foods should be prepared early enough to be refrigerated completely, and then reheated at the picnic or outing site. If cooked food will be served cold, it should be refrigerated until it is below 45 degrees Fahrenheit and kept chilled until time to eat.

When carrying ground beef or other raw meats for a cookout, they should be packed in a cooler inside airtight containers. Although cooking will kill any bacteria in the meat, the same strains of bacteria may contaminate other foods in the cooler that won't be cooled further before being eaten.

If cold-cut sandwiches are part of a hot weather menu, keep the ingredients (including condiments) separate, and prepare the sandwiches at the picnic or other site. If sandwiches must be prepared in advance, use frozen slices of bread and well-chilled cold cuts or spreads, and wrap each sandwich in a plastic sandwich bag that isn't airtight (to avoid condensation).

Remember that during hot weather, cooking meats rare or medium rare may not kill harmful bacteria. Because of the high temperatures, these bacteria may quickly multiply to the point where they become dangerous. Since it takes thorough cooking to kill harmful bacteria, you're taking chances when you eat meat, poultry, fish or eggs that are raw or only partly cooked.

Many people are reluctant to eat chicken salad, potato salad and similar dishes at summer picnics because they've heard that foods made with mayonnaise are the most likely to spoil and cause food poisoning. Scientists, on the other hand, explain that simply adding mayonnaise to a food does not make the dish more dangerous. In fact, foods containing mayonnaise are often safer than those without, because the acid in mayonnaise slows down the growth of bacteria that causes food poisoning. These mixed foods such as egg salad, tuna fish salad and potato salad have gotten bad reputations simply because they undergo a lot of handling during preparation—which by itself increases the odds of contamination somewhere along the line.

OTHER HOT WEATHER SAFEGUARDS

Campers must not drink water that comes from polluted streams or lakes. Harmful protozoon and other "germs" found can cause serious diarrhea and illnesses that will definitely put a damper on camping and outdoor activities. If no approved clean water sources are available, either bring bottled water or water purification tablets, or boil water from nearby sources thoroughly before drinking.

People who take babies along on camping trips should be cautious about preparing and storing infant formula. Although it may be more difficult to transport, canned liquid formula is safer than powdered formula if water to be mixed with the powdered formula comes from an outdoor or unknown source.

HOT-WEATHER SAFETY QUICK CHECKLIST

☐ Protect exposed skin when you go outdoors in the sun. The use of clothing and sunscreens having a sun protection factor (SPF) of at least fifteen is recommended by physicians and sunscreen manufacturers.

☐ Babies should be kept out of strong direct sunlight at all times, and should be protected by clothing and sunscreens at other times.

☐ Avoid the use of indoor sunlamps, tanning parlors and tanning pills.

☐ Examine your skin at least once a month. If you ever notice a change in the appearance of moles, birthmarks or blemishes — in size, shape or color, or a sore that does not heal — see a physician without delay.

☐ Protect your eyes from the midday sun by wearing a good pair of sunglasses designed to block out ultraviolet rays.

☐ To avoid heat illness in hot weather, wear loose, light-colored clothing and a hat. Drink plenty of fluids, rest often, maintain safe salt intake, and stay in the shade or cooled areas whenever possible.

☐ Recognize the signs of heat illness, know how to react to them, and know when to seek medical help.

☐ Never leave children, pets or any passenger in a locked vehicle on a hot day.

☐ Avoid consuming alcohol during hot weather.

☐ Eat light, nutritious meals, preferably cold. Avoid heavy and fatty foods in hot weather.

☐ Keep your distance from unknown or wild animals. Avoid teasing or scaring your own pets during the dog days of summer.

☐ If bitten by a wild animal, wash the wound with plenty of soap and running water and get medical attention right away.

☐ Never leave perishable foods unrefrigerated for over two hours, or even less if exposed to high temperatures.

☐ When preparing a cooler, freeze or chill as many of the foods and drinks as you can before packing them.

☐ Food cooked at home should be thoroughly chilled before being placed in a cooler.

CHAPTER 15

COLD WEATHER SAFETY

Winter. Unless you go for downhill or cross-country skiing, ice-boating, sledding, speed skating, hockey or snowmobile racing, cold weather tends to slow things down. Sleet, snow and ice make driving and walking outdoors difficult and cause a number of winter hazards. Low temperatures, especially when combined with strong winds, can cause serious problems for people who venture outdoors without warm enough clothes. This chapter focuses on some of the special hazards that cold weather conditions bring about, and how to defend yourself against them.

HYPOTHERMIA AND FROSTBITE

You've heard about people living in the country who dash out of doors, garbage in hand, into a whiteout storm, only to be found frozen stiff a half-day later, within calling distance of the front door. And what about hunters or cross-country skiers who lose their way in the big woods, even in relatively mild winter weather, and are found the next morning babbling incoherently, ready for a two-week hospital stay? Hypothermia—also called exposure—is a serious loss of body heat. It's frequently caused by subfreezing weather, but can also occur in surprisingly mild temperatures—the forties and fifties, for example—and even when a person is performing active work or play activities. The most effective treatment is simply early recognition, retreat from the cold, and a change into warm, dry clothes. If allowed to continue, the heat loss can be so great that a victim may no longer be able to produce heat on his own for re-warming, and external heat sources will be needed.

Frostbite is a freezing of uncovered or poorly insulated body tissues. The windchill factor can be a major cause, but so can damp clothing and wet footwear. Frostbite usually affects the fingers, toes, nose, cheeks and earlobes, so keep those extremities insulated and out of the direct wind on subfreezing days. The first sign of frostbite is redness on the cheeks, earlobes, forehead and fingers. As things worsen, those body parts turn white and numb. Don't rub snow on suspected frostbite. Instead, get inside and gently warm the stricken parts by placing them against normal temperature skin or by immersing them in warm, not hot, water. Do not rub hard. If the frostbite is severe, take the victim to a hospital.

The simplest way to avoid hypothermia and frostbite is to stay indoors during frigid weather. Of course, that's not always possible. For most of us, life goes on, wintry weather or not, and we've got to go outside to work, to shop, to pay bills, to shovel driveways, to gas up our vehicles, to pick up our children at school, and to take our dogs for walks. If remaining indoors is not a reasonable option, the only other way to combat the cold is to dress for it.

That means dressing for the elements—dressing to avoid hypothermia and frostbite. It means no wearing clothes that are too light or too heavy. Although clothing made of lightweight, modern materials has come a long way in keeping our bodies warm and dry in cold weather, it must be properly selected and worn. Too much clothing can be as great a hazard as too little. During active work or play the body temperature rises and produces perspiration. "Non-breathable" waterproof outer garments worn at the wrong time can trap this moisture. In turn, dampness reduces the insulating effect of clothing and can result in chills, hypothermia and even pneumonia. Normally, in mild or warm conditions the sweat evaporates, cools the skin, and restores the body temperature to normal levels. That process can still go on in subfreezing temperatures if you select outerwear made of breathable yet water-resistant materials, such as Gore-Tex.

When the weather outside is frightful, a good rule of thumb is to dress appropriately for what you *think* you'll be doing—and also prepare yourself for what you *might actually* be doing. The two could be different from each other. If you're just running outside to jump into the car to drop your child off at school ten blocks away, you may not need the kind of cold weather gear that's designed for hiking the Iditarod Trail. But what would happen if you had a flat tire along the way? It's best to take extra clothing—or keep some in the car in case of an abrupt change of plans.

How Your Body Loses Heat

In cold weather, your body loses heat in a number of different ways: through convection, radiation, evaporation and conduction.

Convective heat loss occurs when cold or cool air currents are heated by your body's warmth. The air currents carry your heat out and away from your body. The best prevention for convective heat loss is several layers of clothing, each of which traps warm air, making it harder for that air to move away from your skin.

Radiant heat is the type of heat you feel on your face and hands from an open fire. Like a fire, your body radiates heat that's generated by various internal processes such as digestion. Several layers of clothing will prevent radiant heat loss, again by trapping warm air as it's generated. Since most radi-

ant heat loss occurs through your head, wearing a hat is critical to staying warm.

Evaporative heat loss is more difficult to control, since your body continues to sweat even in cold weather, especially if you are active. The best strategy is to "wick," or transport, moisture away from the skin to outer layers of clothing where it can evaporate or dissipate without robbing your body of warmth in the process.

Conductive heat loss occurs whenever something cold or wet touches your body. In fact, conductive heat loss occurs over twenty-five times faster when you are wearing wet clothing. The best defense against conductive heat loss is to place layers of dry, insulating clothing, or other barrier items that are low in conductivity between yourself and the cold.

Clothing Guidelines
Dressing in Layers

The concept of dressing in layers for warmth is recommended and has been used for centuries. The idea is that several layers of light, warm clothing are far more practical than a single layer of heavy insulation. Layering allows you to peel off a layer or two according to need, or add layers of different weights for more warmth. Too, individual layers trap air between each other. And air is a good insulator.

To complete a layering outfit, at least the following items should be included: the skin layer (underwear), a middle layer, and an external layer.

The skin layer is your first layer of defense against cold. It should trap a layer of warm air next to your skin while transporting or "wicking" away perspiration your body produces during cold weather activities. To accomplish those ends, the fabric must be nonabsorbent. That rules out cotton and includes fabrics made of certain synthetics, silks and soft-weave wools.

The middle layer offers the most options to choose from, depending on the circumstances. Turtlenecks are good choices when worn beneath a shirt or sweater to protect a wearer from moderately cold weather in which he or she won't be too active. Wool shirts are preferred over chamois or cotton flannel shirts, which may absorb perspiration and become damp. Wool sweaters worn in thin layers are excellent for cold weather pastimes. Synthetic fleece clothing also works well. Down vests and jackets are warm and lightweight. Since your legs don't need as much insulation to feel warm, two layers will often suffice—long underwear and a pair of rugged wool trousers will usually do the job. Feet are a different story. They're equipped with lots of moisture-producing sweat glands that go into full production when covered with socks and shoes or boots that can't breathe. Two layers of socks should be worn. The first or inner layer should wick away moisture as fast as the moisture is produced—they must be made of a nonabsorbent material such as polypropylene. The outer socks should be thicker, designed to hold the moisture that the inner socks have moved from the skin, as well as to insulate and cushion the feet. Wool is a good standby here, but newer synthetics will also work, including acrylics and Orlon polypropylenes.

The external layer of clothing is critical to the overall performance of a cold-weather layering system. It must protect the other two layers from wind and water—the cause of most convective and conductive heat losses. For strenuous activities, the outer shell should be made of a waterproof, yet breathable fabric, such as Gore-Tex. For more sedentary or less active pursuits, coated nylon garments or unlined windbreakers can suffice.

Other Clothing Considerations

Loose clothing tends to be warmer than tight clothing, except for the winter stretch materials that skiers, skaters and joggers find confortable when pursuing their activities.

To conserve body heat, be sure to include a hat with your outfit. Wearing a hat conserves a considerable amount of warmth that would otherwise be given off from the large blood vessel system in your head and neck that radiates heat.

Mittens will keep your hands warmer than gloves will, because gloves have more outside surface area between the fingers where heat can escape.

Sweaters and loosely knitted garments are virtually useless in the wind unless protected by a windbreaker or similar outer layer.

Clothing layers against your skin should be as wearer-friendly as possible, meaning that they'll keep you warm without chafing. Cotton is fine if you will not be exercising vigorously. Again, it absorbs perspiration but gets soaked and gives a "cold" feeling when wet. If you plan to be active enough to work up a healthy sweat, sports enthusiasts and cold weather specialists recommend one of the nonabsorbent synthetic materials such as polypropylene, which allows perspiration to evaporate immediately, or "wick" off of the skin. Wool is also a good choice. It's warmer than cotton and many synthetic materials when wet, and it helps lift moisture away from the skin. Many specialty mail order catalogs designed for hunters, skiers, campers and winter sports enthusiasts feature outdoor clothing made of wool and of fairly high cost, breathable, yet water-resistant materials.

Winter clothes can at times be hazardous in themselves. On children, drawstrings can slip closer to the neck and cause choking. Trailing or loose garment accessories such as scarves or ties can cause choking or tripping.

Because of their size, children are easily affected by cold temperatures. No amount of clothing can be trusted to keep youngsters safe during subzero conditions. Bring youngsters indoors when temperatures or windchill factors approach –20 degrees Fahrenheit.

Lots of people forget about proper foot care during winter. If you're just running out to the curb with the garbage, through a foot of snow, any old pair of boots will do. But if you're going to be spending a full afternoon outdoors, hiking, sledding or ice fishing, select boots constructed from insulated leather or some other breathable material rated for typical winter use. If you'll be sloshing through slush or water, consider boots with rubber bottoms and water-resistant, yet breathable, uppers.

BACK INJURIES

Wintry conditions inevitably bring an increase in back injuries. Ask at any emergency room, or inquire at the office of physicians or trainers who specialize in back rehabilitation. The main causes of cold weather back injury are four: snow shoveling, car pushing, falling, and carrying heavy or bulky items improperly.

Snow Shoveling

For some individuals, shoveling snow can be excellent exercise, *if* the person has already been exercising right along, is dressed for the job, and leisurely goes about his or her business. If not—if someone who has been following a sedentary schedule leaps into a pair of boots and runs outdoors to attack a three-foot snowdrift—that's just asking for back injury and other problems.

If you haven't been active and that first snowstorm deposits more of the white stuff than you can safely handle, consider having a neighbor's youngster shovel your driveway, or call your local automobile club to get a phone number of a wrecker with a plow.

If you decide to shovel by yourself, here are a few pointers to consider. Use a plastic shovel with a slippery blade so wet snow doesn't stick and build up on the surface—you shouldn't have to jerk the snow from the shovel blade. Even slush should slide off easily, with nothing left on the shovel's scoop. Red plastic shovels are best. Their bright color makes them more visible in a snowstorm or at night. Have a few plastic shovels handy, in case one of them breaks.

Find help whenever you can. Get those children out there. They may not be fast, but every little bit will help.

Use common sense. Start early enough to give yourself enough time to clear the driveway, even if it means getting up 45 minutes earlier than usual just to peer out through your blinds to see if it snowed. Instead of trying to burst through deep drifts like a human plow, pace yourself.

Good snow shoveling procedure says to:

- Keep your hands separated widely on the shovel, for maximum leverage (see Figure 15-1).
- Push the snow as often as possible, instead of lifting it.
- When you must lift snow, move only as much as can be handled comfortably.
- Bend your knees slightly and keep your back straight; leg muscles should lift much of the load.

Figure 15-1. Snow shoveling.

- Be careful of pushing back snowdrifts as you lift a shovel full of snow. Don't put any more strain on the upward shovel lift than the weight of the snow in your shovel's scoop.
- Don't twist your body while lifting.
- If there's a lot of shoveling to do, stop and stretch often. It's good for your back and you'll get more done in the long run.
- When stretching, avoid arching your back; instead, reach out your arms.

Pushing Stuck Vehicles

Maybe you used to be able to do it—to help push someone's car out of a snowdrift, or to rock a station wagon out of a snowy rut. In fact, maybe you still can, but is it worth it? To help someone save a few minutes do you really want to risk a back injury that could easily plague you for the rest of your life? A heart attack, stroke, or other disastrous illness could also result. Helping to shovel is something else, but straining to push a vehicle doesn't make sense. Let the person get a tow truck; perhaps she will avoid a similar situation in the future. It's one thing for seven college students push some coed's MG Midget from a two-foot-deep snowdrift, and another for you, by yourself, to strain at the front grill of your neighbor's '78 Chevy station wagon. That's what automobile club memberships are for. And tow trucks. Don't wrench your back out of shape for life, whether to save someone else a few minutes, or a few dollars.

Slipping and Falling

You've seen it a hundred times. Jerry Lewis takes a flop. So does Chevy Chase . . . Laurel and Hardy . . . the Three Stooges . . . or Charlie Chaplin. It may be fun to watch, but it's painful to experience. Walking on icy surfaces without proper footwear or protection is one way to sit out the winter in traction, or in a cast—and an expensive and inconvenient way at that. Why risk injury? During winter, more than any other time of the year, your alertness and sense of balance will help you react safely to numerous slipping and falling hazards you're bound to encounter.

Although slips and falls are the most common winter accidents for people of all ages, youngsters and seniors often receive the worst injuries. Most trips and falls occur on icy driveways, walks or steps, or on wet wood and tile floors. Thinking and taking precautions can save you from painful injury.

Carrying garbage cans and containers, dragging recyclable bags, carrying babies and presents and packages—items that occupy a person's hands while she is walking can cause balance problems and difficulties if a slip occurs. Figure out better and safer ways to do things during winter. Use a sled to transport your garbage. Ask the Christmas tree lot attendant to lift your blue spruce to the roof rack on your station wagon. Arrange for help when carrying packages or the baby. Allocate more time for simple chores. Slow things down.

Use rubber-backed, "walk-off" carpet mats (see Figure 15-2) wherever possible, especially in foyers near front or rear entrances, and in sheds, sun rooms, utility rooms or hallways.

Water-slick tile and wood floors, and greasy salt coverings are cause for caution. Slow down and take smaller steps to maintain your balance.

Irregularly sized front, side or back steps, slanted steps to a patio, or loose wooden stairs that lead to a deck can all present special problems during

Figure 15-2. A walk-off entrance mat.

winter weather. The slightest ice covered sloping surface can send an unsuspecting visitor flying through the air. Keep steps sprinkled with "friendly," non-staining, chemical snow-melt products, not with harsh rock salt that can be tracked through the house. Install handrails on steps that don't have any, and make sure there's good lighting there at night.

Improper Lifting and Carrying Techniques

Back strains and pulls also result from lifting, carrying and dragging items such as large presents, frozen turkeys, Christmas trees, ice huts for ice fishing, wood for fireplaces or stoves, snow tires and other seasonal items. (See the section on proper lifting techniques in chapter three.) Get help when carrying heavy or bulky items. Be aware of slippery walking surfaces. Snow that gets dragged into a kitchen or foyer will melt and get tracked through the house. Basement steps can get wet from boots and other winter gear. It's easier to slip while you're concentrating on lifting and carrying.

SNOWBLOWERS

Snowblowers are great conveniences, but apart from throwing snow, they can easily part a careless owner from anything from her fingertips to something worse. Make sure the store you buy a snowblower at shows you how to operate the unit before you take it home. Ask about and understand all of the safety procedures. Don't force the unit—people have been injured pushing them faster than they were designed to go. Wear hearing protection. Be attentive to where you're throwing the snow. Keep children, spectators and pets away. Be careful with gasoline storage and handling within confined spaces, such as a tightly closed garage.

And be extremely careful about cleaning plugged chutes and blades. *Never reach anywhere near the blades* unless you are certain you have achieved a zero-energy condition with the unit; that is, when you make absolutely certain that the entire unit is shut off and can't be started accidentally, and that the blades are not moving and cannot turn or start on their own. Even then, use a stick or other accessory to free ice or snow between the blades. It's just a good idea never to place your fingers near the blades.

Because snowblowers can be so dangerous, it's always a good idea to get them ready for winter long before the chance of that first snowstorm. Re-read the owner's manual and make sure others in your household who may use the unit do the same. Make sure that everything is running correctly and all of the safety features are working. If repairs are needed, complete them before the snow-throwing season begins—so your dealer won't be rushing the job during the first frenzied weeks of the snow season, when everyone else is clamoring for instant service.

WINTER DRIVING HAZARDS
Drinking and Driving
As if typical wintry driving conditions aren't bad enough, the cold weather season is a well-known time to party. There are end-of-the-year office meetings, dances and dinners. There are family reunions. Children come home for the holidays and go out with their friends. Late night activities such as school plays, sporting events and religious ceremonies draw people out into social gatherings. And there's a whole lot of eating and drinking going on.

You've heard about the tragedies associated with drinking and driving—the innocent and not-so-innocent individuals who are involved in horrible accidents brought about by decreased reaction times, perceptions and motor skills.

What can you do at home? Get plenty of rest before an outing. Tell yourself in advance what you can drink, then stick to your limit. Don't drink on an empty stomach or if depressed or lonely. Designate a driver or take a taxicab, but don't drive. And also, don't rely on someone else to drive if that person will also be drinking.

Unfortunately, all of this does little to protect you from *others* who may be driving while alcohol impaired. The best idea may be to celebrate a week later, or a week in advance, and to stay off the roads during the peak driving times.

Don't forget that the winter holidays are also times when children are out of school and looking for things to do. If alcohol is readily available, many of them, being housebound, are likely to be tempted to try a snort of this or that. It's best to keep the alcohol locked up. You may trust your children, but who knows what other kids will do if they can get their hands on a bottle of whiskey, gin or vodka? You don't want to be an unknowing source or root cause of a drinking problem or accident.

Treacherous Driving Conditions
Treacherous driving conditions include ice, snow, sleet and fog. Every year in most places, during the first few days of winter snow and ice, there is a rash of accidents. Although most are fender benders, some are tragic.

Some people winterize their vehicles during late fall, before winter has an opportunity to strike. They'll get an engine tune-up, put on snow tires, check the antifreeze, toss a shovel and a bag of sand in the trunk, and place a pair of leather mittens and an ice scraper in the glove compartment. Others will take a more reckless approach. They'll face the first freeze with rough-running engines, bald tires, inadequate antifreeze, freezing fingers, and—you guessed it—no scraper. You'll be able to recognize them because they're the ones who slip and slide in traffic, leaning forward at their wheels, noses against the insides of their windshields, peering through the tiny openings they scratched through the ice with their house keys, and driving too fast for conditions because they're attempting to make up for time they lost trying to get going in the first place. What separates the first group from the second is simple preparation.

For yourself and other family members, consider the following points:

Are snow tires on and in good condition? Do the wipers and defroster units work properly? How potent is the battery and charging system? Make sure the vehicle's fluid levels, exhaust system, brake system and lights are in good working order. Re-read your state driver's manual on winter driving.

Keep emergency supplies in the trunk. A cold weather kit should include a shovel, bag of salt, some extra clothing, a few blankets, first-aid supplies, a flashlight, some waterproof matches, flares, and even a box of candy bars. It's also a good idea to carry a set of jumper cables, and know how to use them safely.

Practice skidding and making emergency stops in an empty parking lot. It helps to "get the feel" of winter driving again by practicing panic stops, pumping the brakes and steering sharply.

Drive slowly and approach stop signs and crossings with extreme caution. Drive defensively because someone else may not—and may skid through a stop sign into an intersection. It won't matter if you're right if you get into an accident anyway.

Carry an extra vest or sweater in the car. Always dress for the conditions, even if you'll only be gone for a short time.

Allow extra travel time. Plan for heavier traffic, poor visibility and changing road conditions.

Clean your windows of snow and ice before you start out; don't count on the defroster to clear things up after you've been on the road for ten or fifteen minutes.

Do you get sleepy while driving long distances because of heavy clothes and warm air from the heater? To combat drowsiness, make frequent rest stops, crack the window open, turn down the heat, listen to talk—not music—radio, sing, and make conversation with passengers.

Don't panic if your car starts to skid. Instead, keep your foot off the gas and off the brake if possible. Gently turn in the direction you want the vehicle to go.

Wear your seat belt. Insist that all passengers wear them, too.

DROWNINGS

During winter, parents don't seem to think much about water safety. They figure pool covers will keep children from playing in swimming pools, and sturdy layers of ice will safeguard children from breaking through into ponds and lakes. Not so.

Pool covers alone aren't enough to prevent accidental winter drownings. A pool cover can hide a child who crawls between the cover and the water. Or enough water can collect on the cover's surface for a child to drown in. When a child moves out of your sight, if there's a pool in the area, check it immediately. Keep emergency rescue equipment on hand, such as a ring buoy with an attached line or a long-handled hook. And keep toys away from a pool or hot tub so children won't be attracted to toys that are thrown into or fall into the water.

Never let children—or anyone else for that matter—walk on ice-covered ponds, lakes, rivers or impoundments alone. A surface of ice can be considered safe only if tested by an adult who will be present while the children are playing there. Instruct children never to try to rescue someone else by venturing near the place the person fell through. Too many people have drowned while trying to save others. Instead, have them run for the nearest adult or phone.

Hot tub and whirlpool use increases during the winter months. Hot whirlpool water is especially dangerous to children because youngsters are more susceptible to overheating; their tiny bodies are simpler to affect because they don't have as much insulation and bulk. Be sure to lock the room that the hot tub is in, and fence in outdoor hot tubs and whirlpool baths. Never lose sight of a child in or near them—not even for a few seconds.

FIRES

During winter, pay special attention to Christmas trees and decorations, candles, fireplaces, stoves and space heaters.

Keep heating units away from flammable materials and children away from heating units. Make sure that bedding, draperies and other combustibles are not close to wood-burning stoves, fireplaces or portable heaters. Portable heaters can pose special problems; choose models that will not cause a fire if tipped over. Make sure that all fuels are locked safely away and that extension cords, if they must be used, are not overloading circuits or placed where they can be tripped over. (See chapter one for a detailed discussion of fire prevention.)

POISONING

Cold weather conditions usually mean a variety of poison possibilities. Fuels for snowblowers and recreational vehicles should be stored out of children's reach or locked up. The same goes for antifreeze, which tastes sweet but is deadly poisonous when consumed.

Since family members are more likely to get colds and other ailments during the winter, a variety of medications are usually kept around the house. Make sure prescription medications are placed where children won't be tempted to put them into their mouths, thinking they're candy or vitamins. Also beware of taking someone else's medicine instead of your own. Don't get the containers confused.

One particularly dangerous gas you may encounter during the winter is carbon monoxide, a gas that forms when any fuel is burned without sufficient oxygen present. Small amounts of it are formed whenever oil, kerosene, coal, charcoal, wood, gasoline or natural gas are burned. During winter, when one or more of those fuels is used or burned in an area that does not have adequate ventilation, carbon monoxide levels can build up to critical levels.

You can't taste, smell or see carbon monoxide. It's an invisible killer. That makes it even more dangerous. When too much is present it will foul up your body chemistry, often without warning. It combines with hemoglobin in your red blood cells about 250 times more readily than oxygen—preventing your body from getting the oxygen it needs to stay alive. Symptoms of carbon monoxide poisoning include headaches, dizziness, nausea, coughing, ringing in the ears, muscle weakness, confusion and irregular breathing, which if not taken care of could lead to unconsciousness and even death. At first a victim will appear pale, but may later develop a cherry red color on his lips and ear tips. The most significant symptom is a headache that won't go away.

To prevent carbon monoxide buildup, check your chimney for obstructions, soot deposits, debris and bird nests at least once a year, preferably just before the heating season. Check furnace and water heater vent pipes for rust, corrosion or damage. Replace the pipes if you find any trouble spots. Look at the furnace and water heater exhaust vents. They should be the same size continuously from the unit to where they exit the home. If you're planning to change fuels, let a qualified heating technician make the fuel and equipment conversions. Don't try to do such work yourself.

Also avoid enclosed combustion whenever possible. Don't rely on a gas cooking range to heat a room. Don't burn charcoal inside your home or any other confined area like a shed, recreational vehicle or garage; it releases a large amount of carbon monoxide. If you are burning a fuel in an ice-fishing hut, make sure there's plenty of ventilation to get rid of harmful gases.

Avoid running an automobile engine, lawn mower, snowblower or any other combustion engine in a closed, confined area like a garage or basement. Even if you run an automobile engine in a garage with the big garage door open, make sure the exhaust is escaping outside.

OTHER WINTER CONSIDERATIONS

When conditions are just so, icicles can build up on roof edges, gutters and downspouts. They hold a particular attraction for children who love to try to knock them down with snowballs or sticks. Teach children that they should never stand, walk or play directly beneath icicles. Also be careful of icicles that hang from houses along narrow driveways where the only access to a back or side door is below the icicles. Either remove the icicles safely—knocking them down, if possible, with a long bamboo or other pole, or temporarily use the front door. A long-term solution is to install electrical heat tape, which is simply thin "heat" wires, to prevent ice from forming on roof edges and gutters. Be especially careful of icicles when the weather starts warming up and the weight of an icicle can pull or break the ice where it's attached to the roof or gutter.

Decorative trees and shrubs that are trimmed high enough to allow typical walking headroom height during most of the year, can be dangerous when snow and ice builds up on the ground and people start to walk into stiff branches or thorns. Adults carrying babies and young children are especially susceptible to scratches or eye injuries from brushing past branches. Either trim back the offending foliage or get rid of the snow and ice buildup.

Windchill Factor

You hear it used often by weather forecasters: "the windchill factor." And they frequently scare listeners with numbers as low as –45 degrees Fahrenheit, or –60 degrees. Windchill numbers used by television and radio weathercasters come from charts based on work done by several Antarctic explorers during the early 1940s. Windchill factors are based on the concept that the faster the wind blows warm air from around your body, the quicker the "heated" air molecules dissipate and the quicker the heat escapes. For example, at 10 degrees Fahrenheit, with the wind speeds listed on the chart below, the temperature will feel like the following:

with a 10 mph wind	= –9 degrees
15 mph wind	= –18 degrees
20 mph wind	= –24 degrees
25 mph wind	= –29 degrees
30 mph wind	= –33 degrees
35 mph wind	= –35 degrees
40 mph wind	= –37 degrees

Health Precautions

The winter sun—even during times when temperatures fall below freezing—can damage unprotected eyes and skin. Apply a sunscreen or block with at least a SPF fifteen to skin that will be exposed to late-morning and afternoon sun for a considerable length of time, such as when skiing, skating, hiking, or performing various work tasks outdoors. Full-spectrum sunscreen protects against both ultraviolet A and B rays. Good sunscreens can also help prevent windburn and chapped skin—skin that dries out as result of cold wind blowing against it. Remember to use lip balm to protect tender lips in very cold and windy conditions. Wear UV-screening sunglasses, especially on sunny days when light is reflecting off snow or ice.

During cold weather, more people spend their free time indoors, whether it's in malls, restaurants, movie theaters, or in homes or apartments. The greater the concentration of people anywhere, the greater the likelihood of increased quantities of illness-causing bacteria and viruses. Wash your hands often to reduce transmission of cold viruses. Avoid touching your mouth and nose with your hands. Use disinfectants to remove viruses from frequently handled surfaces. Increase ventilation whenever possible and keep your distance from people who are coughing or sneezing.

Having a cold can increase the risk of other safety hazards. You may not be as alert as usual. You're more apt to get tired easily, and your reaction time will slow down. This can be further accentuated by medicines you take to relieve cold symptoms. The remedies may contain alcohol, antihistamines, or other substances that can impair your ability to react quickly and clearly in an emergency. That's why many medicines carry warnings that they should be taken before bedtime, or when you won't be working or driving a vehicle.

Keep your immune system strong by getting enough rest, relieving stress, exercising regularly, and eating nutritious foods with generous amounts of vitamin C. Studies of vitamin C's effectiveness indicate that although vitamin users may contract about as many colds as the nonusers or control group, the vitamin C group users have significantly milder symptoms.

Moderate amounts of aerobic exercise may enhance a body's immune system, while strenuous activity may depress it.

COLD-WEATHER SAFETY QUICK CHECKLIST

☐ If you're leaving your residence, dress for the weather or at the very least take additional clothing to put on in case you are stranded outdoors, in a vehicle or out in the open.

☐ Protect yourself against cold temperatures and harsh winds.

☐ Recognize the early symptoms of hypothermia and frostbite, and take immediate action if they appear.

☐ If you don't have to go out in subzero conditions, don't.

☐ Dress with wearer-friendly garments next to your skin.

☐ In cold weather, wear a hat to prevent heat loss from your head and neck.

☐ Dress in layers instead of selecting fewer "thick" or heavy items. Loose-fitting clothing is generally warmer than tight-fitting garments.

☐ Wool is an excellent garment fabric choice if you may get wet outdoors.

☐ Avoid dressing children in accessories with drawstrings and scarves that can dangle or choke. If worn, those items should be tucked beneath outside clothing so they won't come loose.

☐ Wear carefully chosen footwear for winter activities.

☐ Don't overexert yourself shoveling snow or pushing stuck vehicles.

☐ When you must shovel by hand, use a plastic snow shovel and try to get some help.

☐ Ice, snow and water make for extremely slippery surfaces. Recognize the numerous slipping hazards that are encountered during typical wintry conditions.

☐ Wear sturdy, nonslip winter shoes or boots.

☐ While using snowblowers, follow all safety procedures. Keep your hands and feet away from the discharge chute and blades.

☐ Never drink and drive; avoid riding with those who drink.

☐ Make sure your vehicles are ready for winter.

OUTDOOR SECURITY QUICK CHECKLIST
(continued)

☐ Keep an emergency safety kit in your car, wagon or truck.

☐ Allow for extra travel time in wintry conditions, and slow down your driving.

☐ Practice defensive driving. Be especially wary of intersections where even a well-meaning driver may slide through.

☐ Teach children to keep away from swimming pools, ponds, reservoirs, lakes, and other bodies of water unless the youngsters are accompanied by a responsible adult.

☐ Keep combustibles away from fireplaces, stoves and space heaters. Store fuels out of children's reach, locked in a cabinet.

☐ Store medicines in their original child-resistant containers placed out of children's reach and sight.

☐ Protect your eyes and skin against bright winter sunrays which may be reflected off snow or ice.

☐ Avoid situations in which carbon monoxide gas could collect within a vehicle, garage, basement or living area.

☐ Avoid walking beneath icicles, and don't let children play beneath them either.

☐ Follow good principles of nutrition during the winter months, when the body's immune system is fully taxed by the weather and by increased concentrations of germs, viruses and bacteria brought about by close contact with family members, friends and strangers.

PART FOUR

HOME SECURITY

Unless you live within the walls or fences of a private association or neighborhood, it's likely that the streets, roads and walks that make up your neighborhood and surround your property are fair game for anyone to pass through at any time of day or night. This section of the book is about the wide range of preventative steps that can be taken to discourage individuals who are either opportunists, professional burglars, thieves or worse. Some locations are safer than others. It's a good bet that you know how safe your neighborhood is, but it's also true that at any given time or place, anything can happen.

Common sense and attention to security can certainly tip the odds in your favor. They can never completely safeguard anyone, but you'll certainly be safer than the typical household by following any number of suggestions from the following chapters.

CHAPTER 16
OUTDOOR SECURITY

The great outdoors, when home security is being considered, is where your first line of defense belongs. Years ago, back in the days when warring tribes or foreign groups staged plundering raids from village to village, outdoor security consisted of castle walls, moats filled with water, deep trenches, wooden forts or sentries stationed from place to place.

Nowadays the danger from separate warring groups has largely passed. During these times we worry about members of our own society who disregard laws and rules of civilized behavior, and who figure they can trespass on someone else's property to steal belongings, or worse yet, to harm the occupants.

Depending on where you live, the probability of facing an intruder within your own residence may be great or small, but it's always present to some extent. The grounds your residence is situated on can and should be made as uninviting to a potential intruder as possible.

Unless you happen to live in a "controlled" or enclosed multi-unit building, neighborhood or area—surrounded by a security wall, fence, natural landscape feature or geographical boundary, and patrolled by a private security outfit—it's likely that you and your neighbors are situated out in the open, only a breath away from the general public at large. While friends and relatives have easy access to your residence, so do total strangers—people passing by. Although most of these individuals are

honest, some may be less than law abiding.

Unfortunately, nonviolent residential crime has been given relatively low priority by most police departments. Squads that deal specifically with burglary, for instance, are generally more concerned with commercial establishments, where large-scale losses can occur. Businesses are easier to monitor, too, because commercial zones are typically more compact and easier to patrol than are sprawling, hard-to-see homesites spread throughout heavily landscaped suburbs. Restaurants, banks, retail stores and other businesses are simply more equipped to combat burglary, and are observable from a passing vehicle. Their lighting is good on the inside and outside, and these buildings are more often than not equipped with sophisticated alarms and systems that detect intruders. Commercial burglary occurs mostly at night, on weekends, or whenever the establishment is closed—unlike residential burglaries, which occur at any time of the day and night, on any day of the week. Officers in a police car cruising through a residential neighborhood during the day may have no idea who is supposed to be there at the time. Is that a jogger running along the sidewalk, casually glancing to and fro? Or is it a cat burglar inspecting the neighborhood for likely homes to enter? Most homes are closed to view, with drapes and blinds drawn, or foliage surrounding the yards. How, possibly, could the police be expected to prevent or catch anyone trying an illegal entry?

HOW DO INTRUDERS GET IN?

Law enforcement agencies estimate that in about 25 percent of burglaries there's no forced entry. An unlocked side or back door or an easy-to-open window provides entrance. That says a lot. It says that all exterior doors, including those leading to an attached garage, should be equipped with dead bolts and reinforced lock plates. Ground floor windows, too, should also have locks. If a simple to open door or window is not available to an intruder, and the intruder believes that no one is home and he's not being observed by anyone, then force is the next most popular means of entry. That usually means kicking in a back or side door, using a pry bar, wrenching off a lock cylinder or door handle, or breaking a window. It's ironic that front doors are generally the most sturdy entryways, but the least likely to be tried by burglars . . . except in one situation: when people are working in their backyards. When at home, most homeowners feel comfortable leaving their doors unlocked, especially in neighborhoods with low crime rates. Similarly, they leave their doors unlocked while they're outside working or playing in the yard. Some burglars specialize in walking through neighborhoods, looking for homeowners who are mowing the lawn, painting, shoveling snow, or having a barbecue in the backyard. Intruders gain entry through the unlocked front door while the homeowner is occupied, or through the back door if the homeowner is in the front yard. A thief needs only a few minutes to rifle through bedroom dressers or closets. And even if nothing of value gets stolen, there's the dangerous opportunity for the thief to be surprised and confronted by the homeowner or another member of the household.

For sure, burglars do not want to spend a lot of time working on illegal entry. And that's the key to preventing intruders from selecting your residence as a target. You've got to place formidable obstacles in a thief's way. Up the odds of his being discovered while he's working on the entry. Make him have to "earn" his burglary. Increase the likelihood that he'll be defeated in his efforts, or that he'll give up shortly after starting to try, or that he'll simply pass by your home for another residence he feels will be easier to enter. The longer a burglar thinks an entry will take, the less the likely he'll want to go for it—unless he can work safely, out of anyone's sight, in complete darkness during the night, hidden from the possibility of accidentally being seen.

One way of inviting trouble is to leave the garage door open when the garage is attached to the house. A burglar can enter the garage and close the doors, giving himself a sheltered, private place to work on the household door, often with tools supplied by the homeowner conveniently stored on a garage workbench.

Of course, it almost goes without saying that doors and windows should be locked, even when you're home. Does that mean you can never have natural ventilation again? No. There are ways of locking doors and windows partway open. See chapter seventeen on doors and windows.

STRANGERS IN THE NIGHT, AND DAY

Who must you protect yourself from? Largely from strangers or from dishonest persons who may want to steal from you or cause you physical or mental harm. Unfortunately, you'd best develop a skeptical attitude toward strangers. Avoid telling the person who delivers your dry cleaning to drop off the clothing in the bedroom, where there could be some jewelry set out on your dresser for a party the next night. It's a temptation for the delivery person. Or he may tell someone else, in all innocence, and the information may then get passed along to yet another person who may think you have expensive tastes and belongings available to be stolen. Things happen like that, odd series of coincidences that lead to unfortunate occurrences—all because a stranger sees the wrong thing, or makes a snap judgement based on what was perceived as an opportunity at your expense.

Keep valuables—at home or on the road—out of sight. Don't tempt fate. Many crimes are acts of opportunity. A person sees something valuable laying in full view, unprotected, and instantly, a decision is made to steal the item because it can be taken with little risk. Don't keep valuable silver, coin collections or crystal on display in or near a window.

Don't fall victim to scams and unfortunate situations at home or away by trusting or trying to help the wrong people. Stories you hear from police and other law enforcement officials are true. If you see someone else having apparent difficulties, consider that if you respond personally on the spot, you may be jeopardizing your own safety. In most situations the safest tactic is to call for help from somewhere safe. Think of the troubles that good samaritans have had. What of carjackers who bump a car from behind and fake an accident? Or how about people who show up at the door, feigning some emergency and wanting to use the phone—and one individual makes the phone call while a partner "needs" to use the bathroom and ends up stealing items from the master bedroom? We freely tell children never to trust strangers, yet time after time adults will let people they hardly know into their homes.

Now that we've addressed who we're protecting ourselves from, what preventive measures can be taken to discourage burglars and other potential intruders from selecting your residence?

LANDSCAPING

The first consideration in outdoor security is how your home is perceived through the eyes of a potential burglar or intruder. Some homes seem to encourage illegal entries, while others do not. One important characteristic is the home's landscaping and how the dwelling sets on the lot. Most of today's homeowners opt to be as far away from the street as possible. Backyards are sacrificed for spacious, wooded front yards. Home buyers are looking for secluded homes, set back from the street, nestled in trees. Unfortunately, that's exactly what professional burglars are looking for, too.

When considering the security of your own home, ask yourself first, if the main entrances to your home and garage are clearly visible from the street or from the homes of neighbors? If the answer is "no" because of a tree, shrub, wall, shed or other feature that could be removed or relocated, then consider removing whatever is in the line of sight. Trimming or removing foliage or other landscaping accents that block an open view of your home's entrances will certainly give you added protection (see Figures 16-1 and 16-2). If a potential intruder feels that he may be seen—even from afar—while

trying to break into a residence, that place will not be as appealing to him.

Privacy or Protection?

Somewhere along the line you've got to come to grips with the privacy/protection issue. What's privacy to you can provide security to a burglar. But there are ways of achieving partial privacy without giving away the farm. Leave openings available through which entrances can be seen; a gap in some hedges, for example. Pick out the easiest, most likely point for an illegal entry and consider how you can make it less appealing to a burglar. Trim trees and shrubs near doors and windows. Again, don't let your residence be overwhelmed and enveloped by foliage that can "creep up" on your house year after year. You've seen houses before where shrubs and trees planted decades ago have literally surrounded the dwellings, so practically nothing of the homes can be seen from the road. Landscape experts keep major trees and vegetation away from the home's perimeter, while locating dwarf and smaller specimens near the home. All vegetation and trees near a house should be kept snugly trimmed. Lower tree branches should be a minimum of seven feet off the ground (see Figure 16-3) so no one can climb the tree easily to get a better view through second story windows or to step onto a second floor deck or through an upper window. Shrubs should be kept to a height of less than three feet, unless planted near a part of the house with no windows or doors. Shrubs and hedges are more intruder resistant if they're of the prickly or thorny variety.

Trim foliage with your neighbor's views in mind as well. Look at the sides and back of your home from your neighbors' locations. Can your back or side door be seen? Again, keep doorways, windows and porches clear when planting tall bushes and flowers.

Think carefully before installing a high wooden fence around a back or side yard. Some high fences are designed to keep intruders out, while others simply conceal intruders from the street or a neighbor. If a fence is higher than forty inches, it's best to use a chain-link design, so it can be seen through. If not, once in your yard, intruders can go

Figure 16-1. Foliage-blocked entrance.

unmolested in an anxiety-free environment while working on an illegal entry.

LIGHTING

As many as half of home burglaries occur during daylight hours. Why during the day? Well, with more people living alone and more working couples, more houses are unoccupied during the day. Simple as that. Nighttime burglars prefer homes that have no outside lighting so they can work unseen. One way to discourage entry is to arrange for good lighting around entrances and other places that an intruder could use to gain access. Adequate lighting, both inside and out, can be a powerful deterrent, and can be well worth the cost of the fixtures and the electricity to run them.

Strategically placed outdoor lighting is extremely important to residential security, because a single-family home, unlike an apartment building, or condominium or other type of residence, offers an intruder a number of potential entry points. These other residences may require lighting at entrances and parking areas, but lighting the exteriors of those places is not usually the residents' responsibility.

Outdoor lighting fixtures should be installed high enough to prevent tampering (see Figure 16-4). Their design should be such that a person can't simply snip a wire or unscrew a bulb to knock a unit out of service. A sixty watt bulb is the minimum suggested strength, unless the fixtures are of a purely decorative nature. Powerful floodlights are also an option. They can illuminate an entire side of a house, yard and all. Whenever possible, strive to have all entryways sufficiently illuminated to make prowlers readily visible from inside the house,

Figure 16-2. Open entrance.

as well as from the street or from homes nearby.

If there aren't any other homes near your residence—if you live in the country, for instance—then lighting, while important, is not as effective a deterrent, especially if a potential intruder believes that no one is home. In that case, more effort must go into burglar proofing the home through mechanical devices, dogs, alarms and similar tactics.

Standard Security Lights

One way to provide added protection is to turn an existing light in your home or yard into an automatic nighttime security light that works without a timer or new wiring of any kind. Screw a "sensor" socket that's available from security companies or lighting stores into the present socket, then insert any standard bulb up to the maximum wattage recommended for the socket. The light will automatically turn on at dusk or whenever light levels reach a low enough intensity (such as during a storm on a heavily overcast day). It will turn off automatically at dawn, or can be switched off and on manually. The brightness of the bulb will be reduced however, when the sensor socket is in place.

When preparing to install sensor sockets, record any model numbers or identification information from the existing fixtures so the electric supply store's representative can check the compatibility of what you are planning to install in your fixtures. Better yet, have an electrician see that you won't be making modifications that could overload a system—especially with older homes on fuse box systems.

In any case, if an electrician will be involved, try to decide on all lighting changes you plan to make in advance, then have the changes completed dur-

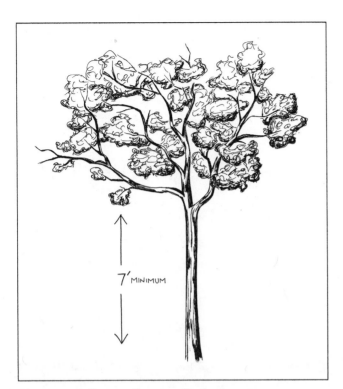

Figure 16-3. Seven-foot tree limb clearance.

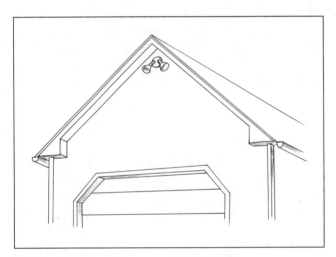

Figure 16-4. Outdoor security light fixture.

ing the same service call. That will prevent the need for additional service calls and you'll be sure that the entire system will work properly and safely on your electrical circuits.

Motion-Sensitive Security Lights

Decorative outdoor lights can also be turned into motion-sensitive fixtures—fixtures that will have potential burglars guessing if there is anyone home when the light turns on as the thief walks into the light's range. Simply purchase a ready-to-go unit

and screw it into the existing socket of an outdoor lighting fixture. A passive infrared sensor turns on the light when motion is detected up to sixty feet away within an arc of about 110 degrees (and covering an area of up to about two-thousand square feet) (see Figure 16-5). It adjusts easily in any direction. The light can be set to stay on for one to twenty minutes, and can be turned on and off manually as well. It takes standard bulbs of up to about seventy-five watts and is prevented from being activated during daylight hours by means of a photoelectric cell that "recognizes" the daylight, and shuts the system down.

These motion detecting lights can be especially effective if mounted away from the house: on the peak of a garage, for example, or on a nearby utility pole ten or more feet off the ground. Bulbs for these fixtures should be covered with shatterproof plastic or wire mesh to prevent damage from rocks or other thrown objects.

Solar-Powered Outdoor Lights

One way of providing inexpensive or "free" lighting is to use solar powered, wireless pathway lights that can provide up to ten hours of light. Replaceable nickel cadmium batteries repeatedly store and supply energy captured from the sun. The batteries provide up to three years of service. These solar lamps are usually installed in the ground on stakes that adjust up to twelve inches high. The units are weatherproof and impact resistant, and because they're wireless, with no cables or wires, they're a safe choice for use around spas, pools, decks or patios, and can be relocated easily. Of course, they aren't a total answer to home security, but they can brighten up walkways (see Figure 16-6) and add a lot of free light to the front, side or backyard of your property.

Vary Your Lighting

A common mistake of many homeowners is to turn on outside lights only when leaving the house. To a burglar that's been casing a home, that could be a positive sign that the owners are gone. A better option would be to give a residence an occupied look at all times by means of remote control timers or photosensitive timers that turn lights off and on automatically. Then periodically

Figure 16-5. A motion-sensitive security light.

change the times that the lights are turned on so no exact patterns can be recognized.

Streetlights

In many single-family neighborhoods, streetlamps cast enough light to take care of the fronts of homes along the way, providing adequate illumination between the street and the front entrances. Naturally, the amount of light is influenced by the amount of setback or distance from the street to the homes,

Figure 16-6. Solar-powered outdoor lights.

and by the general terrain, the foliage, the location of fences and other landscaping features, and the position of the house itself. A well-lighted street or property decreases the chances of a burglary in several ways. Neighbors and people passing by are more likely to see and remember suspicious people, vehicles and behavior if a street is well lit. And the presence of good lighting eases the minds of residents as well, which makes them feel safer. That's a strong point by itself, since persistent fear of crime can be almost as unsettling as crime itself. Report burned out or broken streetlights as soon as you notice them.

Where streetlights are not present, or where they don't provide enough illumination, install porch lights and exterior lights positioned high enough up on the home, perhaps affixed to the roof eaves, so they cannot be tampered with. The same goes for lights over a garage, which will illuminate the driveway area and surroundings as needed to allow adequate visibility from inside the house and for safe walking from the street or garage into the house. Entrances should be bright enough for you to identify callers before you open the door, and potential hiding places nearby should be illuminated.

If streetlight poles are either too far apart or if the landscaping is too dense, you could enlist the aid of your neighbors and together approach your local highway or public works department to improve the situation.

KEYS

Keys. Don't let them fall into a stranger's hands. Avoid attaching your name or your address to your keys. If they're lost or stolen, they can provide easy access for a burglar. If you suspect your entire wallet, gym bag or purse—with your identification and keys—is stolen, immediately have your home and car locks changed. The same goes if you move into a new home or apartment. Avoid giving keys to maintenance or delivery people.

Never leave your house keys and car keys together with attendants at public parking lots or repair garages. Not everyone in the place may be trustworthy. Your house keys can be duplicated quickly while you're at a theater, restaurant or ball game, and your address may be found on something in the glove compartment or back seat.

Some individuals believe they can successfully hide an extra house or car key outdoors or under mats, flowerpots, over moldings, or even in fake rocks. If you can hide it, a burglar may be able to find it. If you want an extra key nearby, leave one with a trusted neighbor.

There are a number of battery-powered key chains on the market that will do more than just hold your keys. One ring, when pulled apart, starts a shrill alarm over one hundred decibels loud. It also converts into a door or window alarm for use at home or on the road, alerting you to possible intruders. If that's not enough, a heat-sensing mechanism and fuse lets the unit act as a portable life-saving fire alarm.

MAILBOX AND HOUSE IDENTIFICATION

Avoid putting your name on your mailbox or other places outside your home, such as on a front door. That can make it too easy for a potential thief to get your phone number, call, and learn when you're not home.

On the other hand, your house number should be easily visible from the street during all hours. If it isn't possible to read your house number from the street at night without using a flashlight, you should consider lighting the number or having a visible number painted on the curb in front of your house. That's mainly so law enforcement and fire agencies can locate your house in an emergency.

Figure 16-7. House identification number.

It's best to use numbers at least six inches high that are made of reflective materials or use black numerals against a white background (see Figure 16-7). Avoid numbers written out in script—they can be confusing. If your house is not visible or is set back far from the street, post the house number at the driveway entrance or on the mailbox. If you live in a corner house, make sure the number faces the street that's named in your address.

LADDERS

In some neighborhoods it's a common practice to store bulky items behind garages. One of those items could be a long ladder. Do not leave ladders loose outdoors. If you cannot store them inside, at least lock them securely. Suggest that your neighbors do the same. Look at the exterior of your home. Are there sturdy trellises that could be climbed? Or any types of landscaping, drainpipes, cables, statues or fixtures that could be scaled to a second story window?

NEIGHBORHOOD SUPPORT

One way that citizens can help make their neighborhoods safer places to live in is through the organization of "block watch," neighborhood patrol, or crime watch groups. These groups have worked well in a variety of housing projects, on city blocks, in trailer parks and other neighborhoods. Contact your local police department or sheriff's office. They'll generally sponsor a neighborhood watch program. Although law and order is a government responsibility, who can deny that today's government can use all the help it can get? Citizens are saying they have had enough—especially in unusually dangerous areas. Together, neighborhood residents can safely provide supplementary protection for their homes and neighborhoods.

Neighborhood crime watches or patrols have a number of advantages.

1. Patrols are relatively inexpensive to maintain. Since they consist of volunteers, no large labor costs are incurred. Police car patrols may be used, but they're rarely efficient, because police departments can't afford to spend a lot of time in such a restricted area. Today's police budgets are inadequate for preventive patrolling of residential areas. There are too many areas and not enough officers, and many of the areas are not visible from a cruising police car. Because the patrolmen on watch must respond to radio calls, they're reluctant to leave their cars except in response to a call. Adding more police to the force solely for patrolling would result in higher taxes than the public is usually willing to pay. By comparison, citizen patrols are relatively inexpensive, because they're not made up of professional policemen or guards. It's important to point out, at the same time, that these patrols are to deter crime, not to apprehend or confront potential intruders or to stop a crime in action.

2. Patrols can be effective in performing surveillance functions. Intensive police training is not really needed to observe suspicious things in a neighborhood. Having residents on the watch is a plus, and if publicly known, is an effective deterrent to potential intruders. Because neighborhood patrols receive plenty of help from residents, the patrols are more likely to be at the right place at the right time. Patrols can write down license plate numbers of any strange car, truck, van or other vehicle seen in a neighborhood.

3. Patrols take advantage of existing behavior patterns. Generally, people tend to come together to take action in response to stressful situations. Patrols are a realistic group action. They use a resource—spare time—that many people have, and they do not require substantial amounts of other resources, such as money, uniforms and other supplies. Patrols are also highly visible and therefore reassuring to those worried about crime.

4. Patrols indirectly improve the individual's ability to deal with crime. Experience on a civilian patrol is likely to make each member more aware of security needs. He or she will be more alert to suspicious behavior or crime within the neighborhood even when not on patrol, and will know how to report a crime and will be more willing to do so.

5. Patrols contribute to other desirable social goals as well. They are likely to result in greater local cohesiveness, which in turn improves the ability of residents to band together in common action to meet other problems. It fosters improved attitudes and cooperation among residents. One other windfall of the neighborhood watch is that everyone is pulling on the same end of the anti-crime rope at all times.

Crime experts are unanimous on one point—the homeowner's best defense against burglars is watchful neighbors. How is such a system installed? Call your police department and ask if they will send out someone to speak about crime prevention if you get some of your neighbors together. Police departments love the help. It will make their jobs a lot easier and it lets them share anti-crime materials with receptive individuals. After a date is set for your first meeting, post flyers around the neighborhood. Include the date, the place and time of the meeting, and encourage people to attend. Then follow the steps recommended by the officer to make homes in your neighborhood less inviting to burglars.

If possible, know your neighbors in the houses around you. Establish a regular meeting time and place to get together with your neighbors for a few minutes. Exchange names, and home and work telephone numbers among the participants. A hand-drawn street map can also be helpful. Or have someone copy one out of the county map book and duplicate it, writing the names and phone numbers of individual residents in the neighborhood. Also place emergency names and phone numbers on the map. Be aware of when residents and neighbors normally come and go, the cars they drive, and what the typical day usually brings. Watch out for one another.

It can also pay to be suspicious. Report to the police any strangers loitering in your neighborhood or people asking strange or vague questions about your neighbors and their whereabouts. Be alert for unusual activities. If you see an unknown person in or around a neighbor's yard, don't be afraid to check his or her identity with your neighbor by phone.

Keep a trusted neighbor informed if your house will be unoccupied for an extended period. It's important to leave him or her a way of reaching you if an emergency should arise. Do the same for your neighbor. This includes collecting one another's mail, newspapers, and other deliveries that could indicate at a glance that no one is home.

Establish and attend regular neighborhood meetings with your local crime prevention officer. Find out about local crime trends and what you can do about them.

Some neighborhoods do not lend themselves well to the concept of patrols. That's because of the general mistrust that's built up over the years. Neighbors may not know who is living next to them. Some families prefer to remain anonymous, and only plan on living in a place for a few years.

It depends on the neighborhood makeup. The areas where people tend to keep to themselves will be likely candidates for alarm systems instead of the more social neighborhood patrols.

WHAT TO DO IF YOU'RE ROBBED

If you come home and see that an illegal entry has occurred, don't go inside. An intruder could still be there.

Call the police immediately from a neighbor's phone. Protect the scene. Don't touch anything, and don't walk around the house, because vital evidence could be destroyed needlessly. Leave everything exactly as you find it. Don't attempt a personal investigation. Let the police handle it.

Provide the police with a detailed, itemized list of stolen property, including any identifying marks. For a small, refundable deposit, you may be able to borrow an electric engraving tool to inscribe an assigned identification number on many of your belongings. (Do not use your social security number; the Social Security Adminstration is prohibited by law from providing information about individual numbers.) The engraving tool may also come with decals for your home's doors to announce to a burglar that your items have already been marked—and are less useful to the burglar.

OUTDOOR SECURITY QUICK CHECKLIST

☐ While you're outdoors in your yard or in the neighborhood, get into the habit of locking the doors you cannot see.

☐ Close and lock your garage doors while you're at home or away.

☐ Keep delivery persons and strangers outside of your residence whenever possible.

☐ Respond to someone else's apparent difficulties (such as a flat tire or broken down vehicle) in a way that guarantees safety for yourself.

☐ The entrances to your home and garage should be clearly visible from the street or from neighbors' homes.

☐ Trim foliage away from your home so it can't be used to hide in or to access a second story level.

☐ Fences higher than forty inches should be of a chain-link design.

☐ Entrances should be well lit at night or, at the very least, the home's perimeter should be covered by motion detector lamps.

☐ Eliminate shadows near the sides of the house.

☐ Some lights inside or outdoors should be operated by a timer to make the residence appear to be occupied when you're not there.

☐ Complex lighting systems should be installed by professionals.

☐ Have outdoor lights mounted out of tampering reach and covered with shatterproof plastic or wire mesh.

☐ Consider using solar-powered "night" lights to illuminate walkways, poolsides or decks with "no-cost" lighting.

☐ Streetlights should adequately illuminate the front yard and entrance of your house.

☐ Illuminate the area outside your garage at night, especially if there's a detached garage.

☐ All of the entrances to your home should be lighted brightly enough for you to identify callers at night before you open the door.

OUTDOOR SECURITY QUICK CHECKLIST

(continued)

☐ Illuminate or eliminate all nearby potential hiding places.

☐ Approach local authorities to improve your street's lighting if needed.

☐ Keep your house keys to yourself. When dropping off your car keys at a mechanic's shop, remove your house keys first.

☐ Never put your phone number and address on your key chain.

☐ Avoid hiding extra keys on the outside of your residence. Give one to a trusted neighbor instead.

☐ Don't put your name on your mailbox or anywhere else on the outside of your home.

☐ Your house number should be easy to read from the street during all hours.

☐ Lock ladders in a garage or inside the house.

☐ Remove trees, trellises, or anything else that could be climbed to enter a second story deck or window.

☐ If possible, help your neighborhood or block organize a crime watch or patrol. Look out for your neighbor's safety and ask them to look out for yours.

☐ Inform a trusted neighbor when you're not going to be home for an extended period, and provide the neighbor with a way to contact you in case of an emergency.

☐ Ask your local crime prevention officer for the latest anti-crime information.

☐ If you come home to an apparent illegal entry, an intruder may be in your residence. Refrain from entering, then call the police from another location.

CHAPTER 17

DOORS, WINDOWS AND LOCKS

Most thieves, burglars and house-breakers are not professionals. Despite being portrayed on television and movies as articulate, multitalented individuals who can pick combination locks with hairpins, scale buildings with grappling hooks, and dress in stylish cat-burglar black leotards and ski masks, in real life they're not that clever. Rather, most house burglars are amateurs, opportunists who can rarely resist the temptation of an unlocked door or open window. They do have some things in common with "career" burglars though—they worry about the same three things:

- Delay in getting into your home
- Being forced to work where they can be observed
- Having to make noise in the process.

In other words, burglars don't want to cause a commotion. They don't want to get caught. That means with both amateur or professional thieves, besides well-designed landscaping, one of the best ways to discourage an unlawful home entry is to have sturdy doors and windows with good locks. Burglars will typically pass by a house that has good door and window locks and other characteristics that will delay or announce their entry.

Discouraging intruders from selecting your home is not just to prevent theft of your belongings, but to prevent injury to yourself or your loved ones. Although crimes of violence occur much less frequently than crimes against property, crimes against property—such as burglary—can quickly turn into crimes of violence if an intruder is discovered and confronted.

DOORS

Doors, of course, are planned points of entry and exit to and from a house or other building. From a security standpoint, types of doors include exterior doors, interior doors, and doors to garages and storage buildings.

Exterior Doors

Most exterior doors are of the "man door" design. With apologies to women and children who use the

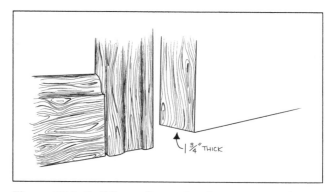

Figure 17-1. Solid wood exterior door construction.

same doors, a man door is any door hinged at one side so it swings open horizontally for people to walk through. In addition to providing privacy and security, exterior doors can serve as effective weather barriers and sound reducers. They're typically about 1¾ inches thick, between 2 feet 8 inches and 3 feet wide, and at least 6 feet 8 inches high (see Figure 17-1). There should always be a secure layer of weather stripping around an exterior door's edges to ensure a tight weather seal. Generally, a safe, high-quality exterior door offers adequate protection if it's installed or "hung" in a well-fitted frame and secured by a quality single-cylinder deadbolt lock. Here are some questions to ask yourself about each of your exterior doors:

- Does it operate easily and reliably?
- Does it close securely?
- Does it permit easy passage of people and objects?
- Will it effectively close off whatever is supposed to be closed off?
- Will it retard the spread of fire?
- Will it permit me to see to the other side?
- Can it cause injury if someone walks into it?

On the other hand, what does a potential intruder look for in an exterior door? Beyond a dark, private work area outside of the door, hidden from view, there are some things a thief knows that you should know. Unlocked doors are easiest to enter, obviously. A flimsy, hollow-core door can be reduced to splinters with a few blows from a claw hammer. A hollow-core exterior door is a security risk, pure and simple. They can be cut, drilled or sawed through with relative ease for direct access to the inner workings of the door's lock.

Rotting doors or doorframes make for easier entry. The areas in a doorframe around lock and hinge areas are extremely important. What good is a strong door and lock if the frame is weak? A burglar can gain entrance by simply prying the frame away from the door.

Prying tools can easily be inserted into wide spaces between a door and its frame. Check the fit of exterior doors while they're closed. There should be no more than one-sixty-fourth of an inch between the door and frame so the door cannot be pried away from the frame (see Figure 17-2). Doors with more "play" should be repaired and rehung or replaced.

Removable hinges positioned on the outside surface of a door will permit the door's removal simply with the removal of a few screws. Or, the pins

Figure 17-2. Exterior door close fit.

on the hinges could simply be pried up and out with a screwdriver. Exterior doors should be hung on three hinges, with extra-long screws. If there's a need for an exterior door to swing outward, nonremovable hinge pins should be used.

To prevent the removal of a door having outside hinge pins, remove the middle screws from each hinge—one from each half of each hinge, both where the screws are fastened to the door and to the doorframe. Then drill one-inch deep holes through the empty hinge screw holes in the door. Next, drive all but one inch of twenty-penny nails into each empty hinge hole in the doorframe, directly opposite the empty, drilled hinge screw holes in the door. Cut the nail heads (not the whole protruding nail part) off with a hacksaw. Then, when the door is closed, the hole in the hinge leaf on the door should close over the protruding nail that's affixed to the frame. After that's accomplished, the closed door cannot be lifted out of place even if its hinge pins are pried loose (see Figure 17-3).

Another method of securing exterior hinge pins is to weld the pins to the hinge. It's effective, but permanent as well.

Glass or plastic panels or panes can be broken

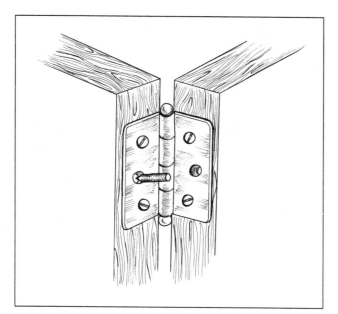

Figure 17-3. A secured hinge.

Figure 17-4. Exterior door peephole.

to permit a burglar to reach in and unlock the door from the inside.

If windows or glass panes are located within forty inches of a doorknob or handle that can be opened from the inside consider changing the arrangement or installing a grill over the glass, using nonremovable screws. A more expensive option is to replace the windowpanes with special shatterproof, see-through, polycarbonate panels. Unfortunately, many homes have a side or rear door with large glass panels. It's a simple matter for a burglar to break a small corner of the glass panel, reach in, and unlock the door. Instead, exterior doors should have quality glass peepholes with a viewing field of 180 degrees (see Figure 17-4). Plastic peephole lenses will fog, scratch or deteriorate in a short while.

Cheaply made combination key-in-the-knob door handles/locks can be snapped off the door by placing a widemouthed section of pipe over the outside doorknob and pushing down on the far end of the pipe. Since about 65 percent of all home burglars enter their prey's households through a door, exterior man doors should be resistant to being forced or "jimmied" open. That leads into a review of their construction. Most exterior doors are made of wood, steel or various composites such as fiberglass, or combinations of those materials.

Exterior Wood Doors

There are two basic styles of exterior wood doors: flush and paneled. A flush door is a simple flat-surfaced door constructed with a particle board or solid lumber core between two outer surfaces of durable wood, such as a high-grade fir. Solid lumber core doors are much stronger—a safer choice, and more expensive. Paneled exterior doors have decorative designs cut into them. The design cuts could, however, considerably weaken individual door panels, and may result in doors that are easier to break into. Although they're attractive to look at, the beveling or cutting that produced the design may make the panels so thin at the edges that they could be shattered loose by a hard kick.

The safest wood doors are solid, flush wood models that are tightly fitted within sturdy frames. But if not taken care of—which means periodically sanding or planing, and then painting or varnishing wood sections—even the strongest solid wood door may expand, warp, crack, shrink, or develop gaps around its doorframe. A wood door is also combustible.

To strengthen exterior doors made of wood, add sheet metal to one side of each door. The finished doors may not be particularly good looking, but they would reduce the likelihood of an illegal entry.

Composite or Fiberglass Exterior Doors

These doors can be made with wood-grain finishes and textures that so closely resemble real wood that it's practically impossible to tell them apart by just looking. Composite doors can combine good features of several materials: the strength of inner hardwood or steel layers and the weather resistant exterior of fiberglass. Fiberglass doors also need little maintenance other than an occasional cleaning.

Steel Exterior Doors

Most steel doors are really part steel and part wood: steel sheets fabricated around a wooden frame in which urethane foam or another insulation material is sandwiched to provide protection against cold and heat.

In general, steel doors are safer and more practical than doors made entirely of wood. Their structural strength makes them difficult to force open, and they're designed to prevent the principal cause of wood door failures—warpage that can result in improper closure and air filtration. They also have fire-resistant qualities that result in excellent safety ratings.

Exterior steel doors come in many styles and finishes and are commonly fitted with glass inserts or peepholes for viewing. The ones with magnetic gaskets along their edges that grip like those on a refrigerator door give the tightest seal against the weather. They're usually pre-hung so the frame and hinges are included with the door as a complete unit—an excellent defense against loosely installed doors that gape between door and frame, where a burglar could insert a prying tool.

When most people think about securing their doors, they may spend a lot of effort on front and back doors, while neglecting other doors and points of entry. Remember to consider garage, storage, side doors and patio doors that lead directly outside or into an area that has an exterior door. These doors are all fair game for an astute burglar. While elaborately designed steel doors are commonly marketed for front entrances, plain metal-clad versions with small viewing windows or peepholes are ideal for those side and "other" exterior doors found in garages, sheds, basements, kitchens and storage areas.

Too, watch out for sidelight windows: narrow glass panes or panels that can run the height of an entrance door, placed at one or both sides for added beauty and natural light. They can be susceptible to intruders, who, if the sidelights are not positioned correctly in relation to the door's locks, can break the glass, then reach inside to unlock the door.

Sliding Glass Doors

Sliding glass doors are usually situated at the back of a home, facing the rear of the property. That can give burglars plenty of confidence. Although most sliding doors consist of two glass panels, usually only one of them is movable. To safe-proof sliders, you must prevent an intruder from sliding the movable door open by force, and prevent him from prying the nonmovable door up and out of its track. A common way to prevent the movable panel's being forced open is to place a long wooden dowel or piece of broomstick in the bottom track. This is not foolproof, however, because it won't prevent someone from simply prying the door away from and out of its track. A special steel or wood bar that locks the sliding track, often called a "Charley bar," will prevent potential housebreakers from prying the panels off the door tracks (see Figure 17-5). The bar is attached to the doorframe and has a locking catch that is attached to the movable sliding door panel. The bar can be swung out of the way to permit normal opening and closing. Charley bars can be purchased at hardware, locksmith or builder's supply stores. In addition, the installation of a simple cylinder lock will pin a bolt through both doors where the doors overlap.

Keyed patio door locks with bolts that go, or are

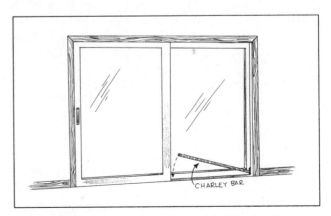

Figure 17-5. Sliding glass door with Charley bar.

"thrown," into a patio doorframe provide additional protection. They can be installed with tamper-proof screws. Other security devices include push-button locking mechanisms that secure the sliding and stationary panels together by pinning them where their two frames overlap (see Figure 17-6).

Figure 17-6. Sliding glass door push-button lock.

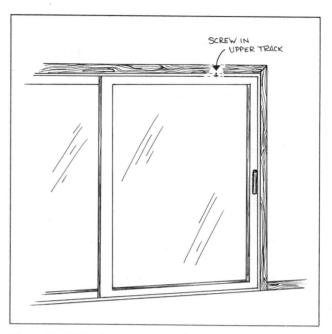

Figure 17-7. Reducing upper door track clearance.

When panels to glass sliding doors are installed, they are lifted into position so their tops slip up and into the top track. This allows the lower part of the door to clear the side of the bottom track, so the door can slide into and be held within the tracks. To prevent a burglar from lifting a panel up and out of the track, "Jimmy plates" or screws can be installed along the upper track to remove any vertical play remaining in the upper track. Although Jimmy plates provide the more secure option, the half-inch or so of upper track play can also be eliminated through the installation of pan-headed sheet-metal screws fastened vertically into the "top" of the upper track of the sliding panel, so there is a narrow clearance between the heads of the screws and the top of the sliding door panel (see Figure 17-7). If an intruder tries to pry or lift the door up and out of the door's bottom track, the screws will not give him enough vertical play to do so.

The quality of construction of sliding doors varies. Inexpensive designs feature malleable, lightweight aluminum frames and tracks that can be bent easily with a crowbar or other prying tool. The locking mechanisms that come with inexpensive doors are also inadequate; some can even be forced open by hand. Others secure only the sliding panel and completely ignore the stationary counterpart.

Garage Doors

An automatic garage bay door opener is the best way to secure a garage door. It will automatically lock the door from the outside. As with all kinds of components, however, some automatic openers are more secure than others. The more inexpensive units may be susceptible to opening from "other" electronic signals, including those from other opener transmitters, from stray radio signals, and from practically any electronic disturbances. The more expensive units are likely to include interference filters to eliminate such problems.

Basement Slanting-Hatch Doors

These old-fashioned doors were typically constructed over stairways leading outdoors from basements. Make sure wood planking, door hinges, old locks and other parts cannot easily be pried open from the outside. Prefabricated steel replacement doors installed in a concrete base offer improved security when used with sturdy locking mechanisms.

Pet Doors

Many homes have pet doors installed next to a side or rear entrance. Several companies manufacture ready-to-install units that are two-way, self-closing, silent, chew proof, energy efficient and even lock-able. But think twice before installing one for your St. Bernard. Small pet doors are fine, as long as they don't permit a slender burglar to enter through them or permit an exterior door to be unlocked from the pet door's opening.

Doors to Outside Storage Sheds and Buildings

If you only store inexpensive lawn maintenance equipment or yard furniture in outbuildings, you may not need tamper resistant locks on the doors. But if the storage building contains various cutting, sawing, prying, hammering, or other demolition-type tools, the door locks better be sturdy. You don't want a potential intruder to have a smorgasbord of burglar tools at her disposal. Ladders also must be kept out of a burglar's hands.

Interior Doors

Interior doors operate in the same way as their exterior cousins, but they aren't exposed to the great outdoors. So you needn't be *as* concerned with locking mechanisms, insulation qualities and weatherproofing. There are several locations where you may want to locate exterior-type doors inside your home. One is the man door leading from a kitchen or other area into a garage. Another is a similar door leading to a basement. If an intruder happens to get into either area, the garage or basement, a low security interior door will not keep him out of the house. But other than those areas, or similar ones, most interior doors are chosen with two major factors in mind: privacy and noise reduction. To be effective, they must be well fitted.

If the house heating system depends on a free flow of air from room to room, interior doors should be undercut by at least a one-half inch above the finished floors to permit air passage. This does not apply to doors bordering areas with their own air supplies and return outlets or doors leading to any unheated areas such as garages, basements and attics.

Interior doors can be built out of wood, plastic, metal or any combination thereof. A solid wood door is a good choice. It's made by sandwiching a wooden core between two sheets of high quality hardwood veneer such as birch, oak, mahogany or

pine. A solid-core door clad with metal is another good option. Lighter duty hollow-core doors can have the same expensive veneer faces, but sheets of wood-grain plastic also make a practical, easy to clean surface. The lowest priced hollow-core models are frequently covered with less durable wood composition board.

If you have a choice, lean toward solid-core flush doors. They provide greater security, better insulation from heat and sound, and more fire resistance and rigidity than hollow-core flush doors.

Interior doors should generally swing into the rooms they close off from hallways. Otherwise they can interfere with hallway traffic. A door at the head of a stairway must—for safety's sake—swing away from the stairs.

WINDOWS

Windows come in all shapes and sizes. They come in single-panes, double-panes and triple-panes. They come in different types of glass and Plexiglas. They come with special coatings and they come plain. They come in wood frames, metal frames, plastic frames and combination frames. Some can be opened. Others can't. Most are see-through clear. Some are partially transparent, or translucent, like "frosted" glass.

A home without windows is difficult to imagine. That's because windows provide a lot of advantages. They allow natural lighting into a home. They admit fresh air for ventilation. They provide access for passive solar-heating sun rays. They provide openings in the house's outer shell for air conditioning units. They allow household members to view the outdoors from inside. And they provide exits to those same outdoors in case of emergencies.

Conversely, windows can turn a house into a goldfish bowl by enabling outsiders to see into the interior living areas. And when not secured properly, windows can provide encouragement to burglars and other intruders. If a window is locked or secured, it's unlikely that a burglar will break the glass to release a lock. Shattering glass attracts attention—just what the burglar wants to avoid.

Although every window should have a way to be locked, it's also important that windows can be opened and closed easily, especially windows located in bedrooms, in case they are needed during a fire or other emergency. If a wood window frame does not slide as easily as it should, rubbing the channel with a piece of paraffin or an old wax candle should help. Another method is to spray the tracks with a silicone lubricant.

Basement Windows

Basement windows are a favorite target of burglars since they are often out of sight and poorly constructed. The glass in basement windows can be replaced with Plexiglas or polycarbonate. Basement windows can also be secured with functional, yet decorative, grilles or bars that have a safety latch for inside opening and with simple latches that can be pinned in a locked position (see Figure 17-8).

Figure 17-8. A basement window lock.

Double-Hung Windows

Double-hung windows are probably the most commonly used today. They operate upward and downward, and lock with a simple metal latch. Approach a locked double-hung window from the outside. Try sticking a knife blade up into the crack between the two halves of the window and see if you can jiggle the latch with it. An experienced housebreaker can open all but the most tight fitting windows in this manner. Older windows often suffer from dry rot around their latches, and the screws that fasten the latch to the wood can easily be pulled out.

You can secure double-hung windows in the

following way: When the window is closed, drill a neat hole through the top piece of the bottom window sash, at one side, all the way through and into the bottom part of the top sash. Then insert a metal bolt or pin (see Figure 17-9). Windows fixed this way are impossible to open from the outside. Make sure the pin or bolt protrudes slightly from its hole so you can remove it easily in case of an emergency. In the summer, when you want fresh air, drill holes into the top sash a few inches above the first hole. The window can then be opened slightly yet remain securely fastened. A rule of thumb is to never leave the window open more than five or six inches.

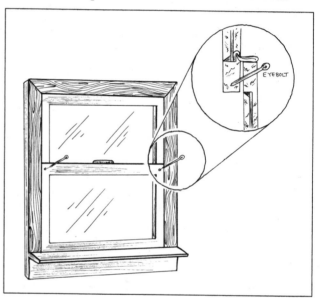

Figure 17-9. Securing a double-hung window.

Casement Windows

Casement windows crank open with handles. They're fairly difficult to open from the outside. Even more security can be achieved by removing the window handle when the window is not in use, and hanging or storing it nearby, more than an arm's length away, so that if someone breaks the glass there's no lever available to open the window. Make sure everyone in the household knows where the lever to each window is kept, in case the windows must be opened during an emergency.

Other Windows and Openings

Louvered windows are a security risk when positioned in an outside wall. They should be replaced.

Window air conditioners can also pose security problems, especially if they're hidden from view by shrubs or trees. Make sure air conditioning units are fastened to their openings and can't be pulled out or pushed in by a strong burglar.

Skylights can offer a burglar a private place to work on an entry, since the roof may not be visible from the street. Replace ordinary glass with a plastic polycarbonate. It has an impact resistance about three hundred times that of standard window glass. Use a strong hasp and padlock on the inside of the skylight sash to secure the sash to the skylight frame. Finally, if you think it's necessary, consider installing bars, grilles or grates on the inside of the frame, in case an intruder gets past the glass and defeats the lock.

Other types of windows can be protected with the installation of security bars that are designed to keep intruders out even if the window glass has been broken. The steel bars are mounted on the inside of the window and secured to the window frame with a three-inch screws. The bars should latch into a mounting bracket in such a way that they can be swung open from the inside if necessary.

Always check the security of windows that can be reached from a porch, garage, fence, tree or other makeshift "ladder."

LOCKS

Years ago, homes and apartments were constructed to last, with doors of thick oak and other hardwoods—sturdy, heavy, impossible to kick in. Unfortunately, their locks were often flimsy by comparison. Many were mortised locks that were recessed into a hole or slot cut from the door's outer edge near the knob. Sometimes their locking bolt fit securely into its frame receptacle, other times not. If the door was "hung loose" or wobbly, often only an eighth of an inch of bolt kept the door locked.

Most of the remaining old-fashioned locks had keyholes, the kind you can look through. They were operated by skeleton keys, the same keys that sell for under a dollar per set in any hardware store. They weren't too secure.

Because skeleton key locks are so easy to defeat (to open through picking or simply by using another skeleton key), many residents installed chain units to supplement their protection. A chain lock is a short chain permanently fastened to the door or doorframe that, when attached to its receiving fixture, prevents the door from being opened more than a few inches. Again, chain locks provide some margin of safety, but not much. All a determined intruder has to do is kick or smash the door with enough force to rip loose the screws holding the chain's receptacle to the door or frame.

Since the days of keyhole locks, other types of locks have been designed and manufactured. Some of them are safer, others are not. Some unsafe locks, in fact, are being used frequently in new construction because they're inexpensive to produce and easy to install.

Key-in-Knob Locks

These relatively new locks are called key-in-knob locks. To open the door from the outside you insert a key directly into a keyhole in the door knob, and turn. To lock it when leaving, you simply push a button on the inside doorknob, or push the inside knob and turn, then slam the door shut. The locking bolt is spring-operated.

A key-in-knob lock is the easiest modern lock to thwart. Unless anti-defeating features are built into the lock, it can be broken into by force or by "loiding." *Loiding* is a new word, invented in honor of the key-in-knob lock. You may not find it in your dictionary yet, but it comes from the word "celluloid." It means to open a lock by inserting a thin plastic strip (like a credit card) between the bolt and door frame or jamb so the plastic strip releases the spring-operated catch.

Most key-in-knob locks are constructed of flimsy materials. As mentioned earlier in the chapter, by placing a piece of widemouth pipe over the outside door handle, the knob can be snapped off. And because its locking bolt is always short and beveled, a crowbar or similar tool can often pry the door open from its frame.

Deadbolt Locks

If any doubts still exist in your mind of the security offered by key-in-knob locks, contact your local police department, and ask them what types of locks your exterior doors should have. They'll probably tell you that deadbolt locks are the best. A single-cylinder deadbolt, operated by a key from outside and a thumb-latch inside, throws a one-inch rectangular (not beveled) bolt into its receptacle, and if installed properly, cannot be pried or loided.

There is a hitch, however; if any glass is situated in or near the door, someone could break the glass from outside then reach in and turn the latch from the inside. If this is the case in your home, you could replace the glass with something sturdier, or you could replace the single-cylinder lock with a double-cylinder model—a lock operated by key from inside and out.

The first option is the safest. That's what most locksmiths and law enforcement agencies recommend. A lock that requires a key on the inside could be hazardous in case of a fire or other emergency.

Doors already equipped with a key-in-knob lock can be made safer by having good single-cylinder deadbolts installed above the key-in-knob lock (see Figure 17-10). Mortised deadbolt locks are probably the most secure since their bolt and locking mechanisms are contained within a metal case that is recessed into the door.

In most cases, strike plates (what the door bolt or latch locks into) should be fastened into the door frame or jamb with long screws, preferably three-inch. This setup will resist heavy blows or force that might otherwise defeat a lock by ripping the strike plate right out of the doorframe.

A lock cylinder with six pins instead of the typical five makes the lock substantially harder to pick open. Also, unusual key designs, such as dimpled faces, are harder to duplicate by illegal means.

Rim Auxiliary Locks

Another way to "strengthen" a door with a key-in-knob lock is to install a rim auxiliary lock (see Figure 17-11). Rim locks are considerably stronger than key-in-knob locks. The strongest rim locks are installed on the inside of a door; they feature through-the-door bolting with vertical or horizontal sliding deadbolts. Vertical deadbolts are best because they defend against an intruder who tries to spread the door from the doorjamb or frame—these models resemble a door hinge and pin. Both the rim lock and

Figure 17-10. Key-in-knob and deadbolt locks.

its mating plate should be installed with long screws (almost as long as the width of the door).

Electronic Locks

One newly marketed door lock can be operated with a transmitter you carry in your pocket or purse, similar to that of a slim garage door opener control. Another lock can be operated with either a key or by turning the knob after a three- or four-digit access code is entered. This means you could never accidentally lock yourself out, ever again.

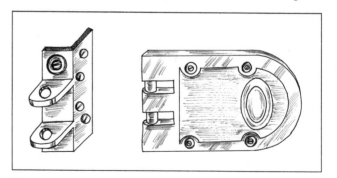

Figure 17-11. A rim-lock.

Temporary access codes can also be set up so guests, servicemen or relatives could let themselves in for some specific purpose without knowing your master code. Various alarm settings are available to scare off intruders who might try to turn the knob while attempting to guess the code.

New locking mechanisms are becoming available all the time. Check with several reputable locksmiths to review their offerings before you replace or add to your own door and window locks.

Other Lock and Key Considerations

Never hide keys outside your home. Burglars have found keys beneath ledges, under doormats, taped beneath downspouts, in hollow trees, beneath rocks in a garden, in birdbaths and other landscaping fixtures and accents.

Don't mark your keys with your name or address. If you're nervous about losing your keys, keep one or two extra sets, one at home, the other with a relative or trusted neighbor.

Get new locks or have lock tumblers re-keyed when you move into a previously occupied dwelling.

Before using a locksmith to do extensive lock work in your home, make sure you know something about his business. Research him as you would any other contractor.

DOOR, WINDOW AND LOCK QUICK CHECKLIST

☐ Exterior doors should be of solid-core wood, fiberglass or metal-clad construction. They should fit well within sturdy frames; there should be no more than a sixty-fourth of an inch between the door and frame. They should also be equipped with quality, single-cylinder deadbolt locks.

☐ Exterior door hinges should be positioned on the indoor side of the door, or nonremovable pins and hinges must be used.

☐ Glass or plastic panes or panels should not be located within forty inches of an exterior doorknob, handle or lock that can be opened from the inside.

☐ All exterior doors should be equipped with quality glass peepholes with a viewing field of 180 degrees.

☐ Children should have the ability to see out of all peepholes, perhaps through the use of a small step stool.

☐ Remember that all exterior doors — front, back, side, garage, storage area, basement and patio doors — must meet similar security specifications.

☐ Sliding glass doors should employ several locking/securing mechanisms, including a Charley bar and a cylinder or push-button lock. Vertical play in the upper door track should be eliminated through the installation of Jimmy plates or sheet-metal screws.

☐ Electric garage door openers should be equipped with interference filters to reduce the possibility of the door being opened by other electronic signals or disturbances.

DOOR, WINDOW AND LOCK QUICK CHECKLIST
(continued)

☐ Store cutting, prying, hammering and other demolition-type tools inside the home, not in a flimsy outside storage building, shed or garage.

☐ Exterior-type doors should be used as man doors leading from a kitchen or other indoor area to a garage, breezeway, sun room or shed.

☐ Solid-core flush interior doors provide greater security, better insulation from heat and sound, and more fire resistance and rigidity than hollow-core flush doors.

☐ Doors at the heads of stairways must swing away from stairs.

☐ Every window in a household should be able to be securely locked, including skylights.

☐ Bedroom windows should unlock and open easily, in case they are needed during a fire or other emergency. Never paint bedroom windows shut. Children should be able to unlock and open bedroom windows.

☐ Basement windows should be secured with grates or bars that can be unlocked and swung open from the inside. Consider replacing basement window glass with Plexiglas or polycarbonate.

☐ Double-hung windows, when opened up to six inches for ventialtion, should be temporarily pinned so they can't be raised further.

☐ Air conditioning window units should be fastened to their openings so the units cannot be pulled out or pushed in by a strong burglar.

☐ Exterior doors with key-in-knob handles and locks should also have single-cylinder deadbolt locks installed as a first line of security.

☐ Consider that the use of a double-cylinder deadbolt lock—which is operated by key on both sides of the door—can be dangerous if someone is trying to exit the house during an emergency.

☐ Keep a spare set of keys with a trusted neighbor, friend or relative instead of trying to hide keys outside your home.

☐ Get new locks or have lock tumblers re-keyed when you move into a previously occupied dwelling.

CHAPTER 18

HOME SECURITY ALARM SYSTEMS

Over the years, home alarm systems have been created or pieced together from a wide variety of components. Indeed, animals have been used for centuries to alert homeowners to strangers, and still are. In rural areas of Europe, flocks of geese are traditionally kept in fenced yards to provide early warning by their honking and hissing at strangers. Dogs, of course, are kept in practically every locale of the world for security. Other, more vicious, alarms once included concealed metal traps, covered pits, and assorted booby-traps. Trip wires or barbed wire that rang bells were also popular for many years.

DO YOU NEED AN ALARM SYSTEM?

Practically any home can benefit from an alarm system, but if your residence is unoccupied for regular intervals — when everyone is at work, for example — or for long periods of time when you're away on weekends or periodic week-long vacations, you should consider acquiring a good system, especially now that costs of reliable electronic alarm systems have dropped substantially. Other reasons for considering an alarm installation are if you live in an affluent neighborhood or keep antiques, coin collections, or other valuables at home, or if you live in a neighborhood where there's been a history of burglaries.

Individuals and families have different needs and lifestyles. A security alarm system should cus-tom-fit the household. A person who is mainly concerned about home protection when no one is at home would most likely need a central monitored alarm system, in which an illegal entry attempt triggers an alarm that is heard and noticed at a central location that's monitored twenty-four hours per day. On the other hand, people who spend more time at home and rarely go out, may want something less elaborate that would still discourage a potential intruder from attempting or continuing an entry, or at least something to keep the illegals out in the yard, with little possible access to the home's interior.

While certain systems can be installed by almost anyone who can read a set of instructions, it's likely that better protection is afforded by a professional installation. Experts know where to place the sensors and how — from past experience — certain situations demand little "tricks" that someone unexperienced would not likely see. Experts can tell in advance where *not* to place sensors, such as where sensors would give weak signals because of factors such as metallic foil in nearby wallpaper. If the installation is slipshod, a knowledgeable burglar can defeat the system a lot easier, by unscrewing outside bulbs, for example, or snipping telephone wires.

Naturally, to have or not to have a security alarm system is a judgement call, similar to buying insurance. The expense of insurance is usually perceived to be worthwhile when something bad happens. Same with security alarms. They're appreciated the most when they foil a burglary or other attempted intrusion. But they can also be kind to the pocketbook in another way: As a financial reward for having a security system, it's likely that you'll be able to save on the cost of your homeowner's insurance, from about 2 to 10 percent, the higher percentages coming mostly from systems with central location monitoring.

In every case, it's recommended that you call professionals first to analyze your security needs. Talk with the local police. Additional assistance may be available from government departments with officers who help taxpayers assess their vulnerability to burglaries and other illegal entries. Next, contact the National Burglar and Fire Alarm Association for a list of members in your area. If your state or area has a chapter, it should be listed in the yellow pages. If not, write to the national headquarters at 1133 15th Street, N.W., Washington, D.C. 20005.

Alarm companies will also do on-site surveys. Compare their products and services. How many clients do they have in your area? How long have they been in business? Can they provide demonstrations of how their systems work under actual field conditions?

TYPES OF ALARM SYSTEMS

Two basic alarm systems make up the lion's share of alarm systems purchased and installed in residential dwellings: in-house monitoring box systems and central monitoring systems.

The main question you'll have to ask yourself when shopping for alarm systems is which of the above is right for you.

In-House Monitoring Box Systems

A monitoring box or unit is located in an out-of-the-way place within the house. When activated by an intruder's entry attempts it will set off a loud horn, siren or bell. This system usually works fine as long as neighbors are close enough to hear and respond to the alarm if you're away. You'll be relying on neighbors or passersby to notify the police when an alarm is heard. What often happens, though, is that whoever hears the alarm ignores it, assuming that it is false. The chance of a police patrol hearing or

responding to the alarm within minutes is very remote indeed. It's more likely that the police will be called quite a while later, if the alarm doesn't stop by itself, after a neighbor finally tires of hearing the sound. In practice, local alarms offer little protection to unoccupied households beyond keeping an intruder from doing further damage.

Central Monitoring Systems

These systems are monitored by a central base outside of the home for a monthly fee. They directly and swiftly summon police, fire or medical emergency assistance. They can also dispatch personnel to respond to, inspect and reset the alarm. They'll notify any other party designated by the homeowner, and can also trigger an outside alarm.

Central monitoring systems can be linked from the home to the central monitoring base in a variety of ways:

They Can Be Directly Connected. Special telephone lines leased specifically for the alarm system also can be tied into the police and fire departments. In addition to alarm signals, these lines can indicate faults or cuts to the lines between the home and the receiving base.

They Can Employ Digital Dialers. These too, send alarm signals over telephone lines to a central monitoring office or to the police department. The difference is that they send the signals over the regular phone lines. Regular lines won't indicate faulty or cut wires. To remedy this situation, a local sounding device should be installed to go off if the telephone line is disturbed or cut.

Automatic Dialers Can Be Used. These dialers deliver a prerecorded message or a coded signal to the alarm company office, to an answering service, to the police station, even to a neighbor, over regular phone lines. This type of alarm should also be equipped with a local sounding device to indicate if telephone line problems or tampering occurs.

Long-Range Radio Signals Are Available. These alarm signals are sent to a central base station direct, by radio transmitter. They avoid the telephone line problems and tampering, but require test signals to be transmitted occasionally to verify if the system is functioning.

Anti-Intrusion Alarms

Alarm systems can be set up to provide three kinds or levels of dwelling protection: perimeter defense, space defense and point defense. Establishing perimeter protection or defense means equipping exterior doors and windows with sensors that will detect unauthorized entry. There are several types of perimeter protection:

• Magnetic switches are attached to doors and windows and adjacent frames. They're wired to signal a control unit when a magnet moves away from its switch.

• Plunger contacts are concealed — recessed into doors or windows. They operate the same way as the hidden light switch on automobile and refrigerator doors.

• Thin ribbons of current-conduction foil are attached to windows, door panels and walls to monitor any breaking of those surfaces. Unless trickily camouflaged by modern decor, the foil is very noticeable.

• Vibration or shock detectors monitor someone or something shaking or breaking through walls, doors or windows.

• Special screens are available to cover windows and other openings. They contain inconspicuous alarm wires to protect against forced entry through the screen material. They're installed so an alarm will also sound if the entire screen is removed from the opening while the system is on.

For internal space protection, several types of motion detectors or other types of sensors can be installed inside the home to guard specific rooms or hallways:

• Simple and effective photoelectric eyes cast an invisible infrared light beam across hallways, rooms, stairs and other areas. When a beam is interrupted or "broken," an alarm sounds.

• Trip wires, when placed across a stairway or hall, will sound an alarm when touched.

• Heat detectors can be installed simply by plugging them into wall outlets, but these units are very sensitive and can result in false alarms more often than other types of monitor sensors, especially if pets are kept in the house. Anything that generates body heat passing near the device is detected by the sensor.

• Pressure switches are flat switches placed beneath floor mats. When someone steps on the mat, the alarm system is triggered.

• Motion detectors similar to those mentioned in the chapter on outdoor security, fill an area with microwaves that are monitored in a specific preset pattern. By entering the area, a person changes the pattern and triggers an alarm. Air conditioning and heat vents, loose-fitting windows, phones, or anything else that might interrupt the microwave pattern could result in faulty alarm soundings.

• Closed-circuit television can be observed from inside a bedroom or any other area of the house. A hidden camera displays an outside view of a doorstep or other exterior area around the house. Of course, this setup is of little use to a homeowner when he or she is asleep or away from home.

Point protection is even more specific. It's used for guarding individual objects or storage areas, and can include many of the arrangements mentioned above. Experts consider perimeter protection to be the most important, but the most effective anti-intrusion systems combine total perimeter door and window coverage with some space protection in places an intruder is most likely to pass through. Point protection comes into play when a residence contains valuable objects or collections, such as expensive artwork, coins, silver, or potentially dangerous items, such as a large gun collection.

Wireless Motion-Sensitive Alarms

Again, these are some of the simplest alarms to install. In fact, they can be up and running in seconds. When mounted on a wall, infrared sensors can detect motion within sixty feet in a 110-degree arc, protecting nearby doors and windows (see Figure 18-1). If anyone does enter the monitored area, a powerful siren will sound to scare off intruders and alert those within hearing distance. Of course, if the sensitivity and volume controls are not set correctly, the alarm also could be triggered by a family pet that's allowed to roam throughout the house.

Disarming the siren is accomplished simply by entering a personal punch-in code number. Or if desired, units can be set with an optional arm/disarm delay feature.

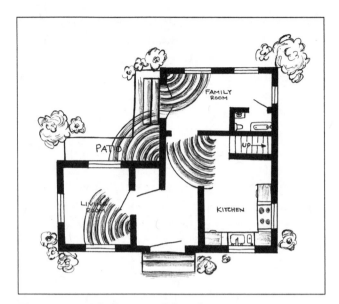

Figure 18-1. Motion-sensitive alarms.

These units can detect intruders, visitors, or children playing in a restricted area—such as near a swimming pool—and instantly alert members of the household. An unlimited number of indoor and outdoor sensor units can be installed at front, side or back doors, at windows, at a fence gate, across a driveway or around a play area. Most of these systems have a receiver console located in the residence. When a sensor on a door, window or fence gate "detects" an entry—or something that blocks the infrared transmissions—that portable module will transmit an alert to the console.

Barking Dog Alarms

They don't have to be fed, watered, groomed, or taken out on freezing December mornings. They don't chew the carpet or shed hairs all over the place either. They're electronic dogs that use infrared technology to detect motion outside of your home. Anyone who approaches your home is greeted with an extremely realistic barking sound that comes from inside your house or garage. When you're at home, the barking sound can be set to chime instead. It includes high/low volume control and sensitivity control to avoid false alarms from pets or small animals. The sensor mounts outside your front door or anywhere else you want to monitor from, and the alarm box plugs into the AC electric outlet of your choice.

Fake Alarms

They look like the real thing, featuring exact replicas of expensive alarm components. They usually include several door alarm panels, one with a key feature and one without. There are plenty of red flashing LEDs and a number of simulated glass break detectors for marking windows and doors to lead potential burglars to believe that an active system is present. The fake main alarm panels take a few AA batteries to keep blinking on and off. The idea is to keep burglars out by making them think the residence is alarmed—without making a "big" investment.

Although the fake alarms are still a viable option, as the costs of sophisticated electronic alarm systems decrease, so do the differences between real and fake systems.

Halogen Solar-Powered Alarms

Even on cloudy days, this security light absorbs enough energy from the sun to be on guard through the evening. It needs no wires, so the unit can be mounted practically anywhere out of reach with a screwdriver and a few simple fasteners. When motion from a nighttime visitor or intruder is detected, the unit floods the area with bright halogen light. During the day a photoelectric cell keeps the light from activating. The adjustable detector senses movement up to about seventy-five feet away, turns on the light for ninety seconds, and continues to turn the light on every time that motion is detected. It features weatherproof ABS construction.

Entry Alert Alarms

These units can be used to protect exterior doors. They install in minutes, with no wiring involved (see Figure 18-2). If an alarmed door is opened—by force or with a key—a powerful 100 decibel alarm will sound. It can be shut off only with a special 4-digit code number. An optional 15-second delay can be programmed into the units to allow for enough time to punch in the code. These alarm units can usually be set to sound a chime instead of a siren alarm. Other features may include a panic button to activate the alarm in emergencies, and a low-battery indicator.

Figure 18-2. Entry alert alarm.

Another use for these entry alert alarms can be to protect a restricted area within a residence from unwelcome guests or children.

Doorstop Alarms

These portable units possess alarm sirens that activate instantly when someone tries to open an alarmed door. One can be placed at the bottom of any door, just as you would place a standard doorstop (see Figure 18-3). The doorstop not only prevents the door from being opened, but it also sets off a loud siren that alerts household members and upsets potential intruders. The doorstop alarm is compact and lightweight, and can travel with you for use in a hotel or guest room. It's about nine inches long and three inches wide, and runs on several AA batteries.

Window Mini Alarms

These small but effective units (see Figure 18-4) provide at least 80 decibels of continuous sound. Because the units are so small—the alarm boxes are only a few inches long—they can be installed in minutes with double-backed tape, and are powered

Figure 18-3. A doorstop alarm.

by several button-cell batteries. They can alert household residents to possible intruders and keeping curious children out of restricted areas.

ALARM FEATURES

As you read this paragraph, new alarm ideas are being turned into prototypes that will one day be featured in the next generation of alarm systems.

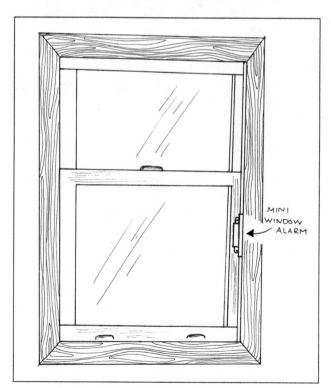

Figure 18-4. A window mini-alarm.

As with all electronic products, constant change is the rule. Here's a sampling of the wide variety of alarm product options currently available. Some can be used by themselves while others come with or must be purchased as part of, or an add-on to, a system.

• Automatic shutoffs ensure that the unit will automatically turn itself off after about five minutes or so. Burglars aren't going to stick around to wait for an alarm to stop and if you're not home you don't want the alarm to sound indefinitely. This feature is particularly beneficial if you're away from home and a false alarm is triggered.

• Area zone coverage is convenient; the main monitor box will reflect various household zones to allow identification of the problem area.

• Glass-break or "shock" sensors detect the sounds of breaking glass or splintering wood. They're generally used for fixed-pane glass such as living-room picture windows. They're practical because once mounted on the frame of a particular window, they can "hear" if other windows in the room are tampered with, too.

• Automatic lighting controls activate illumination when the alarm sounds and during the delay periods before you disarm the system. These controls can also turn on lights during a fire to light an escape route. Strobe lights are available to be mounted on the roof or at an outside window to make your residence easier to find for the police and other emergency services.

• Entry exit and entrance alarm delays will give you enough time to arm and disarm a system without triggering the system when you leave and enter your home.

• Changeable disarming codes provide additional security. You can change the codes if you suspect someone has discovered them.

• Heat detectors may be added to an alarm system to "recognize" intense heat in areas where a smoke detector alone may not sense certain types of fire in time. At the other end of the temperature scale, freeze sensors can be added to protect your home from furnace failure during the winter.

• Hazardous gas detectors that act in the same manner as heat detectors can also be added to an alarm system.

• Automatic digital dialers will automatically call a police or fire station or a central alarm monitoring system and transmit details about the location and nature of the alarm. Medical emergency "panic button" transmitters are also available to activate an automatic dialer programmed to call an emergency room or doctor.

• Loud exterior sirens can warn neighbors of a break-in or fire.

• Self-charging battery-powered backup units can power alarm systems for over twenty-four hours if the regular electric supply fails. These units come with low-battery indicators that tell you when it's time to either recharge or change the backup batteries.

• Instructions for alarm systems should be detailed and legible, so you'll understand the system's operations thoroughly. Be aware of what the system can and cannot do.

• All components should meet requirements of the Underwriters Laboratories and other standards such as Factory Mutual, as well as all applicable local standards, regulations and codes.

EVALUATING ALARM SYSTEMS

The simplest system that will do the job is often the best choice. The more complex the system, the more potential maintenance it may require, the more difficult it may be to operate, and the more expensive it could be to install and maintain. Your system should be only as complex as needed.

Alarm technology has been advancing at a rapid pace. Alarms available today are far more sophisticated and reliable than their earlier counterparts. You can also get a lot more for your money now. Ask if systems you are comparing will be flexible enough to accommodate additional components and sensors at a later date. Can the system be upgraded by changing old electronics for new, in the same way that many personal computers can be upgraded using the latest microprocessors?

Find out how sturdy the installation will be, and how effectively it will resist being tampered with or defeated. Will attempts to defeat the system trigger an alarm? They should. Or will the system automatically reset itself after being tampered with? It shouldn't.

How would the alarm system look in your house? How unobtrusive would the wiring and components be? Surface mounted wiring and sensors may be noticeable.

Will the systems you're looking at comply with local building and other codes? For example, if you're not at home and someone sets off an audible alarm, will the alarm stop sounding within a required period of time?

Does your homeowner's insurance company make any allowances for certain types of alarm systems? Find out if there are any specific requirements for the installation of an alarm system that will result in premium discounts.

ALARM SYSTEM COMPANIES

When evaluating a burglar alarm company, there are a number of factors you should consider. First, request and check references. Favor a well-established company with a record of successful operations. When responding to television, radio, newspaper or phone book ads, don't give out your name, address or phone number right away.

When checking a company's references, find out what bonding organization covers them and for how long. Ask which manufacturers they buy from and find out if those manufacturers have name recognition within the alarm industry. If possible, personally call on people who have purchased installations from the companies you are asking about. Check with the Better Business Bureau, Consumer Protection Agency, Chamber of Commerce and the police to see if any complaints have been filed against the companies in question. Find out how long each company has been in business.

Review the various alarm features available so you know what you need and want. Investigate their approximate cost in advance so you have an idea of what an installation will run before a company's installer arrives at your home.

Once an installer arrives, she should carefully inspect all of your doors, windows, furnishings and floor layouts. The installer should also have a good understanding of any valuables you want to protect, which is necessary so she can recommend the alarm equipment you need for optimum protection. Remember, though, the more elaborate is the system sold, the more profit the installer is likely to make. If the contractor realizes you know little about alarms and what they cost, understands your financial worth and living habits, and perceives that you are fearful of intruders, she may target you for as expensive a system as possible.

Evaluate the service policy. What's warranteed and how long does the coverage last? A quality system should cover parts and labor from both the manufacturer and the contractor for two years from the date of installation.

Components and installation methods must meet the requirements of all applicable local standards, regulations and codes.

Since any system of this type will require service from time to time, be sure that the company you deal with can supply prompt service. Ask what a service call will cost and get the answer in writing.

Insist on receiving verbal as well as written instructions covering all the important details of the system's operation.

When considering overall costs, remember to think about the distance to the alarm company if you're using them as a central monitoring station, the amount of wiring required in and to your home, and the cost of local line rates.

An intruder should not be able to disarm the system easily. The parts and wiring should be concealed as much as possible.

USING ALARM SYSTEMS

Burglar alarm systems are a lot like smoke alarms. How many people go to the trouble and expense to install smoke alarms, then don't follow through with keeping charged batteries in them or testing the units once a week, as recommended in the owner's manual? The same goes for many burglar alarm systems. People have them installed, then fail to consistently turn the systems on. Burglar alarm systems should be turned on whenever possible.

HOME SECURITY ALARM QUICK CHECKLIST

☐ Consider keeping a dog as a combination pet and burglar alarm.

☐ Before making an alarm system decision, have professionals analyze your security needs: first police departments and then lock and alarm companies.

☐ Decide which type of alarm system would be best for you, based upon the professionals' advice, your financial situation, and your level of desired comfort.

☐ Consider the levels of protection the proposed alarm system will provide, including perimeter defenses, space defenses and point defenses.

☐ Review all system features and options available.

☐ The simplest system that will do the job is often the best choice.

☐ Can your homeowner's insurance be discounted with the alarm system you plan to install? If not, which alarm system, if any, would result in lower premiums?

☐ Always check alarm company references before you buy their products and services.

☐ Insist on receiving verbal and written instructions on the system's operation.

☐ Remember to turn alarm systems on whenever you can.

CHAPTER 19

INDOOR SECURITY

There are a number of things you can do to protect yourself, your family members and your belongings beyond what we've discussed so far in the security section.

PROTECTING YOURSELF AND OTHER HOUSEHOLD MEMBERS

Extra Door Protection

In addition to sturdy locks, compact, portable, simple mechanical devices are available to prevent a door from being forced open. Most work by jamming the door against its frame or against the floor—much as a wedge prevents an open door from closing. They can also make sliding glass doors immovable when placed in the door's frame. Likewise, "portable bolts" available in locksmith stores can provide the security of a permanently affixed deadbolt lock. They install quickly and easily between any door that opens inward and its frame. Although these units are marketed primarily for people who spend a lot of time on the road, and who want extra security in hotel and motel rooms or in college dorms, the devices will work in the typical household, too, until permanent installations can be arranged.

Develop Habits of Locking Doors and Windows

The strongest door and window locks won't work unless they're used. Establish a routine to follow in making sure that doors and windows are locked and alarm systems turned on. When working or playing in the backyard, in the basement, attic, or anywhere away from the main house area, don't take a chance. Lock up instead.

Phone Precautions

Voice scramblers are available that plug into any standard telephone line. The scramblers alter vocal pitch. A woman can sound like a man while the scrambler is activated, or a child can sound like an adult. The scrambler can also be used to prepare recorded messages.

Keep a list of emergency phone numbers near each phone. Teach your children how to contact you at work—and make sure your secretary, coworkers or supervisor know how to reach you at all times.

Telephone survey calls and "wrong numbers" are methods used by burglars to case homes. Tell children and baby-sitters never to give any information to strangers over the phone. Burglars try to get people to reveal household members' personal habits, earnings and even vacation plans. If telephone survey takers ask questions you feel are irrelevant, simply hang up.

Report repeated wrong number phone calls or silent calls to your local law enforcement agency.

Other Things You Can Do

Get a large dog, such as a German shepherd. Or *pretend* you have a large dog. Leave a heavy rope or chain with a snap tied to a patio or front yard tree. Place a large pet food bowl filled with water on the kitchen floor. Such signs will give potential intruders the idea that you own a large dog.

Leave a few lights on in the house all night. The safety margin gained by the illumination is well worth the slight cost of electricity.

Don't open your door to strangers, and make certain that children follow the same rule. If children stay home alone, make sure they can access exterior door peepholes and that they know enough never to tell a stranger they're home alone. Make an "emergency" call for someone who says they're in trouble—don't let them in to make their own call.

Weapons

There are a number of philosophies on keeping guns and other deadly weapons in the household for self-protection. One philosophy equates the keeping of guns with the right to self-defense. Another implies that a gun may as easily be turned against its owner by an intruder or provide children with a means to inflict accidental injury or death. Discuss your options with your local law enforcement officials and weigh the pros and cons before making a decision.

PROTECTING YOUR BELONGINGS

What are some other ways you can protect the safety of your belongings, or at the very least, ensure that you'll receive an equivalence in return if they're stolen?

Have you ever applied for a mortgage loan or other loan at a bank? Among numerous questions directed at your financial condition, one is invariably "What is the estimated value of your possessions?" If you're like most individuals, you stop and think for a few moments, then take a wild guess. The loan officer, of course, has no simple way of checking on you, and unless your ballpark figure is wildly low or high, it will remain on your application, becoming a kind of gospel that you'll eventually use over and over, on different loan applications. In the same vein, if you would be "cleaned out" by burglars while you're on vacation, could you prove exactly what's missing?

If push came to shove, could you remember what you own, and what it's worth? A possessions inventory can be a useful tool in establishing realistic insurance coverages. Such an inventory would be invaluable in the unlikely event of a catastrophic loss from a burglary, fire, earthquake or flood. Not even specific replacement cost insurance can save the day without documentation.

There are other reasons for the inventory, too. An accurate, annually updated inventory can serve as proof to the Internal Revenue Service so you can claim a tax deduction in the event of losses. Another function an inventory can serve is, if you move from one residence to another, the list of possessions will serve as record of what the moving company will have to transport and deliver to your new location.

Start by contacting the agent who services your homeowner's insurance policy. Insurance companies, since their homeowner's policies take personal possessions into account, have something at stake here too. The companies often have booklets or pamphlets that can help with your survey. If you have a personal computer at home, that can help as well. Just make sure you keep a copy of the resulting inventory file on a disk or hard copy stored somewhere outside of your residence, in a secure place such as a safe deposit box in a bank. Then once a year—or whenever significant changes occur, update both your in-house and outside copies, and re-date them so the lists are fairly current at all times.

Inventory Methods

There are a number of ways to inventory your items. They include written lists, written lists supported by photographs, and written lists supported by videotapes. The written lists, of course, can be handwritten or typed, or entered into a computer and stored on disk.

While it's difficult to compile a complete inventory list from scratch, it should be done if you don't have one. But first, establish a procedure for yourself and your family members for including newly acquired items to your roster of possessions. Just add each item to a running list of belongings kept by kinds, with individual lists for classifications such as:

- Furniture (beds, couches, chairs, tables, hutches, etc.)

- Electronic appliances (stereos, televisions, VCRs, computers)
- Valuables (jewelry, coin collections, silver, china, artwork, photographs, books, etc.)
- Clothing (furs, coats, dresses, sweaters, shirts, slacks, boots, shoes)
- Sporting goods (guns, scuba gear, racquets, canoes, binoculars)
- Transportation (cars, wagons, vans, boats, motorcycles, trucks)
- Household fixtures (chandeliers, oriental rugs, track lighting, freestanding fireplaces, wood-burning stoves, handcrafted woodwork or doors, stained glass windows, Italian tile, etc.)

You can be as specific or as general with the classifications as you want, but usually, the more specific the groupings, the easier it is to keep track of things. Customize them to concentrate on what you have. Keep the sales receipt, canceled check, or charge card receipt—and make a copy for inclusion with your second list, the list that you'll be storing outside of your residence in a secure place.

Written Lists

A simple written inventory method employs a three-ring loose leaf binder that you can snap open to remove or insert individual pages (see Figure 19-1). Just make sure it's small enough to fit into your bank safe deposit box, if that's where you're going to keep it. Depending on the quantity of items owned, you may need two or more binders. Many binders have pockets in the covers in which you can slip receipts or photos of your most valuable belongings.

Photographic and Video Records

A written inventory backed up with photographs or a videotape is considerably more telling and effective than one without.

The Inventory

After you establish the overall method you're going to use and decide on the categories, go through each room or area of your residence. For each item use at least one line and record a description, date of purchase—estimate one if you're not sure—size,

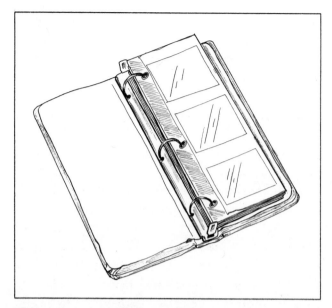

Figure 19-1. An inventory binder.

color, original cost and current value. Again, estimate the original cost and current value if you don't know them exactly. Irreplaceable items and those that have historical value, especially jewelry, silver, antiques and works of art, can be professionally appraised.

Photos or Slides

While a Polaroid instant-print camera can come in handy for certain items, a 35-millimeter camera with a flash unit will result in clearer prints. Make sure you're comfortable with whatever camera you choose, and only use color slide or print film. Color prints or slides will best show the true characteristics and quality of your possessions, but recording belongings on photos is an expensive and painstaking procedure. Costs of print or slide film, with developing, can add up fast.

Video Records

A better visual records option is available through the use of video cameras and tapes. A video of each room in your home, as well as of hallways, porches, attics, basements, garages, gardens and even landscaping will help establish the general appearance and quality of your residence in addition to documenting your personal possessions.

Before starting, call your insurance agent and make sure his company will accept a videotape record. Consider getting his acknowledgment in writing. If you don't own a video camera, look into either contracting the service from someone else, or renting a camera you can use. If you opt to rent a video camera, request a sensitive low-light model because color quality deteriorates easily with other units that are not so sensitive. The camera should also have close-up shooting capabilities, within four inches, for recording small details. Be sure that the rental agent you get the equipment from shows you how to use the camera, and lets you practice shooting for a few minutes in the store. You'll also need a two-hour camera battery, or several, and a tripod to set the camera on for stable closeups and smooth panning (moving the camera from one side of a room to another). A portable video light to illuminate dark corners or small details is recommended, as is a small color monitor or television to check the color accuracy of items such as clothing or works of art, in which color is a significant factor.

Plan your shoot in an orderly way. Start with an outline, a list of items you want to record in the most logical order. Prepare your written inventory in that order, with receipts and serial numbers and descriptions or other information about the possessions you'll be shooting, so you'll be able to describe the items in the tape as you're shooting. You could add a voice-over later, but it's a lot simpler to speak as you shoot. The front microphones on most video cameras work fine; just remember to speak loudly and clearly, and don't rush the commentary. Identify each major item as you go. If the camera has a date/time stamp, use it. If not, say the date and time at the beginning and end of the tape. For additions, note the new time and date where you left off with the old tape. Just add short update video segments as needed.

Plan the actual shoot for daylight hours. Open all draperies, curtains and window shades to let in all available light. Turn the camera to its indoor setting and shoot a quick test recording, taking shots from room to room to check light levels and identify any lighting or color balance problems. If the video camera image darkens as you pan or move across the windows, there may be a backlighting compensation switch you can turn on. If the images look too blue or yellow, try adjusting the camera's color settings to correct them.

Do things systematically. Start with the living room. Brace the camera, preferably with a tripod, and begin each room's shoot with an overall view of one wall from one corner to the other, pausing for about thirty seconds on each main shot or major item that you want to record. Then turn to another wall. Shoot until the entire room's contents is covered, then go to the next room . . . the dining room, perhaps.

First record an overall shot of the dining room, with table and chairs and china hutch. This establishes both details and quality of the room and accessories. Next, focus on the closed cabinet (with the hutch interior light on, if there is one). Open the doors and photograph the contents in place. Next, withdraw several individual pieces. Capture the pattern and china mark in one shot by using two sample plates, one face up and the other face down. While your assistant is handling the plates in the shot, you can be commenting on a description of the number of pieces in the set, the date of purchase, the price, and anything else that should be noted. A variation on this can have someone else videotaping you as you walk through each room describing your belongings.

Remember that if you make mistakes during the taping session, you can simply erase the errors with a new version.

Paintings, crystal, silver, jewelry, and various collections and small valuable items need a scale of reference to indicate size. You can use a ruler or hold items with your hands to show size (see Figure 19-2). Use close-ups if needed to record an artist's signature trademarks or gold or silver content marks. Some small pieces of jewelry, coins, stamps or other items can best be displayed on a table that's covered with a black cloth. It's also a good idea to include your driver's license photo in the same shot, to help establish your ownership.

While you needn't itemize every piece of clothing on tape, at least shoot the insides of all your closets. The cumulative value of closet contents can be considerable.

Collect similar articles into groupings whenever possible. For example, if you own a lot of camping

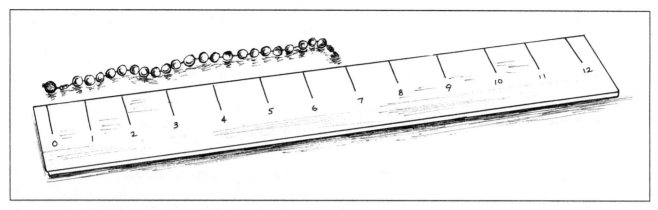

Figure 19-2. Using a ruler to show size scale.

equipment, spread the individual pieces out on a floor, next to each other: tent, sleeping bags, camp stoves, lanterns, tools, expensive camping clothes, binoculars and other items.

Although your basement, garage or attic may not hold valuable items, their contents will probably have to be replaced in the event of a major fire or other loss. Shoot each area, recording items such as landscaping equipment, power tools, laundry appliances and similar belongings.

If you own a second residence, such as a beach house, a summer cabin, a hunting camp or rental property, include a separate inventory for those places.

As you're taking inventory, consider marking valuables such as televisions, video players and cameras with an indelible identification number that will be recognized by the police. Your state's initials plus your driver's license number is one possibility, if you don't plan to move to a different state in the near future. The police department running your local "Operation Identification" program can give you further guidance.

After a few rooms are covered, review what you've shot to see if it's lacking anything important or if there are any technical problems. If not, complete the inventory. When the tape or tapes are finally finished, either break the record-protection tab off the cassette so it cannot be accidentally erased, or put a piece of transparent tape over the tab in case you plan to eventually update or continue on with the same tape as you accumulate more belongings. Then make a copy of the finished tape or tapes. Place the copy, along with a copy of your written inventory, in your safe deposit box or at some other secure place, such as your attorney's office, and keep the originals at home.

Update your records at least annually, and let your insurance agent see them, to make sure you have adequate coverage for what's there.

Last, let burglars know your goods are marked and can be traced. Put "Operation Identification" or similar stickers available from law enforcement agencies on your front window, front door, or any other clearly visible location.

Home Safes

No safe is foolproof, but having one is certainly a lot "safer" than not. There are many ingenious objects that can be used to hide valuables. Floor safes can be bolted to wood or concrete floors, or permanently set in a concrete basement or garage floor and covered with a carpet or mat. Special flowerpots, books, soda cans, mirrors, rocks and other items can double as home safe deposit boxes (see Figure 19-3). There are safes that look like electrical

Figure 19-3. A look-alike safe.

wall outlets, photos, lamps and even ashtrays.

If you need a larger protected space, consider turning a small closet into a "security room" by installing a solid-core door and deadbolt lock. Make sure the door's hinges are inside the closet.

INDOOR SECURITY QUICK CHECKLIST

☐ Contact your homeowner's insurance agent and find out how his company recommends that personal property inventories be kept. Make sure the agent agrees with what you are planning.

☐ Prepare written inventories of your belongings; group individual items by category. For each object or line item, include the description and condition, purchase date and price (keep receipts if you have them), and current value.

☐ Use a personal computer for data entry, if possible.

☐ Prepare video records of your belongings to go along with the written inventories.

☐ Establish a procedure to add new items to your inventory lists.

☐ Make a second copy of your written and video inventories. Keep one set outside of your residence, in a bank safe deposit box or at someone else's home or office.

☐ Periodically update your inventories and review them with your insurance agent to make sure you've got enough homeowner's coverage in case of loss from a burglary, fire, earthquake, flood or other disaster.

CHAPTER 20

PREPARING A RESIDENCE FOR YOUR ABSENCE

Vacations are usually associated with good memories, enjoyable activities, friends and family. They're often times when entire families travel together, a week at a stretch, visiting far-off locations. Some unfortunate vacationers, however, return to households that have been broken into and ransacked. Once a home is violated, feelings of doubt and insecurity gradually undermine the home's reputation as a safe haven for its members. In other words, when a home is broken into, the losses can be far greater than the monetary sum of the goods stolen: It's the stealing away of the family's feelings of security, of their peace of mind, that hurts the most.

For the purposes of this chapter, "vacations" involve individuals or families who travel to different locations for a number of days and nights, leaving a residence unoccupied. Of course, you needn't take a vacation to do that. You could leave town to attend a seminar, to carry out a special project for your company, to visit a sick aunt, or to go house hunting in Minneapolis.

The challenge is how to prevent potential thieves from recognizing that your home is vacant while you're gone, because no matter what precautions you take, your residence is likely to be more vulnerable while you're not there. How to proceed? By either replacing yourself with a short-term tenant or house sitter, or by making your home *look* occupied when it's really not.

USE A HOUSE SITTER

First, consider enlisting a trusted neighbor, relative or close friend who may agree to "work" out of your residence while you're gone. If you have no friendly neighbors, relatives or acquaintances, then house sitters are available, who, for a reasonable fee will live in your home in your absence, and tend to your household. They can even take care of your pets. Students and retirees on flexible daytime schedules who will come and go somewhat unpredictably around the clock are usually the most effective and experienced house sitters. But make sure you personally know the ones you're considering, or that unknown individuals provide you with reasonable references that you can check.

Fill the sitter in on the daily points she needs to know, provide a set of keys, directions on how to use the automatic dishwasher, and a copy of your itinerary with telephone numbers and addresses. That's probably the simplest way to leave your home for an extended period of time.

MAKE YOUR HOME SEEM OCCUPIED

An alternate method is to make your home look occupied while no one is living there. Arrange for some cooperation from an adjacent or across-the-street neighbor or a nearby relative or friend. Give the neighbor your house key, an itinerary, and phone numbers where you can be reached in case of an emergency. Avoid leaving your door key in a mailbox or chute, under a doormat, or on top of a door or windowframe. Burglars will likely check the various places that you consider secure. Instruct your helper neighbor to phone the police if he or she spots a prowler around your house, and to supply an address, description of the prowler, and other pertinent data. Above all, the neighbor should not investigate suspicious activities on his own.

Set up timers (see Figure 20-1) that will automatically turn lights, radios and televisions on and off. Ask your neighbor or helper to change the timers and alter the on and off settings every couple days, so exact patterns cannot be discerned. A burglar may think someone is home when a television or radio can be heard even if no one answers the doorbell. Along those same lines, it's also cheap insurance to leave on a television or radio when you go out for an evening.

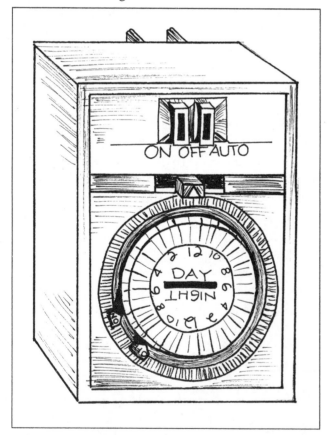

Figure 20-1. A timer.

Arrange for someone to collect your mail, newspapers and other deliveries (see Figure 20-2); again, your immediate neighbor is ideal for this. Some individuals believe that all deliveries should be stopped while family members are out of town.

That can be the case if you're leaving for a few months or more, but if you'll be gone for only a week or two, it's best to continue with mail and newspaper service to avoid drawing attention to the fact that you're gone—due to the absence of routine deliveries. Of course, if you will be gone for a long period of time, your house preparations will be considerably different. Here we're talking about having a week or two or three, to confuse opportunists who, if they recognize that you're gone, may impulsively try to break into your home.

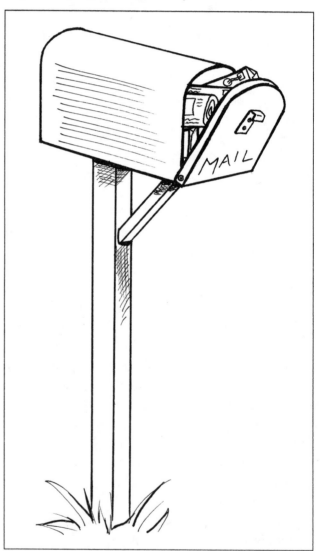

Figure 20-2. Uncollected deliveries.

Ask a neighbor to park one of his or her cars in your driveway occasionally, overnight if possible. Also consider asking your helper to leave commonplace items in your front yard for half-days at a time, such as an inexpensive toy tricycle, an old sled, or a set of lawn chairs—depending on the season—to create the impression that someone is inside your residence.

Hide garbage cans in the basement, garage or storage shed. Cans that are empty when everyone else's are full can tip off a burglar that you're away. Ask a neighbor to put one of his full trash bags or cans in front of your driveway on collection night.

Be sure seasonal chores are taken care of while you're away. In the summer, arrange for someone to cut your lawn if it will need it before you get back. Winter trip preparations can include arranging for someone to keep your driveway and walks shoveled after a snowfall of more than five or six inches, and having a neighbor occasionally pull his vehicle into your driveway and walk up your front and back steps and between the driveway and the house, to leave tracks.

Don't accommodate burglars by taping a "back in two weeks" note to your front or back door. You'd be surprised to learn how many trusting individuals do just that.

OTHER PRECAUTIONS

After receiving permission from your neighbor or helper, provide the police department with your helper's name, address and phone number and explain that the helper will be watching your home while you're gone. If the police need a key to enter the house for any reason, they can get one from the helper. Also provide the police with your departure and return dates and a copy of your itinerary and phone numbers where you can be reached. Tell them how many vehicles will remain in the driveway, with models, colors and license plate numbers. In many cases, such notification may cause the police to make regular inspections of your property while you're away.

Your house number should be clearly visible from the street at all hours of the day and night so the police can easily find your residence if called.

If you have an answering machine, simply collect messages in the usual manner. Don't alter the outgoing message by saying that you're on vacation. Ask your helper to periodically review the messages and pass them along to you, or use a re-

mote unit to tap into the machine from various points along your trip. Make sure your helper knows how to reset the machine or rewind the incoming message tape in case it fills up while you're gone.

Turn down the bell on your telephones if you don't have an answering machine. A nonstop ringing phone can tell a burglar that no one is home.

Pay utility bills in advance, so service won't be interrupted while you're gone. Leave some personal checks with a family member who may need to pay unforseen bills that come due in your absence.

Make sure your home insurance policy is in full effect; don't forget to renew it.

If you don't have an actual security alarm system, at the very least, place home alarm system *decals* on your front and rear doors and first floor windows: Who's to know? A "Beware of Dog" sign, even without the dog to back it up, can also be a significant deterrent.

Place important documents, jewelry, and other small valuables in a bank safe deposit box. At the same time, don't leave extra cash laying around. Deposit surplus dollars into your bank account. Larger portable valuables such as expensive artwork, computers, televisions or stereo units may be temporarily relocated to a cooperative neighbor's home while you're gone.

If you haven't done so already, inquire with the local police to see how to participate in their "Operation Identification" program, in which valuables such as computers, televisions and cameras are indelibly marked with an engraving pen the police provide. Record model and serial numbers of appliances and place Operation Identification stickers facing the outsides of your doors and windows.

Don't flaunt valuables. Expensive cars are best kept behind closed garage doors. Picture windows should not showcase high-priced entertainment centers or family silver. Many burglaries are not committed by professional thieves—rather, they're undertaken by "regular" people from the neighborhood who are easily tempted by what they see.

Since garages are favorite entries for burglars, secure all garage doors and windows and remove or lock up any tools that could be used for gaining entrance into your home. If your cars will be gone during your trip, cover the garage windows so burglars won't know.

Reread chapter sixteen on outdoor security. Pay particular attention to the information on entrance illumination.

Tall shrubbery that blocks windows, doorways or pathways should be trimmed so it doesn't provide hiding and surveillance places for burglars. Branches from large trees should be pruned back away from house windows, decks and roofs. Ladders should not be stored outside.

Secure all potential entry points such as pet doors, old coal chutes, cellar windows and sliding doors.

Weddings, funerals and similar occasions are often announced in newspapers. These situations can be vulnerable times for the people involved, and consequently, burglars can expect to find the main participants away from their homes. If that's your case, ask a neighbor or friend to baby-sit your residence.

Society columns in newspapers can announce your travel plans if you're not careful, letting everyone know about your two-month cruise in the South Pacific. If that happens, you'd better arrange for house-sitting services while you're gone, or change your travel plans to a different time of year.

Be cautious about letting strangers know your daily routine or travel plans in advance, and tell your children not to talk about vacations until *after* the trip, when they're back home. It's best not to tell your mailman, your paper boy, the woman who delivers your dry cleaning, or your barber or beautician, to mention a few. Any time you tell one of them that you'll be leaving home for a lengthy period, you could be asking for trouble. While your barber or beautician may not even think of stealing from you, they may mention your upcoming trip to someone else who can't be trusted and may see your absence as their opportunity. The fewer people who know your plans, the better. Tell the world *after* you return, not before.

You may be driving to and from your vacation or other destination. A breakdown or accident could delay or end your trip, or worse. See that your car(s) are up to the trip. About a week before you leave, pay special attention to fan belts, the cooling system, brakes and tires. Have your mechanic check the essentials:

- batteries
- tires
- air conditioners and heaters
- filters and belts
- cooling systems
- steering systems
- lights
- shock absorbers
- brakes
- exhaust systems
- windshield wipers

If you must leave your car or other vehicle at the airport, remove anything that may have your name, address or phone number on it, such as a gym bag, piece of luggage or school book.

ON THE DAY YOU LEAVE

Unplug electrical appliances such as television sets, stereo systems, irons, washing machines, dryers and fans to prevent possible damage from electrical storms. Make sure all gas appliances are in good working order and that pilot lights are operational.

Set your thermostat so your furnace or air conditioner will maintain a reasonable temperature, about 80 degrees Fahrenheit during summer, and 55 degrees in winter. During winter make certain that outside water faucets are shut off and drained to prevent frozen and burst water pipes.

Shut off the water to automatic washers to prevent possible damage from a broken hose.

Close your fireplace flues to prevent birds or animals from entering.

If you haven't done so already, turn down the volume control on your telephone ringers so they can't be heard from the outside. Collect telephone numbers of relatives, friends, your house-watching neighbors, the police department, your insurance agent, physician, dentist, attorney and other acquaintances in case you need to call someone from out of town.

Put window shades and curtains in their normal daytime positions, arranged so neighbors and police can see into your house. Just make sure that valuables cannot be seen from the outside.

Close and lock windows and sliding doors. Make sure that Charley bars or wooden dowels are placed at the base of sliding doors, and that all screens or storm windows are locked or fastened.

If you're leaving a car or other vehicle in your driveway, see that it's locked, with any portable electric garage door openers locked in the glove compartment.

If you haven't done so already, leave a house key and your itinerary, complete with phone numbers, with the neighbor, friend or relative who will be watching your house while you're gone.

Don't forget your driver's license, car registration, spare keys, a first-aid kit and handbook, and safety equipment such as a flashlight and flares. Also remember your emergency phone number list, your family's hospital insurance and medical cards, traveler's checks and/or credit cards—avoid carrying much cash.

ON THE ROAD

Plan ahead. Try to avoid rush hour traffic. Be aware of weather and traffic conditions that could affect road safety.

If your vehicle is heavily loaded, you'll need to alter your driving style a bit. Acceleration will be slower, stopping distances longer, and sway on curves will be greater. Allow for plenty of time to get where you're going, and plenty of room for passing and stopping.

If you'll be pulling a trailer, practice backing, turning and stopping a day or two before you leave. Make sure the weight ratio of trailer to vehicle is not too high—consult your vehicle's owner's manual. Double-check safety chains and light hookups.

Keep your vehicle doors locked while driving, and everyone should wear safety belts at all times.

Stick to the posted speed limits, or drive slower if conditions warrant (such as in snow or rainstorms). Avoid fatigue at the wheel; every few hours, or when tired, take a break from driving or switch drivers.

✔ **PREPARING YOUR RESIDENCE QUICK CHECKLIST**

☐ Arrange for the services of someone to live in and care for your residence while you're gone.

☐ If you don't have a house-sitter, give a trusted neighbor your house key, your itinerary, and phone numbers you can be reached at in case of an emergency.

☐ Set up timers that will automatically turn lights, radios and televisions on and off; have your helper change the on and off settings every few days.

☐ Have someone collect your mail, newspapers and other deliveries while you're gone.

☐ Ask a neighbor to park one of his or her cars in your driveway occasionally, overnight if possible, in your absence.

☐ Provide the local police department with your departure and return dates and the phone number of your helper in case the police need to contact you or enter your residence while you're away.

PREPARING YOUR RESIDENCE QUICK CHECKLIST
(continued)

☐ Make sure your house number is clearly visible from the street, day and night.

☐ Turn down the bell on your phone so it can't be heard from outside.

☐ Pay utility bills in advance, make sure your homeowner's insurance policy is in effect, and supply your helper with a few signed, blank checks in case funds are needed to pay an unforseen bill.

☐ If you don't have a security alarm system, at least place home alarm system decals outside on your first floor doors and windows.

☐ Consider removing portable valuables and placing them either in bank safe deposit boxes or at someone else's residence.

☐ Participate in an "Operation Identification" program in which appliances and other valuables are indelibly marked with an engraving pen.

☐ Make sure that valuables you're leaving will be placed out of sight.

☐ Illuminate entrances and other possible entry points, and trim encroaching shrubbery and trees.

☐ In summer, have the lawn and landscaping maintained so the property will not look vacant.

☐ In winter, have snow shoveled from walks and driveways. Have your helper pull a vehicle into the driveway after each fresh snowfall, and make tracks walking from the car to the house, and up each lead walk, front and back.

☐ Avoid announcing your trip plans in advance, especially to service people and strangers.

☐ Review the "On the Day You Leave" suggestions in the latter part of this chapter.

Appendix

SAFE JOB ANALYSES

Safe Job Analyses, also referred to as SJAs—or within manufacturing and industrial environments, as Behavioral Job Analyses (BJAs)—are simply written procedures or guidelines on how to safely complete particular jobs. SJAs "realize" that most jobs can be broken down into a number of individual tasks or steps, and that each of those steps may involve specific hazards. SJAs take those hazards into account and prescribe safe behaviors to counter the hazards so the individual steps of a job can be completed safely.

Prepare SJAs for jobs that are routinely or periodically done around and within the home. Sample jobs for which SJAs could be prepared include:

- Cleaning out gutters and downspouts
- Washing the outsides of second story windows
- Putting up awnings
- Pruning large trees or shrubs
- Operating a lawn tractor
- Using a table saw
- Operating a snowblower
- Changing a vehicle's tires

Select jobs that you know entail certain hazards. After SJAs are prepared, thhey can be used to help train others to perform the work safely, as safety reviews or preparations for individuals who have done the jobs in the past, and as guidelines for someone auditing a friend or family member as the job is being done.

Instruction Checklist for Filling Out a Safe Job Analysis Form:

1. Make copies of Figure A-1 and Figure A-2 to use as worksheets and for final versions of your completed SJAs.

2. Gather together the individuals who will be performing the job being discussed. It's important that if your sons or daughters will be doing the job, they be present for the discussion.

3. Write a short title for the job.

4. Determine what personal protective equipment the job requires.

5. Either observe someone else while they perform the job, or think through the complete job, using memory recall. Consult with the appropriate section of this book for additional help, if information on the job is discussed here.

6. Each job can usually be broken down into individual task steps. Identify major task steps. Number and list tasks as they occur, in chronological order, in the first column on the safe job analysis worksheet. They must be observable behaviors.

7. Identify hazards associated with each task step in the middle column of the safe job analysis worksheet. Provide specific information, with short, active statements to describe the hazards.

8. In the third column of the safe job analysis worksheet, specify the required safe behaviors. Specific safe behaviors must correspond to identified hazards. Use concise items, actions or events that are described in behavioral terms. In other words, avoid saying things like "use caution" or "pay attention."

For an example, refer to the sample SJA, "Operating a Riding Lawn Tractor," Figures A-3 and A-4.

HOME SAFETY AUDITS

Because about 85 percent of all accidental injuries result from unsafe behavior, effective safety audits should be undertaken when activities—work or play—are taking place at home.

What to audit? Consider the typical and nontypical activities of children and adults. Here are some examples:

- Bicycle and skateboard riding
- Roller skating
- Cleaning out gutters
- Painting walls and ceilings
- Barbecuing
- Using a swimming pool
- Mowing the lawn

SAFE JOB ANALYSIS

Job Title: _____   Date _____

Personal Protection Equipment Required

Sequence of Steps	Potential Hazards	Safe Operating Procedures/Conditions

Figure A-1. Safe Job Analysis Worksheet.

Sequence of Steps	Potential Hazards	Safe Operating Procedures/Conditions

DESCRIPTION

Job Title: _____

_____

_____

_____

_____

_____

_____

_____

_____

_____

_____

_____

_____

_____

_____

_____

_____

_____

_____

_____

_____

_____

Figure A-2. Safe Job analysis, title and description of job.

SAFE JOB ANALYSIS

Job Title: *Cutting Grass with a Lawn Tractor*   Date 6-20-95

Personal Protection Equipment Required *Safety glasses or goggles, leather work shoes, and work gloves.*

Sequence of Steps	Potential Hazards	Safe Operating Procedures/Conditions
1. Inspect Lawn	– Debris could be struck. – Hidden stumps, roots, or pipes.	– Pick up debris. – Flag stumps, roots, or pipes.
2. Inspect Tractor	– Parts could vibrate off. – Safety features may not work.	– Tighten loose nuts and bolts. – Check kill switch, tires, brakes.
	– Low on fuel or fluids.	– Check fuel, oil, and coolant. – Review operating manual.
3. Operate Tractor	– Tractor could tip over.	– Operate in low gear – Travel at safe speed. – Avoid holes and stationary objects.
		– Reduce speed on slopes. – Turn only on level ground.
		– Cut slopes from top to bottom instead of sideways.
	– Operator struck by low hanging objects	– Trim low-hanging branches. – Avoid riding too close to clothes lines,
		guide wires, and similar obstacles.

Figure A-3. A sample completed Safe Job Analysis Worksheet.

Sequence of Steps	Potential Hazards	Safe Operating Procedures/Conditions
3. Operate Tractor ...continued	—Injury to bystanders or pets.	—No riders. —Keep children, pets, and other adults away. —Look behind you to back up.
	—Injury from blade.	—Never place hands or feet near mower deck while engine is running and parts are still moving.
		—Shut engine off and remove key to unplug chute or blade. —Wear gloves when
		inspecting or removing jammed materials.

- Pruning trees from a ladder
- Trimming shrubs with electric clippers
- Changing a vehicle's flat tire
- Changing a vehicle's motor oil
- Waxing a floor
- Retrieving items from an attic
- Shoveling snow
- Using a snowblower

If a safe job analysis (SJA) has already been prepared on the task or activity, use it as a basis for your audit. Do the behaviors you observe match those that the SJA requires? Or do you see unsafe behaviors? If the activity is performed repeatedly, consider completing a SJA for future reference.

Home Safety Audit Instruction Checklist

- First, make a few dozen copies of the blank Home Safety Audit Form.
- Select another member of your household or a friend to help you audit, and explain how the auditing process works.
- Write your name and her name on the line that says "auditors."
- Fill out the job or activity inspected, and the date (see Figures A-5 and A-6).

There are at least four categories of behavior and conditions you should look at during a home safety audit, including personal protective equipment, tools and other equipment, procedures and housekeeping.

Personal Protective Equipment

- Is the proper PPE is being worn? For example, if a family member is operating a loud, gasoline powered weed trimmer, is she wearing safety goggles, hearing protection, vibration-dampening gloves and sturdy work shoes?
- Is the PPE being worn properly? Is it in good condition?

Tools and Equipment

- Are tools adequate for the job?
- Are they being used properly? For example, if the back of a pipe wrench is being used to hammer a nail, that's improper tool usage.
- Could a particular job be done more safely if tools were used?

- Is equipment being operated with safety guards in place?
- Is it being operated as designed?
- Is it being maintained in safe condition?

Procedures

- Have the people doing the activity been properly trained?
- Is equipment locked out and brought to a state of zero energy before being worked on?
- Do procedures exist for the tasks, and does everyone know and use them?

Housekeeping

- Are materials and tools kept in an orderly fashion?
- Are spills cleaned up immediately?
- Is trash disposed of safely?

In General

- Jot down the most important safe and unsafe behaviors and conditions you notice under the "Safety Observations" section.
- If you see an unsafe action or condition, address it right away, and eliminate the unsafe behavior or hazard.
- Reinforce safe behavior by recognizing and praising it.
- Note if there's follow-up attention needed on the last two lines, and use the back of the sheet if necessary.
- Keep the completed audits in a binder and review them periodically. Some of the completed audits can be used to start SJAs on activities that are repeated with any regularity.

HOME SAFETY MEETING CHECKLIST

There's no doubt about it. Safety meetings work. They inform, they encourage questions and discussion, and they even entertain. Safety meetings are generally a major part of successful industrial and commercial safety management programs. There's no reason they can't work for you at home, too. Use the accompanying home safety meeting form (see Figures A-7 and A-8), and keep notes from the meetings for follow-up and future safety discussions.

- Set aside a day and time for your meetings in

DESCRIPTION

Job Title: *Cutting Grass with a Lawn Tractor*

— Avoid cutting grass when the lawn is wet, or when visibility is poor. Pre-inspect the grass for debris. Remove stones, toys and other objects that could damage the cutting blades or be thrown through the air

— Before starting, inspect the tractor. Check the oil, fuel and radiator fluid. Tighten loose nuts and bolts. See that appropriate cutting-height adjustments are or can be made. With a new or unfamiliar tractor, review the operating manual.

— Always operate the tractor in low gear while cutting, and travel at a safe speed. Never allow riders on a tractor, and never pull anyone or anything other than a mower attachment behind or to the side of a tractor. A lawn tractor is meant for the operator only.

— Be alert and prepared to protect yourself from low-hanging tree branches, pipes, guide wires, clothes lines, and other potential hazards. Watch for holes, roots and rocks in the terrain. Cutting too close to

Figure A-4. A sample completed Safe Job Analysis job title and description.

DESCRIPTION

Job Title: <u>Cutting Grass with a Lawn Tractor (cont.)</u>

stationary objects may knock the tractor out of control.

—Keep children, pets, and other adults away from areas you are cutting. Before placing a tractor in reverse, look behind you. Always be alert and aware of your surroundings.

—When cutting on slopes, reduce your speed and exercise extreme caution. Turn on level ground—not on slopes. In general cut slopes from top to bottom instead of riding sideways on the incline. When possible plant ground cover on steep slopes so those slopes will not have to be mowed.

— If something gets caught in the blades or discharge chute, shut the engine off and remove the key. Before leaving the operator's seat, wait for the engine and attached parts to stop moving. NEVER place your hands or feet under the deck or in the chute while the engine is running. When inspecting or removing a jam under the deck or in the chute, always wear gloves.

HOME SAFETY AUDIT FORM

Auditors: _____

_____

Job Inspected: _____

_____ Date: _____

Types of Observations:

Personal Protective Equipment:
- Eyes and Face
- Ears
- Head
- Hands and Arms
- Feet and Legs
- Respiratory Protection
- Fall Protection

Tools and Equipment:
- Right for Job?
- Used Correctly?
- In Safe Condition?
- Warning Signs Used?

Procedures:
- Safe Procedures Known?
- Safe Procedures Been Written Down?
- Safe Procedures Being Followed?

Housekeeping:
- Slipping/Tripping Hazards Removed?
- Tools and Mtrls. Kept Orderly?
- Waste Properly Disposed Of?

Safety Observations

_____

_____

_____

_____

_____

_____

_____

_____ Follow-Up Required: _____

_____

_____

_____

_____

_____

Figure A-5. A Home Safety Audit Form.

HOME SAFETY AUDIT FORM

Auditors: _Greg_
Jennifer

Job Inspected: _Watched Ronnie trim hedges with gas clippers_ Date: _9-16-94_

Types of Observations:

Personal Protective Equipment:
- Eyes and Face
- Ears
- Head
- Hands and Arms
- Feet and Legs
- Respiratory Protection
- Fall Protection

Tools and Equipment:
- Right for Job?
- Used Correctly?
- In Safe Condition?
- Warning Signs Used?

Procedures:
- Safe Procedures Known?
- Safe Procedures Been Written Down?
- Safe Procedures Being Followed?

Housekeeping:
- Slipping/Tripping Hazards Removed?
- Tools and Mtrls. Kept Orderly?
- Waste Properly Disposed Of?

Safety Observations

Ronnie wore gloves, goggles, and ear plugs. He had quite a bit of trouble starting the gas engine, and had to read the operator's manual. It took over an hour to complete the cutting. Ronnie said next time he will split the work up over 2 days, so his arms and shoulders and lower back won't be as sore.

✓ Follow-Up Required: _Ronnie should read the operator's manual again, and do the work earlier or later in the day, when it's not so hot outside_

Figure A-6. A sample completed Home Safety Audit Form.

HOME SAFETY MEETING FORM

Date: _____

Attendees: _____   _____

_____   _____

_____   _____

Follow-up from previous meetings: _____

_____

_____

_____

_____

Main Topics for Discussion: _____

_____

_____

_____

_____

_____

Follow-up Required: _____

_____

_____

_____

_____

_____

_____

_____

Suggestions for future meeting topics: _____

_____

_____

_____

_____

_____

_____

Figure A-7. A Home Safety Meeting Form.

HOME SAFETY MEETING FORM

Date: _4-2-95_

Attendees: _Ronnie_ _Greg_
Jennifer
Marta

Follow-up from previous meetings: _A hand rail was installed on the steps to the back porch, and the "painted-in" window to Jennifer's room was replaced._

Main Topics for Discussion: _A fire-escape plan, how to use the fire extinguishers kept in the kitchen and in the garage, and how practice fire drills will be handled._

Follow-up Required: _Placing fire department, ambulance, poison control, police, and other emergency phone numbers near each phone extension._

Suggestions for future meeting topics: _What to do if there is a power outage at night._

Figure. A-8. A sample completed Home Safety Meeting Form.

advance. Consider planning a supper, lunch or breakfast meeting.

- If possible, make sure you won't be interrupted during your meeting. Take your phone off the hook or set up an answering machine.
- Fill out the home safety meeting form.
- Prepare your materials.
- Keep the meeting relatively short—don't bore your audience. Use a touch of humor whenever possible.
- Let other household members play a role in the meetings. They can help gather information, take notes, and perform follow-up.

Safety Meeting Topic Checklist

There are plenty of places to find materials to use at home safety meetings. Here are a number of suggestions. Many other possibilities exist.

- Use individual chapters and parts of chapters from this book.
- Borrow or rent safety videos from libraries, video stores, hospitals and law enforcement agencies.
- Discuss pamphlets and other literature that is often available free of charge from government and safety organizations.
- Review operating and safety procedures from owner's manuals to equipment such as snowblowers, lawn mowers, chain saws, garden tractors, trash compactors and other devices.
- Have a brainstorming session about what to do if a natural disaster occurs.
- Review the use and storage of flammables, poisons and other hazardous materials at home.
- Discuss housekeeping, personal protective equipment, material handling, stress management, health topics, food safety, electrical safety and zero energy states, tool and equipment guards, ladders, hand tools, hot weather conditions, cold weather conditions, babysitting or other topics.

Index

More Great Ideas for All Your Do-It-Yourself Projects!